The Role of Law

and

Legal Institutions

in

Asian Economic Development

1960 - 1995

KATHARINA PISTOR AND PHILIP A. WELLONS

with

Jeffrey D. Sachs and Hal S. Scott
Senior Advisors

and

Fan Gang and Xin Chunying
People's Republic of China

T.C.A. Anant and N.L. Mitra
India

Hideki Kanda and Kazuo Ueda
Japan

Seung-Wha Chang and Kwang-Shik Shin
Republic of Korea

Wong Sau Ngan and Jomo K. Sundaram
Malaysia

Tain-Jy Chen and Lawrence S. Liu
Taipei, China

OXFORD

UNIVERSITY PRESS

Oxford University Press is a department of the University of Oxford.
It furthers the University's objective of excellence in research, scholarship,
and education by publishing worldwide in

Oxford New York

Athens Auckland Bangkok Bogotá Buenos Aires Calcutta
Cape Town Chennai Dar es Salaam Delhi Florence Hong Kong Istanbul
Karachi Kuala Lumpur Madrid Melbourne Mexico City Mumbai
Nairobi Paris São Paulo Singapore Taipei Tokyo Toronto Warsaw

with associated companies in Berlin Ibadan

Oxford is a registered trade mark of Oxford University Press

First published 1999
This impression (lowest digit)
1 3 5 7 9 10 8 6 4 2

Published in the United States
by Oxford University Press, New York

Published for the Asian Development Bank by
Oxford University Press

British Library Cataloguing in Publication Data
available

Library of Congress Cataloguing in Publication Data
The Role of Law and Legal Institutions in Asian Economic Development 1960-1995
p.cm.
Studies initiated by a regional technical assistance grant from the Asian Development Bank.
Includes bibliographical references and index.
ISBN 0-19-590983-6

Printed in Hong Kong
Published by Oxford University Press (China) Ltd
18th Floor Warwick House East, Taikoo Place, 979 King's Road, Quarry Bay
Hong Kong

CONTRIBUTORS

Authors:

Katharina Pistor	Harvard Institute for International Development
Philip A. Wellons	Program on International Financial Systems (Harvard Law School)

Senior Advisors:

Jeffrey D. Sachs	Harvard Institute for International Development
Hal S. Scott	Program on International Financial Systems (Harvard Law School)

Team Leaders:

PEOPLE'S REPUBLIC OF CHINA

Fan Gang	National Economic Research Institute, China Reform Foundation
Xin Chunying	Chinese Academy of Social Sciences, Institute of Law

INDIA

T. C. A. Anant	Delhi School of Economics, Centre for Development Economics
N. L. Mitra	National Law School of India University

JAPAN

Hideki Kanda	University of Tokyo, Faculty of Law
Kazuo Ueda	University of Tokyo, Faculty of Economics

REPUBLIC OF KOREA

Seung-Wha Chang	Seoul National University, College of Law
Kwang-Shik Shin	Korean Development Institute

MALAYSIA

Wong Sau Ngan	Securities Commission, Kuala Lumpur, Malaysia
Jomo K. Sundaram	University of Malaya, Faculty of Economics

TAIPEI,CHINA

Tain-Jy Chen	Chun-Hua Institute for Economic Research, International Division
Lawrence S. Liu	Lee and Li

ABBREVIATIONS

DSIs	dispute settlement institutions
FDI	foreign direct investment
EBRD	European Bank for Reconstruction and Development
EC	European Community
GDI	gross domestic investment
GDP	gross domestic product
GNP	gross national product
IGFs	intermediate growth factors
IPRs	intellectual property rights
MITI	Ministry of International Trade and Industry
PMP	per million people
PRC	People's Republic of China
SOEs	state owned enterprise
UK	United Kingdom
US	United States

FOREWORD

The dramatic economic progress of the "East Asian miracle economies" during the last four decades of the twentieth century has been extensively studied by economists and other social scientists. Such studies, including the Asian Development Bank's 1997 study, *Emerging Asia: Changes and Challenges*, and the World Bank's 1993 study, *The East Asian Miracle: Economic Growth and Public Policy*, have emphasized the importance of sound government economic policies, but have also observed—without extended analysis—that the "miracle economies" were characterized, generally, by reasonably effective legal institutions which encouraged private sector development and by reasonably effective governmental institutions.

The past decade has seen significant attention to legal reform by many developing countries, particularly among the "transition economies" moving from central planning to market economics. The decade has also seen a dramatic expansion of assistance by international financial institutions, such as the Asian Development Bank, to the legal reform efforts of Asian governments and to capacity-building among their legal institutions.

This book examines the role which legal systems played in six Asian economies—People's Republic of China, India, Japan, Republic of Korea, Malaysia and Taipei, China—during a 35-year period of dynamic economic growth, from 1960 to 1995. It presents the results of a major comparative study commissioned by the Asian Development Bank in 1996[1]. The purpose of the study was to come to a better understanding of the relationships between legal and economic change in Asia, with the belief that such an understanding would inform and influence government legal reform and economic development policies and the assistance provided by international financial institutions and other development agencies in support of such policies.

The study documents the manner in which laws and legal institutions have made important contributions to the economic development of the six economies, particularly as each turned towards greater reliance on market oriented economic policies in the 1980s. The similarity in the changing patterns of legal development across most of the six economies during the 35-year period of the study is striking. Patterns of convergence in substantive law and in the operation of legal institutions can be seen across the six economies and towards Western legal systems, though the patterns are

---

[1] Technical Assistance for the Role of Law and Legal Institutions in Asian Economic Development (T.A. No. 5665-REG, approved on 22 December 1995).

incomplete, show significant variances in different substantive areas of law, and are least clear in areas of procedural law and in the operation of legal institutions. The importance of the compatibility of economic law and government economic policy to the effective operation of such laws emerges as an important theme. Changes in economic policy have been seen most often to initiate changes in economic law, though changes in such laws have often been necessary to ensure the realization of the economic policy.

While historical in its perspective, the importance of the issues addressed in the study has been reinforced as a number of the East Asian miracle economies moved in 1997 from "miracle" to "meltdown". As governments, international financial institutions, and other analysts attempt to understand the causes of the regional financial crisis, the legal systems of the affected economies have been identified as one contributing factor. Deficiencies in corporate governance, corporate financial disclosure, and corporate regulation, deficiencies in the governance and regulation of financial institutions, inadequacies in collateral security and bankruptcy laws, and corruption in government and the judiciary have all been highlighted. Significant legal and institutional reforms are a part of the responses of the governments concerned, and development agencies' assistance is being marshalled in support of such reform programs. The experience of the previous 35 years as to how economic law reform has evolved in Asia and as to the efficacy of such reforms is the subject of this study. Such experience is of direct relevance to our efforts to craft solutions to the new set of economic challenges now facing the region.

The study represents a seminal contribution to our understanding of the relationships between law and economic development. It has been described by one commentator as the single most ambitious exploration of the subject since the work of Max Weber. In addition to the study's relevance to government policymakers and development agency officials, we look forward to it serving as a stimulus for further research into those critical relationships.

BARRY METZGER
General Counsel
Asian Development Bank
Manila, Philippines
October 1998

ACKNOWLEDGMENTS

This study is the result of a collaborative, interdisciplinary, multinational research effort. It was conceived, sponsored, and actively assisted by the Office of the General Counsel at the Asian Development Bank. Scholars in each of the six economies carried out the analysis, drawing on deep experience in their respective home economies and their knowledge of Western economic and legal systems. Led by the senior lawyers and economists named in the list of contributors, the teams produced from the marriage of two disciplines a unique set of data and insights. We would like to thank them, and also their home institutions for the technical help and additional research time this project warranted for all involved.

The conceptual framework for the research was developed, in collaboration with the teams, by the authors and Professors Jeffrey D. Sachs and Hal S. Scott, the two senior advisors, at the Harvard Institute for International Development and the Program on International Financial Systems at Harvard Law School. In this endeavor and in the subsequent analysis of the findings of the teams, the authors benefited from discussions with a panel of academic advisors, including Professors William Alford, Dwight Perkins, and Ezra Vogel, who brought a deep knowledge of the history, legal systems, and socioeconomic development of the Asian economies included in this study. The advisors helped shape the authors' views and prevented them from committing the most egregious errors. Those that remain are solely the responsibility of the authors.

Barry Metzger and Jeremy Hovland from the Bank commented on many occasions both on the design of the research and our analysis of the findings. The study greatly benefited from their knowledge of law and legal development in Asia and their lively interest in a research undertaking that was both academic and designed to provide new insights for policymakers.

The findings of this study were first presented at a Symposium held at the Bank in Manila in September 1997. The participants included Bank staff, scholars, and policy advisors from around the world. Their discussions, comments, and suggestions made important contributions to our revision of the comparative report after the Symposium.

The authors of the study relied heavily on technical and administrative support at their respective home institutions. We would particularly like to thank Debra Mattina, Anni Pirinen-Valme, and Wendy Whiteaker for their administrative and secretarial help.

Jenepher Moseley edited the study and Alex McLellan prepared the tables and figures. R. Rajan at the ADB's publication office and his staff prepared the report for publication. To all of them our thanks for their thoroughness and commitment.

The views and opinions expressed in this volume are those of the authors and do not necessarily reflect the views and policies of the Bank.

Use of the term "country" does not imply any judgment by the authors or the Bank as to the legal or other status of any territorial entity.

KATHARINA PISTOR and PHILIP A. WELLONS

TABLE OF CONTENTS

Chapter 1

OVERVIEW

Law played an important role in Asia's remarkable economic growth during the second half of the twentieth century. This role has been largely ignored, even disputed as irrelevant. This book, the result of an interdisciplinary research effort by legal and economic experts from Asia and the West, offers a different perspective. We test competing theories about law and its relation to economic development against the experience of six Asian economies over 35 years, between 1960 and 1995. The results suggest that far from being irrelevant, law made an important contribution to Asia's economic development and was most effective when it was congruent with economic policies. During the development process, the context, action, and nature of law changed over time and with changes in economic policies. Overall, we suggest that law and legal institutions tended to converge among the six economies and with the institutions of the West with economic development, although the extent of convergence differs from country to country and for different areas of the law.

Beginning in about 1960, Asia changed on a scale unprecedented in history. Industrialization, urbanization, and the increasing division of labor altered society, the economy, and politics across the region. The success of the Asian tigers and dragons prompted other economies in Asia to try to emulate it. The Asian Development Bank's Emerging Asia suggests that the experience of these early reformers bears important policy lessons for other newly emerging markets (ADB 1997). This "East Asian miracle" captured the attention of policymakers and scholars around the world (see, for example, World Bank 1993).

The analysts' neglect of the role of law in this transformation is puzzling. Most focus on economics, some refer to the institutional environment, but few attend to the development of law and the relationship between legal and socioeconomic change in Asia. This neglect is the more puzzling since some of the most influential social theories about the process of industrialization and modernization in the West asserted a key role for law. Max Weber (1980 [1921, first German edition]) noted that the development of a rational legal system was a significant factor in facilitating the development of capitalism. Emile Durkheim (1984 [1893, first French edition]) described the impact of the division of labor on the nature of legal rules. Adam Smith and Karl Marx observed the close relation between the complexity of economic relations and the complexity of legal systems (Stein 1980).

One possible reason for analysts to ignore law in Asia may be a widely held view that because Asia differs from the West, law plays a fundamentally different role in Asian development. If correct, this observation would be significant. It would suggest that the prevailing social theories, which were derived from the experience of economic development in the West, cannot be generalized. It would also caution against the use of legal technical assistance programs as an instrument to stimulate and support economic growth and development.

Against this backdrop, our study explores the role of mostly economic law and the legal institutions through which it operates in Asian economic development. The study draws on the experience of six Asian economies: the People's Republic of China (PRC), India, Japan, Republic of Korea, Malaysia, and Taipei,China.

The study is the first of its kind that tries to investigate the interaction between legal and economic change on a comparative basis using empirical data. This analysis proffers important new insights. The empirical analysis of law and legal institutions also confronts substantial data as well as methodological problems. We hope that our findings will stimulate further research in Asia and elsewhere and provide the basis for systematic research and data gathering in law and economic development.

The study focuses on the period from 1960 to 1995. Taking 1960 as a starting point for our analysis is well justified when comparing economic growth rates in Asia before and after 1960. As figure 1.1 below demonstrates

Figure 1.1   Economic Growth in Asia, 1820–1992

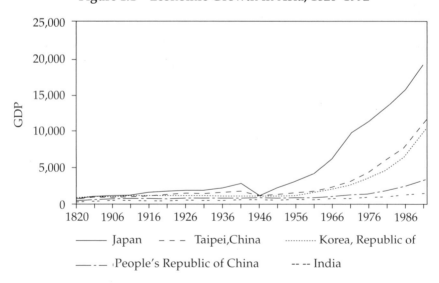

Source: Maddison (1995).

for five of the six economies in our sample, growth rates were low for most of the nineteenth and early twentieth centuries.[1] Japan is a partial exception, since its economy began to grow several decades earlier than the others. But prior to World War II, Japan did not achieve growth rates on the scale experienced since the mid-1950s. The data in the figure reflect the success of Japan, Republic of Korea, and Taipei,China for the entire period between 1960 and 1995. They also show that the two Asian giants, the PRC and India, trail far behind the early reformers, although the PRC in particular appears to be poised to emulate its neighbors.

In contrast, legal development in the six economies would not, by itself, justify starting our analysis in 1960. Legal modernization long predates the period of dynamic growth and development. Nineteenth century Western imperialism brought Western law to Asia by way of colonization or through the comprehensive adoption of Western law by economies trying to protect their legal sovereignty against Western powers. India and Malaysia came under colonial rule. Japan modernized its legal system in the late nineteen hundreds using continental European, in particular German, law as a model. Japan transferred this law to Korea and the island of Taiwan when they came under its rule. China used various models to modernize its legal system in the first decades of the twentieth century, with particular emphasis on the Japanese/German models. When the PRC embarked on a renewed legal reform effort after 1978, it further diversified and copied from various economies · with different legal systems.

The disparate sequencing of legal reforms and economic growth reveals little about the causal relation between the legal system and the economy. It was only decades after legal reforms were implemented that the economies of our survey embarked on fast track growth and development. This long hiatus may be largely due to external factors, such as the two world wars and the intervening worldwide economic recession in the 1920s. Historical circumstance prevents us from simply relating legal modernization to growth and development. We must content ourselves with an analysis of the use of the existing legal framework as well as legal changes in the period when economic development took off.

By the early 1960s, all the economies but the PRC had comprehensive legal systems in place which encompassed both public and private law. After World War II, legislative activity in the years leading up to 1960 had been intense. Economies that had been occupied by colonial powers asserted their legal sovereignty, repealed overtly colonial rules, and added laws and institutions to the inherited legal system. However, in most cases the basic frame-

---

[1] Historical data for Malaysia have not been available.

work of private law, including contracts, property rights, and the law governing business organizations, was not fundamentally affected by these changes. Following major revisions under American occupation, basic laws remained largely untouched in Japan. Malaysia enacted a new company law, borrowing heavily from Australia, which in turn relied on English law. In the Republic of Korea, the civil and commercial codes underwent major revisions, but were not significantly altered in substance. The most far reaching changes occurred in India, where the new social order after independence affected the substance of economic laws. An example is the Company Law of 1956, which expanded state control rights over private investors and entrepreneurs.

In comparison with this earlier activity, the period between 1960 and 1995 witnessed little modification to formal law. Reform was piecemeal rather than comprehensive. A notable exception is the PRC, where the introduction of economic reforms in 1978 set the stage for the creation of a new formal legal system virtually from scratch.

DIMENSIONS OF LEGAL CHANGE, 1960–1995

Despite the absence of major formal law reform in most economies, the legal systems changed significantly between 1960 and 1995. This change cannot be captured by focusing only on the enactment or amendment of major codes. Legal change over the 35 years was less visible because it often took place at the level of administrative rule making or practice rather than the enactment of new major codes. However, these changes had important implications for the functioning of the laws that were already on the books.

To capture these shifts, we define law as a complex set of rules and institutions. It consists not only of the formal law enshrined in the constitutions, statutes, or precedents, but includes the legal practices that may or may not follow the formal law. To capture change in the legal system, we distinguish two dimensions of legal systems, allocative and procedural. The *allocative dimension* determines whether the power to make decisions over the allocation of resources is vested in the state or is left to the market. The *procedural dimension* reflects whether decisions are primarily rule-based or discretionary. Each dimension is a continuum, but both are cross-cutting and combine in four ways. One may speak of a legal system as (a) market/rule-based, (b) market/discretionary, (c) state/rule-based, or (d) state/discretionary. Each combination is an ideal type into which no economy falls unambiguously. We are interested in how Asian legal systems have evolved along these two dimensions.

Allocative Dimension

Along the allocative dimension the state, in contrast to the market, played a very important and even dominant role in the six economies for much of the period between 1960 and 1995. The state actively exercised the power to allocate resources in the economy, albeit to a different degree in the six economies and over the course of the years. When state controls were extensive, the legal framework for market transactions and resource allocation, already on the books, played only a marginal role for economic transactions and by inference for economic development. At such times, this framework was superseded by new rules that expanded the control of the state and provided substantial discretion for state agents. Where state ownership prevailed, rules governing private property rights were marginalized or even became irrelevant. Although some state enterprises were incorporated under the existing company law, shareholder rights and management responsibilities were of little significance for the relationship between government departments and managers.

Even where state control fell short of direct control through ownership, it provided substitutes for legal mechanisms. For example, under state led development strategies the provisions of corporate law played only a marginal role in determining the governance of firms. This can be attributed, at least in part, to the fact that company managers were more likely to turn to bureaucrats than to shareholders for approval (Milhaupt 1996). Similarly, when the government allocated credit to targeted industries for policy considerations, loan contracts and security interests may have been used, but their function was altered from their market based sources. Because of the policy objective, breaches of contract were frequently ignored and security interests of creditors were left unenforced. By implication, these mechanisms were degraded to formalities. Government credit policies also skewed the patterns of corporate finance with further implications for the influence of shareholders, creditors, and company insiders on the governance of firms. As long as external finance was available at low cost from banks, which allocated credits according to official credit policies, companies had to make little effort to raise capital in the market in the form of equity. This in turn undercut the rights that the company law allocated to each group of interested parties, in particular to outside shareholders.

When economic policies changed and provided greater scope for market activities, as they did in most economies around 1980, market-based law became more important. We found that throughout the 1980s market-allocative law gained ground against state-allocative law in five of the six economies. The relevance of market-allocative laws that were already on the books, but had rarely been used in previous policy periods, increased as economic agents turned to formal law to enhance the predictability and enforceability of market transactions. The rapid growth of these transactions also created a demand for new laws. Our findings suggest that during this latter period, legislative activities increased in areas such as company law, securities market regulations, anti-trust rules, and other areas of economic law.

Procedural Dimension

Along the procedural dimension, the same overlay of discretionary law that augmented the states' allocative powers also displaced the transplanted formal legal processes for making, administering, and enforcing the law. In fact, many of these processes had never been fully put to use, at least not with respect to the local population, as colonial authorities ignored them when it suited their objectives, and warfare and civil unrest provided further justification for a more discretionary use of law. Following World War II, most economies further expanded the state bureaucracy's authority to make rules and regulations. Even where a country followed the principle that basic legal rules had to be established by legislation, the laws rarely limited the bureaucracy's authority to issue interpretative regulations or use administrative guidance to influence business behavior. Administrative rules, decrees, and informal guidance often prevailed over underlying laws. Moreover, courts were limited in their review of administrative action, whether by their own choice, by law, or by the raw political power of the executive. Economic agents could not choose between the two different sets of rules, but had to adapt their business activities to the expanding framework of a more state-allocative and more discretionary law.

The extent to which the state allocated resources and applied discretionary procedures varied across economies and over time. In 1960, Malaysia had the closest of the six to a market/rule-based legal system, since the state's allocative role and discretionary power was relatively limited. In Japan, the state-owned-enterprise sector was small and it controlled few business institutions directly, but through administrative guidance the government had wide procedural discretion and allocative control over key economic resources. India, Republic of Korea and Taipei,China had already begun a process to vest increasing legal power in the executive. During the 10-15 years after 1960, all but Japan operated periodically under emergency rules that gave the executive extraordinary allocative and procedural powers even in economic matters.

The PRC is a special case among the economies in our sample. The PRC had probably the closest to a pure state/discretionary legal system in 1960. The state owned the major means of production and implemented an economic planning system replacing contracts among nonstate parties with economic plans that allocated resources. Change occurred only after the introduction of economic reforms in 1978. In all other economies, state-allocative law did not completely displace market-allocative law, but it dominated for at least a decade at or soon after 1960.

The trend away from state-allocative law that occurred in most economies around 1980, in Japan about a decade earlier, was accompanied by greater emphasis on rule-based as opposed to discretionary laws and legal processes. Legal recourse against state acts was expanded or permitted for the first time. The independence of state agencies, such as antitrust committees, was enhanced. Moreover, the extensive lawmaking power that had been allocated to the executive during earlier policy periods was circumscribed by providing specification for the scope of the executive's lawmaking authority in laws that were passed by the legislature. This substantially reduced the discretion of individual bureaucrats. A partial exception to this general trend is Malaysia, where the independence of the judiciary was curtailed in the second half of the 1980s.

This trend in the 1980s appears to be a signal change in the Asian legal tradition. State control has for centuries been a hallmark of the legal tradition in East Asia and India. In all that time, law was perceived mainly as a way to administer the country and punish deviant behavior. Economic matters were the subject of administrative rules or criminal law. Economic law, including the rules governing contracts and the organization of firms, developed for the most part outside the realm of formal legislation enacted by the state. The use of bureaucratic controls over economic activities at least in part reflects the traditional role of the state in Asia. In addition, development strategies and the notion of a welfare state that prevailed in the decades following World War II favored a stronger role of the state in the economy in many countries around the world. Against this background, one should not be surprised that the countries expanded the allocative function of the state. The remarkable act is the state's choice after 1980 to withdraw gradually from managing economic activity. This change has been accompanied by greater emphasis on rule-based procedures. State officials were made increasingly accountable to the law by limiting their discretionary power and vesting nonstate agents with the right to judicial review of administrative acts.

CAUSES OF LEGAL CHANGE

Changes in the allocative dimension of law took place primarily because of corresponding changes in the basic development strategy of each economy, and secondarily because changes in the structure of the economy led to changes in the demand for law. Early in our period, economic strategies that were adopted by policymakers increasingly emphasized a direct state role in the economy and the legal system adjusted to accommodate this role. As a result, many of the essentially market-allocative laws that had earlier been copied from Western sources, including company laws, laws governing credit and security, as well as property law, were superseded by a new layer of mostly administrative rules that gave to the state greater allocative power. Later, around the 1980s for most economies and the 1970s for Japan, new economic strategies reduced the role of the state in the economy, which led to the important changes in the legal systems. Typically, the changes, rather than emerging from the legal system itself, were primarily top down, induced by government policy. Economic policies played the key role in initiating the trend first toward and then away from state-allocative law. The greater scope for market-based transactions these policy changes created enhanced the relevance of formal law for economic transactions. While previously state policies and bureaucratic guidance provided business with a high level of certainty, this function now had to be provided by the legal system. In this sense, the demand for formal law may be said to have increased.

Changes in Development Strategy

The changes in the economic strategies and the legal system in the Republic of Korea illustrate the close relationship between economic policies and law that prevailed in Asia. The Republic of Korea had four major policy periods over the 35 years. In 1961, the new government adopted a strategy of export led growth, nationalizing key industries, relying on cheap labor, liberalizing imports, and allowing foreign direct investment (FDI). In 1973, the oil shock prompted it to shift to import substitution in chemical and heavy industries, targeting key industries and firms for import protection, cheap credit from state banks, and tax benefits. In the process, the government became much more directly involved in economic decisions than it had in the first phase. The strategy accelerated growth and industrial development but also produced considerable costs to the economy Therefore, in 1980 the government switched to a policy that would contain inflation and promote exports by rationalizing problem industries, training, and supporting research and development. Around 1985, the Republic of Korea began to open its economy, liberalizing imports and capital and shifting its promotion policies away from light industries.

The Republic of Korea's legal system changed to support the policies in each period. In the first policy period, 1961–1972, the legal system became increasingly state-allocative as well as discretionary. Executive authority was centralized, the constitution was rewritten, labor laws augmented government authority and reduced union power, a list of acceptable industries for FDI was drawn, and laws delegated substantial power to bureaucrats to give incentives to key industries and firms. Citizens' power to seek redress for government action was reduced and government officials operated almost with impunity. The second policy period (1973–1979) saw government control tighten further, even to the point of amending the constitution to give economic development priority over labor's rights. But beginning with the stabilization policies of the third period (1980–1985), the legal system became less discretionary and more market-allocative. Numerous economic laws were amended. Intellectual property laws and competition laws were strengthened and began to be enforced. Industry specific laws were relaxed. Laws were enacted that liberalized foreign direct investment. The bureaucracy's power began to narrow, contracting, for example, the discretion to determine permissible FDI. The number of judges was deliberately raised. This trend accelerated in the fourth policy period (1986–1995), as the Republic of Korea further liberalized economic activities. Most significant was a 1987 constitution designed to eliminate authoritarianism. Change was not complete by 1995. Moreover, even to the extent policy changes were implemented, the adaptation of the legal and institutional framework to meet the challenges of these new policies has been slow. These weaknesses appear to have exacerbated the financial crisis that the country found itself in late 1997.

Striking parallels with developments in the Republic of Korea emerge from a comparison of policy periods and changes in the legal systems in each country of the survey. Although the precise timing of the periods and their content vary by country, each country was liberalizing its economy by mid-1985. The important points about the changes in the law are that the process is iterative, much occurs without legislation, and change is usually qualitative in the last decade but not complete by 1995. To put it graphically, the overlay of state-allocative/discretionary law was being peeled back so that the existing set of market-allocative laws came to apply in practice. This trend was further supported by rules that reduced the discretionary power of the state and by augmenting resources available to the legal institutions that enforce contracts, property rights, and rights against state agents. Still, not all economies were far advanced by 1995. In Malaysia, for example, the substantive laws governing economic transactions became more market-allocative in the later policy periods, but the legal process became more rather than less discretionary. The PRC's efforts in rebuilding a comprehensive legal system that supports market based activities after 1978 are impressive. Between 1978 and 1995, a basic legal framework for most relevant areas of substantive law was put in place. However, many of these laws continued to allocate extensive discretion to the bureaucracy. Many laws are still missing and the remaining gaps are filled by the executive as well as by the Communist Party.

Changes in Economic Structure

Economic development was a secondary but important factor in the transformation of legal systems. Both income growth and structural change in the economy directly prompted the trend from state- to market-allocative law. By causing fundamental changes in economic policy, they had an indirect effect in prompting the change in the legal system. Japan was a developed economy in 1960, but its per capita income still lagged the United States (US), for example, substantially. Republic of Korea, Malaysia, and Taipei,China were low-income economies in 1960. The Republic of Korea had recently ranked as one of the poorest economies in the world. However, like most economies in our survey, it experienced impressive growth rates after 1960. Annual real per capita growth rates between 4 and 9 percent before the economic policy shift reveal a substantial economic change during the early part of the survey period (see table 1.1 below). By 1980, four of the six economies had made the transition to middle income economies. The PRC and India grew at a much slower pace and were left far behind their neighbors.

It should be clear that a relatively high level of state involvement was compatible with, and perhaps even conducive to, economic growth. The growth data in table 1.1 report economic performance during the periods of active government involvement in the economy. However, the performance of the PRC and India demonstrates that too much state control is counterproductive.

Table 1.1   Economic Development in Survey Economies Prior to Policy Shift

Economy	Year of policy change	Average real GDP per capita growth rate between 1960 and year of policy change
PRC	1978	3.4
India	1980	1.3
Japan	1971	8.9
Korea, Republic of	1980	6.9
Malaysia	1985	4.1
Taipei,China	1985	6.8

Source: World Bank (1997); for Taipei,China: Government statistical yearbook (various issues).

Around 1980, despite the success of the earlier development strategies, all economies began to change their economic policies. The most important reason was that the earlier strategies had created costs that threatened their long-term sustainability. Most economies experienced problems balancing their budgets shortly before implementing policy change. State-owned enterprises frequently failed to keep up with set performance targets. Industrial policies had produced large industry sectors, but changes in the demand for their products created huge losses for companies and financial institutions that had provided much of the capital for the development drive.

To a government official schooled in 1960s' state-allocative and often discretionary law, the perverse effects of this growth must have been startling. One effect was to create conditions that fostered change. The economies became increasingly complex: urbanization rates increased, the labor force shifted from agriculture into manufacturing and services, markets expanded, and the enterprise sector grew. Vesting so much discretion in bureaucrats came to be seen as a mistake. Forces of supply and demand became harder to manage, confronting firms with risks that the old system could no longer resolve. The failings of the old economic policies generated opposition to the system of state-allocative law, and added costs that the emerging economy did not need to bear. Governments lacked the fiscal clout to continue to absorb the costs themselves. Trading partners, like the US government, began to pressure specifically for changes toward market-allocative laws, sometimes to the point of specifying the particulars of compliance with an administrative law. Newly powerful groups, such as consumers with wealth and economic power they had lacked in the earlier periods, wanted the protection by the legal system that would come with market/rule-based laws. Thus, economic development itself undermined state-allocative/discretionary law.

The combined effect of changes in basic economic policies and in the economy prompted what can best be described as demand led evolution in the law. Economic actors demanded change in aspects of the legal system that affected them. The shift was not simply a matter of those in charge of law supplying more market-allocative law on their own initiative.

Hindsight allows us to identify these factors as turning points in the legal and economic development of the six economies. The initial changes were often incremental rather than radical. However, they began to unravel the existing legal system and led to a chain reaction that resulted in most countries' legal systems being much more market-allocative as well as rule-based in 1995 than they had been before these changes. We do not want to overstate the extent of the change, since it varies by country and room exists in all for much more change to take place, but the difference remains striking.

As bureaucratic controls relaxed and the scope of markets increased, a bottom up demand for legal change and for a new role for the state in the economy developed. The relaxation of entry requirements increased competition. Market forces rather than bureaucratic guidance became the primary focus of attention for many entrepreneurs. Indeed, continued state tutelage increasingly turned from a source of support into a source of constraint.

Market developments also created a need for new forms of state intervention in the form of regulatory oversight of markets rather than direct control. This is apparent in various fields. As securities markets developed, for example, rampant misuse of investors' rights led to calls for improvements in market oversight and legal protection for investors. Governments in some countries responded by reducing their own role in evaluating risks, ostensibly to protect investors, and increasingly shifting responsibility for risk evaluation to the investors. Market developments also prompted groups to use existing law that they had previously ignored or avoided. As consumers became wealthier, they could use land as security for loans, making them concerned about the ability of the legal system to protect their interests.

The structural effects of the old interventionist strategies sometimes impeded the development of market-allocative law. Limited competition was one effect. Entrenched interests delayed Japanese and Korean reform of anti-monopoly laws until after the paradigm shift in economic policies and kept actual enforcement of these laws weak. Strong reliance on direct state controls through ownership of enterprises and financial institutions also had structural consequences. Economies that had primarily relied on direct state controls were less able to scale back state involvement in the economy than economies that had relied more on indirect control measures, such as trade and credit controls. The speed and magnitude of the development towards market-allocative law was thus partly a function of the economic structure that itself reflected earlier economic strategy.

Overall, the general pattern of change was similar in all economies. The initial policy change created a new incentive structure for nonstate parties, which they used to expand their activities.

THE RELEVANCE OF LAW TO ASIAN ECONOMIC DEVELOPMENT

Law did indeed matter for economic development in the period after the policy shift, though its costs and benefits must be weighed as part of an assessment of overall economic policies. One cannot simply measure a shift from state-allocative to market-allocative law, for example, against overall growth rates. To do so for these six states would reveal divergent trends: extraordinarily high growth rates for the PRC and Malaysia and lower rates compared with the past in other economies. These lower growth rates were in part the result of the inevitable slowdown in economic growth as economies matured and became rich, and in part the legacy left by the earlier state led economic strategies, which proved to be unsustainable in the long term. The increasing complexity of the economies and their integration into the world market required economic strategies that were more adaptable to the changing environment. These changes also demanded a legal framework that would provide flexibility for market agents and stable institutions to enforce contracts and property rights and enhance the predictability, transparency, and accountability of state actions.

Law leads or lags economic development depending on the type of legal rules. During the earlier period, legal rules that gave state agents substantial allocative powers were used as an instrument of economic policies pursued by the state. They typically led economic development and served a primarily utilitarian function. In some jurisdictions, such as the PRC, such legal practices entirely lacked a rule-based legal framework. In others, basic laws were in place, but they typically delegated substantial discretionary powers to state agencies and officials.

By contrast, legal rules that empower nonstate agents with allocative decision-making powers tend to be less powerful as tools for implementing socioeconomic change. For these rules to become effective in legal practice there must be a demand. Several factors can enhance this demand, including socioeconomic development, the withdrawal of the state from making allocative decisions in the economy, and limits on the discretionary power of the state. In other words, the shift from state- to market-allocative law is self-reinforcing. The clearest expressions of this trend towards market-allocative law are extensive privatization and the expansion of legal procedures that allow nonstate agents to take state officials to court and hold them accountable to the law.

IS ASIA DIFFERENT?

Comparisons between "Asia" and the "West" tend to focus on differences in culture, history, and tradition. These differences and their implications for legal systems should not be underestimated. Legal systems are embedded in the social, economic, and political life of a people, and are therefore influenced by their culture, history, and tradition. However, we need to weigh the relevance of culture in the context of other factors that shape a legal system.

In 1960, at the outset of the period investigated in this research project, factors other than culture made Asia look quite different from the West at the beginning of its industrialization. Except in the PRC, a basic legal framework for market based economic transactions was already in place and had been in place for decades in most economies. By contrast, the development of law and legal institutions in the West took place in parallel with the process of industrialization and economic development. The roots of the laws and legal institutions that were enacted, codified, and systematized in the West through-out the late eighteenth and nineteenth centuries dated back many centuries. But it was only in the nineteenth century that the corporate form was made accessible at low cost for large-scale private investments, and commercial rules were harmonized across regions in the newly formed nation states.

The general perception, not only in Asia but also in the West, about the role the state should play in economic development was markedly different in the 1950s and 1960s from that of nineteenth century Europe. In both areas, the notion of a welfare state, of a state that uses its coercive power to engage in extensive redistribution, or a state that actively shapes and guides economic development, evolved only in the twentieth century. The UK and the US are prototypes of a market led industrialization strategy that started in the nine-teenth century; the state played a role in business only peripherally even during the period of greatest state involvement in social welfare after World War II. In Germany and France and other late industrializing economies of the West, the state played a more active role during the period of the catch up in the early part of the twentieth century. In much of the developing world, development strategies that focused on the guiding role of the state became dominant following World War II. Although they may have been less strong in the six Asian economies included in this study than in other parts of the world, they were indeed influential.

Over time we see strong signs of convergence of legal systems in Asia and in the West. Three related factors contribute most to convergence. First is the internationalization of law since the late 1940s, notably in the norma-tive rules and due process for international commercial transactions. Sec-ond is a kind of political convergence, as authoritarian governments lift martial law and give way to democracy. Third is the trend towards global and international markets over the past decade. These three factors rein-force one another. Globalization and democratization made existing inter-national standards even more relevant to commerce. International agree-ments, along with conditions imposed by multilateral agencies, support glo-balization. These international rules and market forces generally curtail the discretion of national actors.

A fourth factor prompting legal convergence is a fundamental change in the perception of the state's role in economic development since the 1960s. In developed as well as in developing economies, the allocative power of the state has been reduced and the scope of markets increased. As a result, market-allocative rules gain in importance. The extent of change differs from economy to economy, but the direction appears to be the same.

With respect to the domestic legal systems of the six jurisdictions sampled in this study, these trends are reflected in two selected areas of economic law which are analyzed in detail in this study: the laws on business governance and capital formation, and credit and security. Evidence is less strong for legal institutions and processes, as our analysis of dispute settlement demonstrates, but we find change even here.

BUSINESS GOVERNANCE AND CAPITAL FORMATION

Firms occupy a key role in the process of capital formation, the expansion of markets, and technological progress. Their ability to raise capital and put it to productive use is an important element in economic development and the competitiveness of economies. This ability in turn depends on the confidence of investors that they can obtain adequate returns on their investment. The legal framework for the governance of firms is an important factor in generating this credibility.

An important finding of the World Bank's *The East Asian Miracle* (1993) was that in the high performing Asian economies high investment rates, in particular in the private sector, greatly contributed to their economic success. This raises the question of whether the corporate form, which has played an important role in the process of private capital formation in the West, was also important in the context of Asian economic development.

All countries in our sample, except for the PRC, had a basic framework for company law in place in 1960. This framework changed very little for most of the period. Most changes occurred only over the past ten years, after the policy shifts we noted above. This timing again shows that policy change and legal development closely interact. It also confirms that the need for legal change arose only after changes in economic strategies provided a basis for these laws to become relevant for business practice.

The major economic attributes of the corporate form are limited liability for investors and the corresponding ability of a firm to raise capital from a large pool of investors. Our findings suggest that to the extent economic policies promoted capital formation within the private sector, the corporate form greatly contributed to the process. Where such policies were in place, the share of the private corporate sector in total capital formation tended to be larger than the share of either the private unincorporated sector or the state sector.

The ability to raise finance from a large pool of investors was less important for most of the period after 1960. During periods of state controls over financial resource allocation, companies relied heavily on internal finance and bank credits. The market for equity remained underdeveloped. This changed only in recent years. Since the middle to late 1980s, capital markets developed in all six economies. They facilitated initial public offerings and the trading of shares. Although these are relatively recent developments, they suggest the increasing importance of the legislative framework for raising finance in the form of equity.

CREDIT AND SECURITY INTERESTS

Credit, an essential link between savings and investment, allocates resources to productive use. The level of lending is important for development. Creditors can reduce their risk by relying on collateral, or security interest, that can be realized if the debtor defaults.

The factors that affected the impact of the security interest regime included the economic policy of the government, the performance of the overall economy, and substitutes for security interests. The economic policy was significant for the use of collateral to secure credits. When banks must follow government directives about the volume and cost of loans, supported by official refinancing and other funding schemes, they expect the government to make good the losses they bear as a result either directly or indirectly by supporting the borrower. Under these circumstances, even if the banks take security they do not rely on it to reduce risk as much as they would in market conditions. To a large extent, this seems to have been true of the economies in our study. At the end of the period, however, governments were less able or inclined to provide that essential support. Market oriented mechanisms such as security interests became important when markets were allowed to work. Events in the macroeconomy affected supply and demand conditions for loans, hence the relative economic power of lenders and borrowers and the capacity of lenders to insist on secured lending.

Substitutes for security interests became important when they rendered security interests unnecessary or relatively more costly. Substitutes include ownership relations that promote trust or give informational advantages, criminal sanctions for default, guarantees, and delayed transfer of title to the goods whose purchase is being financed. We found evidence that the loss of a major substitute (criminal sanctions for default) drove lenders to greater use of secured loans. Ownership relations did not necessarily reduce the use of security interests; indeed, in the context of certain government strategies, relationships increased the use of security. Each of these substitutes relied on law: relational lending on equity ownership, guarantees on contract law, sanctions for bouncing checks or promissory notes on the criminal code, and delayed transfers of ownership on special laws creating, for example, conditional sales. For this reason, we treat the substitutes for security interests as a part of the legal system.

The basic story seems to be that Asian lenders used security interests as one of several ways to reduce the risk of default and loan losses, and that they shifted to greater reliance on security interests when alternatives became *relatively* less effective as markets replaced government management of the economy. By contrast, security interests do appear to become important when markets are allowed to work.

DISPUTE SETTLEMENT INSTITUTIONS

Although we see a significant shift towards market/rule-based law especially after 1980, legal processes and legal institutions have not been equally affected. This does not imply that policies are irrelevant for legal institutions. India provides an example of how economic and social policies that are enshrined in the constitution influence the role of the legal system, including courts, in enforcing these policies.

Courts and judicial procedures were part of the comprehensive transplantation of entire legal systems during the nineteenth and early twentieth centuries. Courts were important institutions for the reception and further development of common law deriving from England in India and Malaysia. The transplantation of European-based civil law systems to the Far East included not only the three codes of substantive law, the civil code, the commercial code, and the criminal code, but also the civil and criminal procedure codes as well as laws governing the organization of courts.

These imported laws did not fundamentally alter the role of courts in the receiving economies. State courts were not new institutions in Asia. A formal state court system existed in PRC, Japan, and Republic of Korea, and parts of Malaysia had a well established system of Islamic courts. The primary task of the new state courts and the existing formal system was to uphold law and order and to enforce the existing criminal and administrative formal law. By comparison, courts played a less important role in settling commercial disputes among nonstate parties, and claims by nonstate parties against the state were virtually unheard of.

Social theory predicts that with growing markets and increasing division of labor, traditional means of enforcing contracts become less effective. In light of high urbanization rates and a substantial shift from employment in agriculture to employment in manufacturing and services, which is indicative of increases in the division of labor, we would expect an increasing demand for formal dispute settlement institutions provided by the state. Our data show tentative support for this proposition, as in most economies we find a positive correlation between the number of civil and commercial cases per capita that were filed in the court system and gross domestic product (GDP) growth rates. However, several puzzles remain. Litigation rates in Japan have remained low despite the country's economic development and high levels of division of labor. By contrast, civil litigation in the Republic of Korea and Taipei,China has surged. In some economies, relatively low litigation rates on a per capita basis may be the result of a severely understaffed judiciary. In others, business appears to avoid the courts or displays preference for settling disputes through negotiations. Future research would need to collect company level data to throw light on these matters

A more striking finding is the increase in administrative litigation in recent years. It is evidence of the greater commitment to rule-based legal systems that today all six countries have procedures in place that allow nonstate (private) parties to sue the state for allegedly wrongful acts. This change in the supply side of legal processes has met an increasing demand, as market agents sought to reduce the economic costs of state interference. Interestingly, the number of cases where courts reversed agency adjudication has increased. This reflects a greater confidence on the part of the judiciary and may improve the credibility of administrative litigation. It is also likely to enhance the accountability of state officials to the law.

Other legal institutions, such as securities and exchange commissions or antitrust agencies, revealed great institutional inertia. In countries where these state agencies were established during periods when a state led economic development strategy dominated, they were designed to fit the prevailing policy considerations. Even where countries borrowed from Western institutions, their independence, power to enforce the law, and methods of enforcement differed markedly from the original models. However, to the extent the functioning of these institutions reflects primarily their adaptation to prevailing policies, one may expect that in the future they will align more with the new economic and legal policies. In some countries there are already signs of such a trend. In the Republic of Korea, the fair trade commission became independent from government ministries in 1994. In Taipei,China, a newly established fair trade commission started with much more independence than its counterparts in other Asian economies.

CONCLUSION

Law and legal institutions in Asia changed in response to economic policies. When economic policies were introduced that gave nonstate actors a greater role in making allocative decisions, the law and its role in Asian economic development became increasingly similar to the West. Not only substantive laws, but also legal processes and institutions responded to these changes, even though the process of convergence with respect to the latter was much slower. This suggests that the relationship between law and economic development can hardly be explained without factoring in the state. It is the state that defines the economic policies and legal rights. By its lawmaking power it establishes the role of state versus markets in making allocative decisions and creates the rules that determine the extent of the state's discretionary powers or its adherence to legal rules and processes that further its accountability to the law. Likewise, the state determines the jurisdiction of courts, their independence, and the amount of human and other resources made available for establishing a well functioning and credible court system. Without a political commitment to provide these institutions with resources and to ensure their effectiveness, they become dysfunctional.

A key finding of this research project therefore is that law and legal institutions should not be viewed as technical tools that once adopted will produce the desired outcome. The point that law is embedded in culture has often been made especially with respect to the Asian economies. We would add that to be effective law has to be embedded in the overall economic policy framework. This finding cautions against the blind transplantation of legal institutions without due consideration for the relevant economic framework within which they shall operate. It also suggests that law reform projects should be assessed not in isolation, but within a broader context of economic policies. Finally this conclusion calls for a closer interaction between policymakers and legal reformers as well as between policy and legal advisers in designing legal reform projects.

Chapter 2

FRAMEWORK OF ANALYSIS

Does law matter for economic development? Is Asia different? These two questions, framed in the last chapter, have guided the research project whose results are presented in this study. To address these questions we will explore four hypotheses about the relationship between legal and economic development, some or all of which may have some bearing on our questions.

• *Convergence Hypothesis.* Laws and legal institutions converge with economic development. This occurs across economies as domestic economic development interacts with the growing internationalization of markets to produce law and legal institutions that, if not identical on paper, perform largely similar functions.

• *Divergence Hypothesis.* Each economy follows a distinct path of legal development. The laws and legal institutions of different economies vary not only in design, but also in function. Some may be more conducive to economic growth, others less.

• *Irrelevance Hypothesis.* Law as a formal legal system is irrelevant for economic and social development; no detectable link between different legal arrangements and intermediate economic growth factors has been found.

• *Differentiation Hypothesis.* Different parts of an economy's legal system behave differently in response to economic development; some parts show signs of convergence, and others develop along an idiosyncratic path. This may be the result of the socioeconomic environment in which law is situated, weak law enforcement, or cultural or other factors.

The importance of law for economic development has long been asserted by scholars, including legal scholars, social theorists, and economists. Although not strongly promoted in Asia, this widely held view has influenced policymakers, advisers, and international lending institutions. Legal reforms have become an important element in economic reform efforts around the world. In most cases, emerging market economies or developing economies are encouraged to copy legal models from economies that appear to be more advanced in legal and economic development. The implicit assumption behind these efforts is that legal systems converge with economic development and that law can promote this process of convergence (Convergence Hypothesis).

Available evidence shows rather mixed results from legal technical assistance projects. There are few data that demonstrate unambiguously a positive impact of legal reform on subsequent economic development. This seems to suggest that law has little relevance for economic development

(Irrelevance Hypothesis). In part, the lack of evidence appears to be due to the absence of systematic comparative studies based on empirical evidence. Existing case, as opposed to comparative, studies typically reflect the idiosyncrasies of a particular economy and focus on a relatively short period of time. Although they provide important insights about the functioning of a legal system, the findings can usually not be generalized. To show whether or not law matters for economic development, we must choose a sample size that is sufficiently large to allow some generalizations, but small enough to allow a sufficiently detailed analysis to account for the complexity of law and legal institutions. Moreover, we need to cover a long enough time span to capture the usually slow change of institutional behavior over time. To meet these requirements in this study, we analyze the legal development of six jurisdictions over the course of 35 years that were critical to their economic development — from the year 1960 to 1995.

The focus of this research project is on Asia, or rather six economies in Asia. Asia is often characterized as fundamentally different from the West. The major factors typically identified to account for this difference are culture, history, and tradition. As legal systems are shaped by a country's history and culture, this would imply that Asia's path of legal development differs from the West (Divergence Hypothesis). However, there is insufficient evidence to make that assumption. We lack comprehensive studies about the role of law in the economic development accompanying the process of industrialization in the West. As a point of reference we therefore take the prevailing social theories that are based on the experience of the West, rather than empirically tested propositions. Where data from Western economies are available, we present them. This lack of comparative empirical research on legal development in the West exposes a major gap in existing research. We hope that this research on Asia will stimulate similar research undertakings in other parts of the world and enhance the collection of data that are relevant for studying law and legal institutions.

THE SAMPLE

The study includes six Asian economies: PRC, India, Japan, Republic of Korea, Malaysia, and Taipei,China. Four of these six economies belong to the group that has experienced unprecedented economic growth rates for most of the period between 1960 and 1995. It is the group commonly considered responsible for the "East Asian miracle" (World Bank 1993). The four economies are Japan, Republic of Korea, Malaysia, and Taipei,China. The recent history of economic growth and development in all six, particularly in the PRC and—to a lesser extent—in India, suggests that all of these economies could make a significant contribution to another remarkable growth experience.

With respect to their legal history, the six economies have characteristics in common but also reveal important differences. When modernizing their legal system, all six economies borrowed extensively from theWest. Comprehensive law reforms during the nineteenth and early twentieth century borrowed heavily fromWestern legal systems. Two economies, India and Malaysia, received common law from England. The other four economies received legal transplants from the civil law economies of continental Europe, primarily from France and Germany. In addition, three of the economies share a history of administrative guidance, and two economies have experienced state controls that were more extensive than in the other four economies.We present an overview of the similarities and the economies that share these similarities in table 2.1 below.

Table 2.1   Structural Similarities across Six Asian Economies

Similarity	Economies sharing similarities
Early high economic performers	Japan; Republic of Korea; Malaysia; Taipei,China
Latecomers in high economic performance	PRC; India
Common law tradition	India; Malaysia
Civil law tradition	PRC; Japan; Republic of Korea; Taipei,China
Tradition of administrative guidance	Japan; Republic of Korea; Taipei,China
Recent history of extensive state control and state administration of the economy	PRC; India

Source: Authors' compilation.

These similarities should not disguise the fact that in other respects the six economies differ substantially from each other. The most obvious difference is in their size, both in terms of geography and population. The PRC and India are the two giants of Asia; the other four economies are small by comparison. Other differences concern their histories, policies, and rates of development. In 1960, Japan was already a well developed economy, but all the others were in the early stages of economic development. The Republic of Korea had been one of the poorest economies in the world ten years earlier, in 1950.The PRC was a socialist planned economy until 1978. Although India shared a preference for socialist policies for most of the period after independence, it stopped short of full economic planning, nationalization, or the collectivization of agriculture. Finally, each of the six economies has a different political history. Even today they have substantially different political regimes in place.

Each of the factors mentioned above is likely to have a different influence on the role of law in economic development. We have not been able to control for all these factors at all times. By spelling them out up front we hope to draw attention to the complexity of law and the factors that may account for the differences we observe across economies. This also explains why we frequently include individual sections that describe the specific features that are relevant for the analysis separately for each economy.

DESIGN OF THE RESEARCH FRAMEWORK

The comparative findings presented in this report are the results of an interdisciplinary research effort undertaken by legal and economic experts from the six Asian economies as well as the West. The research was based on an outline developed at the outset of the project. In designing the research outline we attempted to address the particular challenges posed by specific economic and legal developments in Asia without losing sight of the general question about the importance of law for economic development. In addressing these issues we looked at both the effect of law on the economy and of the economy on law, starting from a number of premises that are crucial for understanding our approach and the findings.

Effect of Law on the Economy

A key premise was that economic growth is a complex phenomenon. It is the result of the interaction of multiple variables. Macroeconomic growth analyses have made important inroads in assessing the explanatory power of basic growth factors. Basic growth factors represent the underlying fundamentals of economic growth. They may be determined by basic political choices, such as government savings rates, the trade and investment regime, or investments in education and infrastructure. Alternatively they may be determined by natural conditions, including natural resource endowment or geographical location, the latter being important in determining access to other markets. Economic analyses of the sources of growth in Asia have stressed the importance of policy variables for the success of the high performing economies over the past decades (ADB 1997). They have shown that the combined effect of differences in key policy variables such as government savings rates, openness, and institutional quality, accounted for

2.1 percentage points worth of the difference between growth rates in East and South Asia. All three policy variables affect our subject, and we are interested both in the rules that directly reflect the prevailing economic policies and in the basic framework for economic transactions. Moreover, we seek to understand the relation between the two.

The difficulty of doing this is enhanced by the complexity both of economic growth and development and of legal systems with their incremental laws and institutions. The openness of an economy is undoubtedly largely determined by laws and regulations that establish the conditions for cross-border trade and investment. However, this says little about the functioning of an economy's contract law or the effectiveness of legal institutions in enforcing contracts and property rights. It is widely held, especially among foreign investors, that these factors matter, despite the fact that economic growth analyses for the region have said little about the role of law and legal institutions in economic growth and development,.

Foreign investors are typically the most outspoken advocates for strengthening legal institutions and for legal reform. But most economies caught in the development process make substantial efforts to reform their legal framework, not only to please foreign investors, but also to enhance the prospects of domestic entrepreneurs. To account for the apparent importance of law and legal institutions for trade and investment, economists have used survey results of businesses around the world and included them in cross-economy regression analyses (Barro 1994; Knack and Keefer 1994; Mauro 1995; Sachs and Warner 1995). The European Bank for Reconstruction and Development (EBRD) conducts an annual survey, based on the assessment of the legal infrastructure in transition economies by domestic and foreign legal professionals. The results of the statistical analysis show a positive and statistically significant correlation between the effectiveness of the legal system and economic growth. Analysis based on the EBRD data suggests that economies with well functioning legal systems are also among the most successful economic reformers.

These studies provide some evidence about the importance of law in economic growth. Still, many questions remain unanswered. Most surveys are of recent date. We therefore lack time series data to quantify the effect of major changes in the legal system over time. Moreover, survey data reveal the perception of a legal system in the eyes of entrepreneurs, but they say little about the functioning of individual laws or legal institutions and how they affect economic growth factors. To address these questions we have designed our study to include an analysis of the change in legal systems over time and in relation to changes in economic policies. The focus is on the period from 1960 to 1995, but a review of earlier legal reform efforts is included in the analysis. To the broad or macroanalysis of legal and economic change we have added a more detailed microanalysis of laws and related institutions for which we have singled out three areas of the law: business governance, credit and security, and dispute settlement.

Effect of the Economy on Law

A second premise of this study was that to understand the role of law in economic development we needed to understand not only the impact of law on the economy, but also the effect of the economy on law. Social theories have long stressed the importance of the socioeconomic environment for a country's legal system. It has even been stated that the legal system can serve as a mirror of an economy's development or a country's political governance structure. The fact that legal systems grow more complex in the development process has long been noted, and this proposition seems to be supported by the experience in many economies.

The legal development in Asia over the last century reinforces the importance of studying the effect of economic development on law. The reason is that the major legal reforms establishing comprehensive formal legal systems modeled largely on Western law occurred long before Asia's economic takeoff. This makes it difficult to construct a causal relationship between legal and economic development. It also poses numerous questions about the process of assimilating the transplanted laws and institutions into Asian legal and business practice. We propose that the process of socioeconomic change in the period under survey may have facilitated assimilation of largely foreign legal systems that had remained for the most part dormant until that time. To test this proposition, we needed to investigate the impact of socioeconomic change on legal development.

Norms and Rules

A third premise was that the norms and rules that are accepted as "law" differ across economies. We used a broad definition of the term "law" in order to avoid falling into the trap of calling law only what looks like law from a Western perspective. Using such a broad definition proved to be more difficult than expected, because of the lack of empirical data. A broad definition of law should include not only statutory law and legal precedents, but also informal law, including trade practices, informal administrative processes, and traditional norms of behavior. Time constraints and the breadth of the project did not permit us to investigate in detail the extent to which informal rules influence business practice in Asia. We therefore limited the analysis to formal law. Formal law in our analysis includes not only case law and statutory acts passed by the legislature in established procedures, but the whole array of normative pronouncements by the state, including the state administration.

THE DIMENSIONS OF LAW

Even though the study aims to be comprehensive, a detailed analysis of the entire legal system and its relationship to economic development was not possible. We are interested primarily in two dimensions of law. One, which we term the allocative dimension of law, refers to legal rules that stipulate who determines the allocation of economic resources in society. Broadly speaking, this may be either the state or the market. The second dimension of law captures how law is to be promulgated and enforced as well as the functioning of legal and administrative institutions that support the enforcement of law. We call this function the procedural function of law. Lawmaking and law enforcing may be rule-based or discretionary. Rule-based means that state action is bound by law and to be valid, pre-established legal procedures about rule making and rule enforcement have to be complied with. Moreover, in cases where these principles are violated, nonstate actors have recourse to legal review. Discretionary law, by contrast, allows state agents to set rules and enforce them without significant legal constraints. Each dimension of law, allocative and procedural, is continuous.

Lawyers typically use other categories to define different areas of the law. Private or civil law, for example, includes contract, corporate, and property law, or the legal framework for market based transactions. In our two-dimensional classification, these are allocative laws. However, the allocation of resources is determined to a large extent also by rules that are commonly classified as public or administrative laws. These are rules that govern the relationship between the state and citizens or entities and include everything from zoning rules to environmental legislation. These rules limit the extent to which private parties may decide the allocation of resources based on market principles alone and therefore have an allocative dimension. For other areas of the law, the classification of either private or state has become increasingly difficult. An example is antitrust law. The purpose of antitrust rules is primarily to ensure the allocation of resources through competitive markets. To achieve this goal, the relevant state agency has broad authority to intervene in markets, and in some jurisdictions may even force companies to divest. In our classification, antitrust rules are closer to market than to state-allocative law, but they are certainly not simply market-allocative.

Another distinction that is commonly used by lawyers is the distinction between substantive and procedural law. The former refers to laws that define the scope of legal rights and obligations. For example, a company law defines and limits the rights and obligations of shareholders, bestowing on them, among other things, limited liability. Procedural law refers to the rules establishing legal mechanisms needed to enforce these rights and obligations. An administrative law, for example, establishes procedures by which private parties can challenge or compel government action. Obviously, procedural law is a major component of our procedural dimension of law, although we would add that, apart from the formal law itself, the procedural dimension also captures the use and functioning of these mechanisms in practice. There are also overlaps between substantive law and our allocative dimension of law, but the two are not identical. Criminal law and traffic rules are examples of substantive law that would not be captured in our allocative dimension.

For the purpose of our analysis, we will stick primarily to the allocative and procedural dimension of law. However, the use of some technical terms cannot be avoided. For example, all economies have different laws in place that regulate litigation between private parties on the one hand and between private parties and the state on the other hand. The former are referred to as civil litigation, the latter as administrative litigation. We use these terms only descriptively. They themselves say little about where these laws are located along our two dimensions of law. Thus, administrative law may be rule-based or discretionary. Even rules governing administrative litigation may be discretionary rather than rule-based, if, for example, a claimant has little access to these procedures and access is determined by arbitrary rules.

MACROANALYSIS OF LEGAL AND ECONOMIC CHANGE

Chapters 3 and 4 of this book present the macroanalysis of legal and economic change. Chapter 3 is devoted to the concepts used in the analysis and traces the historical roots of the legal systems in the six economies. Chapter 4 describes the major features of the legal system in each economy as of 1960, identifies the major changes in the legal system between 1960 and 1995, and relates these changes to the evolution of the economy during this period.

For each economy we identify major economic policy periods. While one may dispute the exact timing of the beginning of a policy period for a given economy, the policy periods in general follow commonly accepted definitions, such as the period of the heavy and chemical industry drive in the Republic of Korea, or the period of new economic policy in Malaysia. For each economy we analyze the process of legal change and the nature of the laws that were newly adopted, repealed, or enforced perhaps for the first time during this period.

Legal change is not only expressed in the enactment of major new codes. Although this has been the hallmark of the period of legal modernization and reception of Western law, legal change in the period from 1960 to 1995 has been much more incremental. Existing laws were often not repealed, but were altered or superseded by new rules that changed the scope of applicability of the already existing rules.

For the economic analysis, we have used different measures of economic change: economic growth rates, variables that reflect the structural features of the six economies. The variables include the extent of direct state controls over the economy as measured by government expenditures and the size of the state-owned sector; state controls over the allocation of financial resources, including state ownership of financial institutions, interest rate controls, and the use of policy credits; and the extent of state controls over cross-border trade as indicated by exports and imports as well as foreign exchange controls.

MICROANALYSIS OF LEGAL AND ECONOMIC CHANGE

In chapters 5 through 7, we shift the analysis of the relationship between law and economic development from the macro level to a level of analysis with relatively less complexity. We look for links between (a) specific laws and legal institutions and (b) economic growth factors below the macroeconomic level. We refer to these indicators as "intermediate growth factors" (IGFs).

The relationship between the legal system, individual laws and legal institutions, IGFs, and economic development is depicted in figure 2.1 below.

When considering the relevance of the role of law to economic growth, IGFs are attractive, because the link between IGFs and economic growth has been well established both theoretically and empirically and can therefore be assumed. The importance of capital formation and capital allocation, for example, has been detailed by scholars such as Raymond W. Goldsmith (1969), Ronald I. McKinnon (1973), and Joseph Stiglitz (1989). Douglass North (1981, 1990) has provided important evidence for the historical significance of secure property rights for long-term economic growth—rights that result from state policies, especially from the creation of effective property laws. The fact that economic growth is closely associated with an increasing division of labor has been recognized since Adam Smith, and the social implications of this finding were first analyzed systematically by Emile Durkheim.

For economic development in Asia, the World Bank's study of the "East Asian miracle" (1993) provides detailed empirical evidence of the role IGFs play in the economic development of the high performing Asian economies. The study identified several IGFs as important determinants for the success of these economies and identified key elements of the IGFs that we have used in our study. For example, the World Bank's study revealed that high growth rates of physical capital are an integral part of capital formation. Its high rates of domestic savings are an important element of financial intermediation and capital formation. Secure property rights were identified by the World Bank study as a basic condition for the impressive accumulation of physical and human capital in the high-performing Asian economies. The study found that "better technology, better organization, gains from specialization, and innovations on the shop floor" contributed to higher total factor productivity, which refers to the combined effect of capital formation, the division of labor, and secure property rights.

The advantage of using IGFs also becomes apparent when we analyze the reverse causal relationship, or the effect of a country's socioeconomic development on its legal system. For example, secure property rights can be seen as resulting from a historical development that created a constituency demanding better protection of its rights. The IGF division of labor also illuminates the causal link from socioeconomics to law. In complex market economies—by definition, characterized by greater division of labor—laws and legal institutions are more numerous and complex than in preindustrial settings. It has also been suggested that the nature of law changes as a result of the increased division of labor. According to Durkheim (1984 [1893, first French edition]), in societies with a low division of labor, repressive law that relies mostly on punitive sanctions predominates. With an increasing division of labor, these rules are replaced by cooperative rules. Legal sanctions change from being restitutional and become reciprocal. Henry Maine (1977 [1874, first edition]) had earlier recognized a similar change in the nature of law in his now famous quote "from status to contract." These theories are not undisputed. However, the core of these theories, namely, that socioeconomic development influences the nature and contents of law and legal institutions, is widely accepted.

The three areas of the law we have selected for our microanalysis of the role of law in the economic development of Asian economies are business governance, credit and security, and dispute settlement. They represent areas of the law that played a crucial role in the economic development of the West. The organization of firms and, in particular, the emergence of private corporations is closely associated with the spurt in capital formation after industrialization. The growing importance of capital markets has prompted legal reforms aimed at enhancing investors' rights. Credit has been termed the most important invention for capitalism, and the ability to secure credits that are extended to previously unrelated individuals or firms is an important legal underpinning. Legal devices, such as security interests and bankruptcy laws, may reduce the risks creditors face. Finally, institutions that are capable of settling disputes and enforcing their rulings among private parties irrespective of their geographical location, ethnic or professional affiliations, or previous relations have been recognized as an important element of the legal and administrative infrastructure for economic growth and development. At the same time, all three categories involve areas of law that are widely perceived to be different in Asia and the West. They therefore provide excellent cases to test the hypotheses spelled out at the beginning of this chapter. The corresponding IGFs we use for our analysis are capital formation for business governance, lending volume for security interests, and the division of labor for dispute settlement.

Figure 2.1   Relating Legal and Economic Indicators

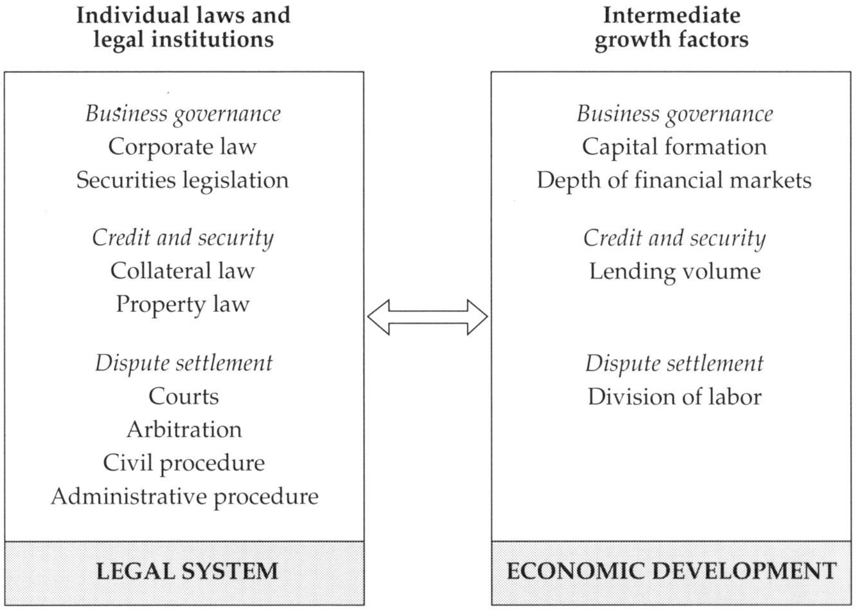

Individual laws and legal institutions	Intermediate growth factors
Business governance Corporate law Securities legislation	*Business governance* Capital formation Depth of financial markets
Credit and security Collateral law Property law	*Credit and security* Lending volume
Dispute settlement Courts Arbitration Civil procedure Administrative procedure	*Dispute settlement* Division of labor
LEGAL SYSTEM	**ECONOMIC DEVELOPMENT**

Source: Authors' compilation.

Chapter 3

LAW AND SOCIOECONOMIC CHANGE

The relationship between law and socioeconomic change has been the subject of much theorizing. In this chapter we review some of the theories. We also point out a major difference in legal development between Asia and the West. Finally, we review existing typologies of legal systems and develop a simplified model that serves as a conceptual framework throughout this report.

MAJOR THEORIES ON LAW AND ECONOMIC CHANGE

Although we lack substantial empirical evidence on the role of law in economic development, there has been a lot of theorizing about this issue. The most influential theories on the role of law in economic development were developed in Europe and assumed an important role during the Enlightenment (Stein 1980; Kelly 1992). In Asia, by contrast, theories on law, legal evolution, and the interaction between legal and economic development played a far less important role. One obvious reason for this is that the most dramatic change in legal and economic relations, the development of capitalism, took place in the West and influenced the world view of Western scholars. Moreover, theories on law are closely related to the concept of authority, and Eastern concepts of authority differ substantially from those in the West (Moore 1966).

Although differing considerably from each other, the major Asian religions and philosophies—Confucianism, Hinduism, and Islam—share similar concepts about the origins and purpose of power. "The dominant view has been that idealized authority existed at the dawn of history and that the main danger of primitive power lies ahead, when there may be a breakdown of established authority"(Pye and Pye 1985). It is the task of the established authority to maintain order. An important implication of the concept that perfect order, under a godlike authority, existed in the past is the idealization of authority in general. Power is a desirable necessity for upholding order. This idea of authority reflects a static view of social order that was reinforced by the preeminence of united central authorities, such as the "Son of Heaven" in China and the godlike ruler of India. In Western thinking, on the other hand, the creation of the state and the emergence of law is viewed as a positive progression from an anarchic state of nature to more refined systems of authority in which the state itself increasingly becomes subject to legal controls.

From the many theories and statements that have been made by Western philosophers and scholars of law, sociology, anthropology, and economics we may distill three core theories that have greatly influenced the current thinking about law and socioeconomic development in their tendency to converge both with each other and between economies or cultures.

Evolutionary Theory

First, there is a wide range of evolutionary theory predicting that law develops over time and in interaction with changes in the socioeconomic environment. Classic proponents of this view include Adam Smith, Henry Maine, Max Weber and Emile Durkheim.[1] The core of these theories is most closely associated with Weber and Durkheim. In Weber's view, one can identify four important factors that contribute to the emergence of capitalism in the West: (1) private appropriation of all the means of production; (2) freedom of labor; (3) free movement of goods without noneconomic or irrational restrictions; and (4) a calculable law, both in adjudication and public administration. In Weber's analysis, it is the bureaucratic system rather than economic conditions that precedes change and facilitates the development of capitalism. Weber also recognized the importance of culture and tradition in legal development and the functioning of state bureaucracies and legal institutions. With respect to China, for example, he noted that the administration of justice in traditional China was a type of patriarchal obliteration of the line between justice and administration.

Durkheim's analysis provides a different view of the relationship between legal and economic development. He hypothesized that the division of labor resulting from economic development leads to a high ratio of cooperative legal rules over penal and repressive legal rules and raises the demand for rules and institutions that facilitate dispute settlement among previously unrelated parties.

Douglass North's theory of institutional change and economic performance (North 1990) is a modern version of evolutionary theory that leans away from convergence. North draws a picture of evolutionary change and continuity which does not exclude the possibility of convergence between economies, but which suggests that a high level of continuity may result from constraints imposed by path dependent institutional change. Increasing returns for some institutional arrangements as opposed to others may ensure that economies with different institutional arrangements diverge persistently.

---

[1]   A summary of Western legal theory can be found in Kelly (1992) and Stein (1980). See also Trubek (1972) for a detailed analysis of Weber's thinking on law and economic development.

Some institutional arrangements may be conducive to economic prosperity, while others may diminish an economy's prospect for growth.

Cultural Theory

Other theories view cultural factors as the major determinants for legal systems. A number of theorists and philosophers, foremost among them Montesquieu, have suggested that law and legal evolution are part of the idiosyncratic historical development of a country, and that they are determined by multiple factors, including culture, geography, climate, and religion. Although law is by no means static, legal evolution in each country is distinct and will produce vastly different outcomes. Far from converging over time, legal institutions remain different. The idea that law is culturally distinct applies as much to the law governing private transactions ("les lois civiles") as to "les lois politiques"—constitutional law, administrative law, and judicial procedural law—the legal processes that define the relation between the state and citizens. The same idea is also reflected in the writings of the German scholar Friedrich Carl von Savigny (1814), who argued that the soul of the people, the "Volksgeist," shapes political and legal institutions. Theories that view cultural differences as the cause of Asia's distinct path to economic success and proponents of the distinct Asian approach to law also represent this view.

Utilitarian Theory

Finally, utilitarian theorists see law as an instrument to be used to promote economic development. Since Jeremy Bentham's writings in the early nineteenth century, law has been increasingly viewed not as the result of socioeconomic development, but as a tool for governments to initiate and shape economic development. The most famous proponent of this school of thought is John Stuart Mill, who coined the term "utilitarianism (Stein, 1980)." According to his theory, law can and should be designed to enhance efficiency and to reduce transaction costs, ultimately promoting growth. This theory assumes that legal change has a direct impact on the behavior of economic agents and therefore on economic development.

The evolutionary, cultural, and utilitarian theories are not mutually exclusive. Different areas of the law may develop along different paths. Some may converge in form and substance, and may in the long term even lead to similar legal practice between economies. Others may be more path dependent and slow to change. Opinions on which areas of the law would experience convergence have changed over time. Family law, for example, which is closely associated with culture, has witnessed an unprecedented period of convergence especially after World War II. This convergence is largely attributed to socioeconomic change. In analyzing the reasons for the patterns of continuity and change affecting different areas of the law, comparative scholars have begun to shift their attention from culturally embedded laws to politically embedded laws. Kahn-Freund (1974), for example, argued that in most substantive areas of the law we are witnessing a "flattening out of economic and cultural diversity." By contrast, in Kahn-Freund's view, countries continue to diverge with respect to laws that "are designed to allocate power, rule making, decision making, above all, policymaking power." However, the areas of the law he singled out as an example for persistent divergence, including individual and collective labor law, have witnessed substantial convergence since (de Roo and Jagtenberg 1994).

Moreover, some laws may lend themselves better than others to a utilitarian approach of using law as a tool to achieve socioeconomic change and improve efficiency. Changes in tax laws, customs regulations, and laws that govern the inflow of foreign investments have measurable impact on economic growth variables. By contrast, changes in contract law or property rights may change behavior only in the long term.

Finally, law may turn out to be incidental to economic development. Formal legal systems may be only one of several mechanisms that govern transactions among economic agents, or the relationship between the state and its citizens. Others include family ties, or a paternalistic state which promotes economic development, but whose power remains de jure or de facto unconstrained by law.

LEGAL EVOLUTION AND LEGAL TRANSPLANTS IN ASIAN ECONOMIC DEVELOPMENT

The theories about law and social change mentioned view the process of legal change primarily as an evolutionary process that interacts with a similarly evolutionary process of social and economic development. This view is based primarily on the European experience, although even there, it is not always congruent with historical facts. Much of the modern European law developed over centuries in interaction with the expansion of markets and innovations in the organization and financing of firms. The reception of Roman law has been part of this development. It denotes the process by which the classic Roman law, in particular the compilation of the writings of the classical Roman jurists into the *Digestes* under Justinian (527–65 CE) were rediscovered in the twelfth century and came to influence legal scholarship and legal practice. The church played a crucial role in the reception of Roman law as the rulings of the ecclesiastical authority (canon law) were system-atized in accordance with Roman legal principles. Because of the extensive jurisdiction of the church not only over matters related to marriage and fam-ily, but also over matters of economic importance, such as succession, this greatly influenced legal practice. Thus, Roman law became influential long before the enactment of the great codifications in the nineteenth century, which made explicit use of this historical source of law. However, the codifications also drew heavily from actual legal practice. For many areas of the law the actual contribution of Roman law was less its content, but its organization of legal principles into a consistent and comprehensive system. Although much of Europe's legal history was evolutionary, Europe also experienced more radical changes in legal systems. An example is the enactment of the Napole-onic codes in much of central and east Europe as a consequence of Napole-onic invasion. In many countries, these codes remained in place even after the troops were withdrawn.

In contrast to continental Europe, but also to Scotland, the influence of Roman law on England's legal development has been more attenuated. The hallmark of English common law is the absence of systematic codifications of the type introduced in continental Europe in the nineteenth and twentieth centuries, and the reliance on cases as a primary source of law. As a result, courts have traditionally played a much more influential role in English com-mon law than in civil law systems. The difference between case law and statu-tory law appears to be diminishing as common law countries are increasingly adopting statutory laws and civil law countries discover the need for exten-sive interpretations of existing positive law. However, differences in legal pro-cesses that result from the different role legal institutions, such as the courts and the legal profession have traditionally played in common as opposed to civil law systems, still characterize the two major Western legal systems (Merryman 1985).

In Asia, the evolutionary process of legal and socioeconomic develop-ment was disrupted in the last century as the result of imperialism. The cre-ation of colonial empires led to a proliferation of Western legal systems in Asia. Other Asian countries, which had not been colonized, responded to the threat posed by the Western powers by modernizing their legal systems. In this process they borrowed heavily from the West.

As a result, much of the formal legal framework of the six Asian econo-mies in our sample is derived from Western law. The reception of foreign law is not unique to Asia. The history of legal transplants is as old as law itself (Watson 1974). However, the transplantation of entire legal systems within a relatively short period of time to countries with a very different cultural, eco-nomic, and sociopolitical background was unprecedented. Even though many adaptations were made in the process of enacting laws that were modeled after Western laws, the formal legal systems of many countries today look fairly familiar to a lawyer trained in Western law.

LEGAL TRANSPLANTS BEFORE 1960

The reception of Western law by Asian countries took place in the second half of the nineteenth and the first half of the twentieth centuries. Political factors, which included the military and economic conquest by Western powers, greatly influenced not only the source of law but the scope of legal change. The history until 1960 of legal transplants in each country in our sample is outlined in a series of tables attached to this chapter as an appendix.

Two of the economies in our sample, India and Malaysia, received English law after British administration was established over their territories (appendix tables 3A.1 and 3A.2). By contrast, Japan independently adopted Western law primarily from French and German sources in an attempt to modernize its legal system and to fend off foreign pressure (appendix table 3A.3). From Japan, this new law was transferred to the island of Taiwan, which came under Japanese occupation in 1895 and to Korea where Japan established a protectorate in 1905 and subsequently colonial rule in 1910 (appendix tables 3A.4 and 3A.5). China, in a move similar to Japan's, made a major effort first at the very beginning of this century during the ultimately failed restoration and then again during the 1920s to transplant codifications from the West (appendix table 3A.6). Continental European and in particular German law again served as the primary source for these transplants. In all cases, legal transplants were quite comprehensive. They included not only substantive laws, but also laws on legal institutions and processes, such as court organization and judicial procedural laws.

The reception of foreign law was not a new phenomenon in southeast Asia. Indian law prior to British rule, for example, was influenced by Roman legal forms and principles and Islamic law dominated many of the territories that were later to become Malaysia.

The transfer of legal institutions and processes as opposed to the transfer of substantive law has often been decisive in changing the existing legal system. This can be demonstrated in the case of Malaysia. In contrast to India and many other British colonies, a comprehensive transfer of substantive English law did not take place at the time the territories that comprise Malaysia came under British rule. However, subject to the treaties that established British rule, a court system was established. These courts, staffed with British jurists often refused to apply local law, in particular Islamic law, and instead relied on English precedents and rules (Hooker 1988). In addition, British influence in the state and federal councils ensured the incorporation of English laws in the promulgation of new statutory law. A more comprehensive transfer of English substantive law took place only shortly before independence in 1957.

The emphasis on the judiciary and legal procedures is more pronounced in common law jurisdictions, where the judiciary is allowed to take more initiative in the lawmaking process than in civil law countries. To some extent, these different traditions are reflected in the Asian countries that received Western law from different sources. With respect to the contents of economic law, by contrast, the distinction between common law and civil law has had little bearing on the development of the legal systems in Asia. We therefore refer to the specific country source and refrain from grouping countries into legal families as proposed by the comparative law tradition.

Among the countries that chose to adopt Western law, Japan set a first example for radical and far reaching law reform, which included laws on the government and judicial institutions. The choice of the model for legal transplants, both for substantive law and for legal processes and institutions, was largely determined by the functioning of the latter in the model country. Japan had already drafted a civil code based on French models, but it subsequently shifted to German law. An important reason for this turnaround was the political development in France in the 1870s—the establishment of the Paris Commune and the renewed quest for democracy—which stood in contrast to the conservative and stable constitutional monarchy in Germany where the parliament exercised comparatively little control over the monarch (Oda 1992). The fact that Germany had just completed a first draft of its civil code facilitated the transfer. The clearest evidence for the importance of political considerations for the choice of the model country is that the Prussian constitution of 1850, which sought to restore the authority of the monarchy subsequent to the revolutionary events of 1848, was chosen as a model for the new Japanese constitution of 1889.

From Japan, the new laws were transferred to other parts of Asia as part of Japan's own efforts to establish a colonial empire. The island of Taiwan was ceded to Japan in 1895. As of 1989, the laws in force in Japan generally applied, although the governor had the authority to issue additional rules and regulations that served the colonial power. It took until the early 1920s for the entire body of commercial law to become applicable on the island. Significantly, independent courts or administrative legal procedures, which Japan had also received from the West, were not part of the legal transplantation. Similarly, Korea received European civil law via Japan. This process had begun already in the decade prior to the establishment of Japanese colonial rule in Korea and accelerated after 1910.

In China, first efforts to modernize the legal system drew heavily on legal experts from Japan and elsewhere. However, the committees in charge of drafting the civil, criminal, and commercial codes that were finally enacted in the early 1930s were staffed primarily with Chinese legal experts. They referred to many foreign sources, but tried to integrate them with long established Chinese legal principles. Overall, the influence of German/Japanese civil law appears to have been dominant in China until the PRC was established in 1949.

The comprehensive reception of Western law influenced the formal legal system in all six countries prior to World War II. The contents of substantive economic laws and legal processes were determined initially by the source of these transplants. Subsequently, the influence of the original donor country has become less important as countries began to borrow from multiple sources. Malaysia, for example, sought to distance itself from colonial law by increasingly borrowing from other common law sources. US law was brought to Japan under American occupation following World War II. From there it was transferred to the Republic of Korea, which used Japanese models when revising its own laws.

LEGAL CHANGE AND LEGAL TRANSPLANTS, 1960–1995

Between 1960 and 1995, the legal systems of the six economies underwent major changes. The most fundamental change occurred in the PRC where, after the introduction of economic reforms in 1978, a new legal system was created virtually from scratch. China had modernized its legal system during the 1920s and 1930s (as noted above). Most of these laws were abolished when the PRC was established. During the first years of communist rule in the PRC a substantial amount of legal reform took place based on revolutionary Chinese and Soviet models. However, this trend was reversed with the Antirightist Campaign in the late 1950s. By 1960, the PRC had successfully dismantled much of its legal system. The new legal system created after 1978 relied to some extent on the legal reforms introduced during the first decades of communist rule. The PRC also made substantial use of laws and legal concepts of various other countries with different legal systems, including common law and civil law systems.

In the other five economies of the study, as the process of legal borrowing from foreign sources continued after the earlier wholesale transplant of legal systems, such economies' borrowings from foreign sources were primarily supplementary. They occurred mostly after World War II and augmented new areas of the law for which a legal framework had not yet been established, or areas where earlier laws proved ineffective. The areas of law most affected by legal borrowing in the period from 1960 to 1995 include antimonopoly rules (competition), environmental and consumer protection (including product liability), the law governing intellectual property rights (IPRs), and securities and exchange regulations. The reasons for the introduction of these legal innovations differ from country to country and for different areas of the law. In some cases, legal transfers were imported as part of technical assistance programs. In others, law reform was initiated after crisis situations, such as environmental disasters or blatant misuses of monopoly power, that created an awareness of structural problems that needed to be addressed. A striking feature of the history of these legal transplants is that most of them were left unenforced for years after they had been enacted. This is true for the antimonopoly legislation first introduced in Japan in 1947, for the securities and exchange rules that were enacted in Taipei,China and the Republic of Korea in the 1960s, and for the earlier enactment of laws governing IPRs. Domestic policies at times favored industry concentration and therefore bypassed existing antitrust rules or led to a change of these rules. Governments favored a financial system that was centered around banks, which were often controlled by the state, rather than markets; the effect was to reduce the attractiveness of capital markets. Finally, environmental protection legislation passed to comply with international treaties also tended to be weakly enforced. A turning point in the enforcement of these recent legal transplants in most countries was when domestic interests called for the enforcement, and often for extensive revisions, of these laws. Even then, the effectiveness of law enforcement often depended on political support. In the sections that follow we review the history of legal reforms after 1960 that involved transplants in the four areas of the law under discussion. Their chronology is summarized, with their sources, in table 3.1 below.

Competition Law

Industry concentration and the misuse of monopolistic power was not an issue of great concern in most economies for much of the time after 1960. The first antitrust law in the region, the Japanese Antimonopoly Act, was introduced in 1947 under American occupation. It was part of the American strategy to ensure that the efforts to decartellize the economy by dissolving the large family centered business conglomerates (zaibatsu) would have long lasting effect. Not only did this law remain unenforced, but Japan substantially amended the law in 1953, in order to adapt it to Japanese circumstances. More than 20 years later, in 1976, the Antimonopoly Act was amended again, this time primarily in response to domestic forces seeking improved antitrust enforcement in the wake of the oil cartel cases of the early 1970s. Many provisions were strengthened, but the actual enforcement of the law remained

Table 3.1 Major Legal Transplants, 1960–1995

Economy	Antitrust		Product Liability		IPR		SEC	
	Year	Source of law	Year	Source of law	Year	Source of law	Year	Source of law
PRC	—	—	—	—	1982	G	1992	Multiple
							1960	E
							1988	US
India	1970	E	—	—	1968	E	1992	US
	1947	US						
	1953	US						
Japan	1977	US	1986	US, EC	1990s	Int'l A	1950	US
							1963	US
							1977	US
							1983	US
Korea, Republic of	1980	US, G, J	—		1986	Int'l A	1988	US
					1969	N	1973	E/A
Malaysia	—		1975	E	1986	Int'l A	1993	US
		G, US, J		US			1960	US
Taipei,China	1992	K	1994	EC, J	1983–1995	Int'l A	1988	US

— = not available
Index: A = Australia; G = Germany; E = England; EC = European Community; I = India; Int'l A = International Agreement; J = Japan; K = Republic of Korea; N = Nigeria; US = United States.
Source: Team reports.

weak. By 1985 the total number of criminal prosecutions initiated by the Japanese Fair Trade Commission amounted to not more than six cases, only two of which were directed against cartels (Ramseyer 1985).

In India, the constitution provided that the state should counter the concentration of wealth and means of production to the benefit of the common good. In pursuance of this objective, India adopted the Monopolies and Restrictive Trade Practices Act in 1969 and established a commission to enforce it. The purpose of the law was to prevent the concentration of power in the economy. However, government undertakings, including state-owned enterprises, which played an increasingly important role in the Indian economy, were explicitly excluded from this law. In light of the expanding state ownership and other forms of state control this meant that large parts of the economy were in fact exempted from the application of the law. This was not changed in subsequent revisions of the law.

The Republic of Korea first enacted a law dealing with unfair and restrictive business practice—the Price Stabilization and Fair Trade Act—in 1975. The primary emphasis of this law was on price stabilization enforced through price controls. In addition, the law prohibited unfair trade practices such as the hoarding and cornering of staple goods, and provided a legal basis for the government to monitor and intervene in individual product markets. However, the law was not used to counter monopolistic tendencies in the economy. In fact, the concentration of economic power increased rather than decreased after the enactment of the 1975 law. The legal basis for antitrust enforcement was substantially improved with the adoption of a new law after the concentration of economic power had become a political concern at the end of the heavy chemical and industry drive. The 1980 Monopoly Regulation and Fair Trade Act borrowed from several sources including the US, Germany, and Japan. It was the first true antitrust law and was primarily the result of domestic developments. Nevertheless, the actual enforcement of the law did not meet expectations. Additional changes were introduced in 1986, 1990, 1992, 1994, and most recently in 1996. Most significant was the 1986 amendment, which inserted provisions into the law that were designed to restrict the diversification and expansion of big Korean conglomerates (chaebol). Provisions aimed at ensuring greater independence for the Korean Fair Trade Commission were incorporated in the statute in the 1994 amendment. Over the last years, enforcement practice appears to have been improved, but the signs of a more effective enforcement of antimonopoly legislation are still tentative.

The other economies have followed suit only much later. Taipei,China enacted its first fair trade law in 1992. This law borrowed not only from Western countries, but also from Japan and the Republic of Korea. It also established a fair trade commission to administer fines and initiate criminal investigations. Certain acts of state-owned enterprises were exempted from the application of the law. However, this exemption expired in 1996. The effectiveness of this law and the political commitment to antitrust policies remain to be tested. In the PRC, a law on unfair competition was enacted in 1993. However, this law does not address the problem of counteracting monopolistic tendencies. Finally, Malaysia to this date does not have an antimonopoly law in place. First initiatives to enact such a law were launched as late as 1994.

Environmental and Consumer Protection Law

Domestic events were primarily responsible for the transplantation of laws for environmental and consumer protection, including product liability. The effects of industrialization, including water and air pollution and safety issues of new products placed on the markets, were seen to call for legislative intervention. Many countries reacted to ecological and human disasters by enacting their first comprehensive environmental protection legislation. The most vivid example is India, where the Bhopal tragedy of 1984 led to the inclusion in the Factories Act of 1987 of a whole chapter dealing with hazardous processes. Additional rules concerning environmental protection were also passed: theWater Protection Act (1974), the Environmental Protection Act (1986), and the Air Pollution Act (1981). Product liability rules were included in the 1986 Consumer Protection Act.

Similarly, the incidence of damage caused by new products increased with the introduction of mass production and the release of a greater number of new products. Japan was the first country to enact a comprehensive consumer protection act in 1968 that established health and safety standards. Legislative changes that allowed consumers to take direct action against producers followed in 1986. These changes were enacted in response to domestic demands. Substantial support was provided by the enactment of the European Community (EC) directive on product liability, as this mitigated Japanese fears that the country would place itself at a comparative disadvantage vis-a-vis the EC with the adoption of product liability legislation. The new law borrowed from the EC directive as well as from US law.[2] Consumer protection was not limited to establishing health standards and providing consumers with effective remedies against defective products. Many countries in theWest increasingly sought to protect consumers against aggressive marketing strategies, including doorstep deals and installment sales. Japan followed this trend and enacted relevant laws in the first part of the 1970s.

In 1980, the Republic of Korea enacted its consumer protection act and the Monopoly Regulation and Fair Trade Act. The two together signaled the

---

[2]   In the US, product liability law developed primarily through case law.

Republic of Korea's departure from a primarily growth oriented development strategy to a market economy based on competition and on the interests of consumers rather than producers. Indeed, the legislation can be seen as a response to the emergence of a mass production society and as a sign of the increasing affluence of consumers. Additional consumer protection legislation was enacted after 1980. It included rules governing bargain sales, the offering of premiums, aggressive marketing practices, and mail order sales. Like the Japanese laws, the Republic of Korea's legislation relies primarily on bureaucratic means to enforce the interests of consumers. The national and local governments are mandated to enact new laws and regulations, and to establish administrative organizations whose purpose is to protect the interests of consumers. Moreover, governments are obliged to establish and operate a consumer compensation system. The two major institutions established for realizing the Consumer Protection Law, for example, were the Consumer Policy Deliberation Committee and the Consumer Protection Board (CPB). Within the CPB a special arbitration tribunal for disputes concerning consumer interests was established, which also provides a procedural right for consumers who seek recourse against businesses. Apparently, direct recourse by consumers is more frequently invoked than government sponsored compensation schemes.

In Taipei,China the first environmental protection law was passed in 1975 with the adoption of the Air Pollution Act. Beginning in the early 1980s, several other laws to reduce water pollution and noise and to improve waste management were also adopted. In 1987, an environmental protection agency was established, and in 1994 a comprehensive law on environmental protection was adopted. A consumer protection law was adopted in 1994 borrowing from Western models. The law provides, among other things, for strict liability for product and safety defects, and product recall. Moreover, it allows the government to take legal action as a representative of consumers.

For other areas of the law, the stimulus to enact new laws came primarily from outside. This is the case for the early securities and exchange legislation in several countries in our sample, as well as for comprehensive revisions and additions to the laws governing the protection of IPRs.

Intellectual Property Law

With respect to IPRs, all six economies had a basic legal framework on the books before 1960. However, in many countries, as with other laws, these were not enforced. This was the case particularly in PRC, India, and Republic of Korea. The enforcement of these laws was perceived to benefit primarily foreign investors and to disadvantage the domestic industry. For this reason, some countries narrowed the scope of the legal rights that transplanted laws had offered or they provided only weak enforcement. India and the Republic of Korea, for example, explicitly excluded pharmaceutical substances from the application of patent laws, although processes could be patented. Moreover, India amended the Patent and Design Act in 1968 to provide that the central government may interfere to delay the grant of a patent in the public interest. Further amendments in 1970s narrowed the definition of patentable inventions. Nevertheless, subsequent change occurred often in response to pressure from trading partners and in order to comply with international treaties. Furthermore, in the case of the Republic of Korea the growing domestic demand for the protection of IPRs was of at least equal importance for the strengthening of the IPR regime in 1986. In India, a comprehensive amendment to the Copyright Act was passed in 1995, paving the way for improved protection of IPRs.

Taipei,China's history of improving IPR protection is similar. Until the mid-1980s, it was not a major concern. Although counterfeiting was not uncommon, it only became a problem when Taipei,China emerged as a major exporter and the economy sought to improve its competitive edge in high-tech products. For trading partners, this required the effective protection of IPRs. The proceedings of the Uruguay Round added to the pressure for change. Between 1983 and 1995 the existing legal framework for IPRs, which had been put in place between 1928 and 1944, was revised and new laws were added to meet these standards.

Japan had already strengthened the legal regime for IPRs in the early 1970s, at least partly as a result of domestic pressures as Japanese producers sought to protect their innovations. Another important revision was introduced in early 1990s in order to comply with revisions of international treaties.

The main reason for the reform of IPR law in Malaysia in1969 was to unify the different laws that were in force in the Federation of Malaysia at that time. The Federated Malay States had adopted a copyright act in 1911 based on early English models. Sarawak and North Borneo used the UK Copyright Act of 1956 before becoming part of the Federation of Malaysia in 1963. The new unified law for the federation was modeled closely after the Nigerian copyright bill. Subsequently, this law was amended to comply with evolving international standards for the protection of IPRs, and to satisfy foreign investors who were using Malaysia as a processing and reexporting base and demanded effective protection of technology transfers.

The PRC enacted a trademark law in 1982 and a patent law in 1984. The trademark law was amended in the early 1990s and, in addition, a copyright law was adopted. These changes appear to have been primarily targeted at foreign investors who demanded better protection (Alford 1995). In India, the development of the legal regime for IPRs has lagged far behind. First signs that the official position concerning the protection of IPRs is changing appeared in 1995 with an announcement by the prime minister vowing to improve patent protection. However, so far this has not been reflected in legislative change.

Securities Law

The transplantation of the legal framework for securities and exchange regulations in the six economies came in two waves. First, in the early decades of the Cold War, the US tried to endow Japan, Republic of Korea, and Taipei,China with the institutional frameworks that would allow them to embark on a market based capitalist economic development path; as part of this effort, the US transplanted securities and exchange regulations to these three economies. Only in Japan had a stock market existed already prior to American occupation, and its exchange started to play an important role in the 1970s. Stock market development in the Republic of Korea and Taipei,China was slow and accelerated only after 1980. Both economies then moved to amend their laws to support this trend. In this process they again borrowed from foreign sources, primarily from the US. India already had a basic framework for stock market regulations in place in 1960, based on English law. In Malaysia, a new legal framework relying primarily on English law was established in 1960. However, both economies changed their legal regime substantially after the mid-1980s. They centralized the state's oversight over capital markets and vested it with a newly created state agency, similar to the US model. Thus the second wave of regulatory transplants occurred after the markets became more important both domestically and internationally, as economies increasingly competed to attract foreign portfolio investment.

Several patterns emerge from this overview. First, the US played a key role as a source of law particularly for securities market regulations, and also for antitrust law and product liability rules. The impact of US sources is even stronger if we consider that German antitrust law, the major non-Asian source that was used as a model for antitrust law, had also borrowed extensively from the US following World War II. Similarly, the EC directive on product liability was influenced by American product liability law.

Second, countries have not only borrowed from the West, but also from countries in other regions, including other Asian countries. These models offered adaptations of Western legislation to the circumstances in Asia or in other developing economies. A case in point is the antimonopoly legislation of the Republic of Korea and Taipei,China. The Republic of Korea, which adopted its first major antimonopoly law in 1980, borrowed from the US and Germany, as well as from Japan. Taipei,China, which followed suit in 1992, also incorporated elements of the Korean law. When adopting its product liability law, Taipei,China copied not only from the US and the EC, but also from Japan, which had earlier enacted a similar law, borrowing from the US and EC sources. Another interesting example is Malaysia. After independence, it turned increasingly to common law countries other than the UK for reforming its legal system. Australian law became a major source of Malaysian law for company and banking legislation. For the 1969 copyright law, the Nigerian copyrights bill served as a model, after earlier drafts relying on the laws of the UK and New Zealand had been discarded.

Third, a comparison of the preference for different sources of law across economies shows that although civil law economies have increasingly borrowed from non-civil-law economies, in particular the US, the reverse has not been the case. This does not seem to be the result of particular features of either common law or civil law systems, but reflects the fact that for many new areas of the law developed in modern industrialized nations the US has been at the forefront of legal innovation. Although many of the new legal principles were first developed by case law, they were ultimately incorporated into statutory law, which facilitated their transferability. Finally, IPR law has become primarily a matter of international law. With the finalization of the Uruguay Round, the formal law has converged across countries, even though the enforcement of this law may differ considerably from country to country.

The history of legal transplants in Asia both before and after 1960 reveals interesting variations in practice in the pattern of transplantation and assimilation. Laws can be transplanted for a variety of reasons and external factors have played an important role in promoting transplantation. Foreign occupation— or the threat of foreign occupation—played an important role in the earlier transplantation of legal systems. Since 1960, technical legal assistance programs and compliance with international treaties have become more important. Moreover, after 1960 domestic forces have become more prevalent in legal change that made use of foreign sources. In many cases legal transplants have remained dormant for a long time. This is the case for the transplants of legal systems at the end of the nineteenth and early twentieth centuries, as well as for the transplantation of antitrust and securities exchange laws in some of the economies in our sample in the 1950s and 1960s. A lack of domestic demand for these laws appears to be largely responsible for this. It has often been suggested that the Western origin of these rules prevented their assimilation in Asian legal practice. Although this may be true to some extent, our results suggest that prevailing economic policies often stood in the way of the assimilation process. With changes in economic policies and subsequent economic development, a demand for formal legal rules and institutions to enforce them developed. Throughout much of Asia's legal history, legal change preceded economic development. The fact that many transplanted laws lay dormant for years appears to be less an indicator of cultural differences between East and West than of an economic environment that was not at all times conducive to providing a legal framework for market based transactions. With changes in economic policies, the process of assimilating formal law into practice has caught on.

TYPOLOGIES OF LEGAL SYSTEMS

Taken at face value, the fact that Asian legal development was heavily influenced by the reception of Western law may suggest convergence of legal systems. However, such an assessment would assume that the body of law that was copied and incorporated into the Asian legal system not only influenced the specific rules that were transplanted, but transformed the entire legal system. We define a legal system as a complex set of substantive rules, legal processes, and legal institutions. Not only does it consist of the formal law enshrined in the constitutions, statutes, and precedents, but it also includes the legal practices by state and nonstate agents that may or may not follow the formal law. To assess the real impact of transplanted laws we need to analyze change beyond selected legal rules in the entire legal system.

Existing Typologies of Legal Systems

Scholars, among them Emile Durkheim (1984 [1893 first edition in French]), Max Weber (1980 [1921 first edition in German]), and more recently, Roberto M. Unger (1976), have long sought to explain the relationship between legal systems and socioeconomic change using various typologies that go beyond the schematic classification of private and public law.[3]

Durkheim's analysis rests primarily on the distinction between "repressive" and "restitutory" law. Overall, less developed societies appear to have a higher proportion of repressive law characterized by criminal sanctions. In complex societies with substantial division of labor, restitutory law dominates. Restitutory law is characterized by cooperative rules, the development of which is a result of the division of labor. Cooperative rules are not limited to contractual law, but also apply to family, commercial, administrative, and constitutional laws. Thus, not the area of the law but its nature determines the classification of law. Both private and public law can be either restitutory or repressive and both types of law typically coexist. However, one type typically dominates, which can be largely attributed to the process of socioeconomic change.

---

[3] For a critique of the application of typologies derived from Western theories, especially Unger's view of Chinese legal history in Asia, see Alford (1986).

In his analysis of the sociology of law, Weber links the nature of law to the political governance structure rather than to economic conditions. A rational legal system is closely related to the emergence of a rational, well trained, and fully professional bureaucracy. The link to economic factors is more indirect. Ever more complex economic relations require the professionalization of the bureaucracy as well as the legal profession, thus reinforcing the trend toward rationalization of law. Basic elements of rational law include the generality of legal norms and their organization into a logical system without major gaps or contradictions. To determine the rationality of a legal system, the way in which law is applied is as important as the contents. Irrationality of law can be the result of irrational formal procedures, as is the case when factors that are beyond reasoning—such as oracles—are used to apply a legal rule. The irrationality of law can also be the result of substantive irrationality; that is, when, instead of general norms, ethical, emotional, or political circumstances become the basis for legal decisions. A rational legal system is characterized by its formal legality. Such a rational legal system may consist of legal norms that can be prescriptive, prohibitive, or permissive. Prescriptive norms attempt to achieve a certain behavior; prohibitive norms seek to prevent one from doing something; permissive norms endow one with the legal right to do certain things. According to Weber, for the development of capitalism, permissive legal rules, which are also referred to as contractual law, were crucial. They enabled economic agents to conclude contracts for a variety of purposes either in their own name or as representatives for others. This has facilitated the diversification of economic activities.

The prevalence of permissive, or contractual, law in Weber's view is not simply the product of economic development. "Economic conditions do not automatically give birth to new legal reforms, but provide only a chance for a legal invention which once made will proliferate" (Weber 1980 [1921], p. 412). To Weber, the important modern legal invention was the rationalization of the political governance structure, which gave recognition to formal equality before the law. This facilitated the rationalization of the entire legal system and the professionalization of law.

The extent to which different countries have achieved a rational legal system is, according to Weber, largely dependent on the existing political governance structure (*Herrschaftsstruktur*). Governance structures, such as autocracies, theocracies, and some forms of democracy, are not conducive to the development of a rational legal system because they do not accept formal constraints, including constraints they may have established themselves. The motives for the lack of accepted formal constraints may vary. They are different in the patrimonial welfare state—exemplified by Prussia of Frederick the Great—than in theocratic India or in the democratic theories of socialist revolutionaries. The emphasis on formal, or legal, constraints on power is also important for the assessment of the bureaucratic governance structure. Weber acknowledges the danger of self-perpetuating bureaucracy which thrives on its accumulation of information and regulatory power. The major constraints on the power of bureaucracies of this type are coalitions among other branches of the state (e.g., between the constitutional monarch and the legislature), and the private economy whose knowledge in economic matters far exceeds that of the bureaucracy.

In his critique of the classic social theorists Roberto Unger distinguishes three concepts of law: customary law; bureaucratic, or regulatory law; and legal order. Customary law is defined as "any recurring mode of interaction among individuals and groups, together with the more or less explicit acknowledgment by these groups and individuals that such patterns of interaction produce reciprocal expectations of conduct that ought to be satisfied" (Unger 1976, p. 49). Customs are not in writing (not positive) and are typically inarticulate. This type of law is contrasted with regulatory, or bureaucratic, law that is both positive and expressive. The existence of bureaucratic law presupposes the existence of a state with rulemaking and rule-enforcing capacity. The state, or interest groups that control the state, can use law as an instrument of power. Bureaucratic law is not encompassing, but coexists with customary law as well as with the third concept of law, the legal order. This third concept of law in Unger's classification refers to the emergence of the liberal state and its adherence to the generality in lawmaking and uniformity in the application of law. The autonomy of the legal system gives it the appearance of independence from the political and economic system. Specialized institutions make, apply, and enforce the law and offer recourse against unlawful action. Legal order results not simply from the political interests of rulers, but presupposes and reinforces the existence of a pluralistic society. It reflects the often antagonistic interests that exist in such a society.

While Durkheim and Weber in their own times heralded the advent of what Unger calls legal order, Unger's critique in the early 1970s is based on his assessment of the postliberal order. He emphasizes the discrepancy between the ideal of the rule of law, its autonomy and generality, on the one hand, and, on the other, the reality of life, which reflects a society divided into interest groups with different access to political and economic power. Unger concludes that the major features of a legal order based on the rule of law, including the generality of lawmaking and the division of power, are not inherently democratic, but "can help promote an oligarchic or dictatorial monopoly of power" (Unger 1976, p. 191). In the postliberal society the emergence of the welfare state leads to the disintegration of the rule of law. The inclusion of open-ended norms that leave substantial discretion to the state officials in charge of applying and implementing these norms requires value judgments on the part of the judiciary rather than the formal deduction of legal principles.

It also places greater emphasis on substantive justice or what Weber calls the "substantive irrationality" of law. Evidence for the strengthening of substantive justice cited by Unger is the development of product liability rules and a general trend to "extend liability in response to equitable considerations" (Unger 1976, p. 199). As a result of these trends, formal legal reasoning is replaced by economic and/or political considerations. A second factor that, in his view, undermines the legal order is the corporatist state. The most important implication of the emergence of the corporatist state is the blurring of the boundaries between the private and the public sphere. Administrative law, labor law, and in some countries corporate law, in his view, became part of a new body of social law that is both public and private.

Traditionalistic societies that incorporate the legal order developed in the West provide another example of a deviation from the ideal rule of law. An example given by Unger is Japan from the Meiji Restoration to the present. The law of this period is described as "a sprawling body of bureaucratic law that mainly regulates the economy. The law is often designed to circumvent the central legal system, which is perceived as remote and rigid or as committed to procedures, interests, and ideals opposed by the dominant elite" (Unger 1976, p. 288). The third example of the disintegration of the rule of law is the revolutionary socialist society. Old institutions are destroyed and new institutions, to be used in establishing a new social order in the future, are created.

All of these social theories share a common view that important links exist between the type of legal system and social and economic change. Weber and Unger place even more emphasis on the political governance structure than on the stage of economic development. Many differences in the theories can be attributed to the time when they were conceived. Weber wrote his sociology of law at a time when the socialist planned economy did not yet exist and the welfare state had not developed beyond the Prussian paternalistic model of the late eighteenth century. By contrast, Unger's writing clearly reflects the development of socialism and the modern welfare state in the twentieth century. However, since the publication of Unger's theory, important changes in socioeconomics and law have taken place affecting many countries around the globe. The socialist system in the former Soviet Union and Eastern Europe has collapsed and many countries have sought to reduce the role of the state in managing economic activities. Many countries that could rightly have been classified as traditionalistic societies 20 years ago have made the transition to more open and pluralistic societies. Nevertheless, many features of the legal systems described by these theorists are still valid for analyzing legal systems past and present. In the following section we attempt to develop a classification of legal systems that builds on these theories. We seek to simplify the analysis while still accounting for the potential of different configurations of legal systems across time and space.

A Simplified Model of Legal Systems

Legal systems can be classified according to the nature of sanctions that follow from legal rules or according to who is empowered to make decisions over the allocation of resources in society. Durkheim's distinction between repressive and restitutory law is an example of the former; Weber's categories of permissive, prescriptive, and prohibitive law exemplify the latter. Permissive law, which Weber also refers to as contractual law, leaves to the market the decision on how resources are allocated and with whom parties contract. By contrast, prescriptive and prohibitive laws vest the state with the power to make such decisions.

For the purpose of our analysis we identify two dimensions of a legal system, an allocative and a procedural dimension. These were defined in chapter 2 and are further developed here in light of the discussion in the previous section. We distinguish legal systems that leave the power to make decisions over the allocation of economic resources primarily to the market on the one hand, and those that leave these decisions primarily to the state, on the other. The second important dimension for classifying legal systems is the procedural dimension. In Weberian terms this addresses the rationality of a legal system. Legal systems that are primarily rule-based and leave little discretion to those in charge of enforcing the law are termed rule-based legal systems. They may not always fulfill Weber's demands for both formally and substantively rational legal systems, as many norms may incorporate open terms that require value judgments. However, in a rule-based legal system these norms will not be pervasive. The contrast with a rule-based legal system is a legal system that leaves wide discretion to those who are in charge of implementing and enforcing the law. The way in which discretion is used may differ, but the important point is that the law itself provides few formal constraints on the use of discretionary power.

The reduction of a legal system to allocative and procedural dimensions leaves out many other features. It does not directly address the question of the political governance structure, which features prominently both in Weber's and in Unger's writings. A detailed analysis of changes in the political governance structure in the six countries that may have brought about changes in the allocative and procedural dimension of legal systems would go beyond the scope of this research project. However, we do propose that the political governance structure is closely related to the two dimensions of legal systems and we provide examples in the discussion of dispute settlement institutions that clearly reflect this close interaction.[4]

---

[4] See the section on administrative litigation in chapter 7.

The two-dimensional approach also does not allow us to clearly differentiate the procedural dimension for laws that govern market transactions on the one hand, and those that relate to the state, including public administration, on the other hand. Thus, a legal system may leave the power to make allocative decisions primarily to markets and the rules governing market transactions may be primarily rule based. This does not necessarily imply that administrative law, or law that deals with political as opposed to economic rights, is also primarily rule based. Indeed, there are many examples around the world of legal systems that provide rule-based enclaves only for foreign or domestic entrepreneurs and investors. As this research project deals primarily with economic law, we do not specifically address the different quality of rules that deal with noneconomic matters, even though they are linked.

The different dimensions are depicted in figure 3.1 below.

The combination of the allocative and the procedural dimensions of legal rules or legal systems gives us four typologies; market/rule-based; state/rule based; market/discretionary and state/discretionary. It is important to recognize that the two dimensions used to derive these four typologies are continuous rather than distinct categories. The ideal of a strictly rule-based or rational legal system is hardly ever realized on the books, much less in practice. The distinction between state and market is more pronounced, although considerable overlaps exist even here.

The typology of legal systems developed above may also be used to classify individual legal rules. The fact that laws may be more rule-based while others are more discretionary is therefore compatible with this model. Still, the classification of a legal system in one of the four typologies of law is not simply the sum of the classification of all legal rules, as not all rules are of equal importance. By the same token, the classification of individual rules may differ from the overall classification of the entire legal system.

In the next chapter we present an overview of policy periods and legal change in the six economies using this typology of legal systems.

Figure 3.1   Four Typologies of Cross-Cutting Legal Dimensions

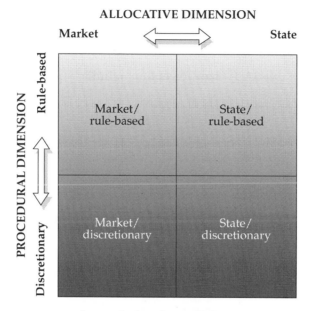

Source: Authors' compilation.

APPENDIX 3A:

LAW RECEPTION IN THE SIX SURVEY ECONOMIES

Table 3A.1   Law Reception in India before 1960

Period	Legal change	Source of law
Precolonial	Trade, commerce, family, and inheritance matters	Indian customary law
	Reception of Western law	
British Control (1772–1947)		
1726	English law (common law and statute) introduced in the settlements of Calcutta, Bombay and Madras by Charter	English law
1772	Courts established by East India Company apply law	English law
1773	First supreme (crown) court established in Calcutta	English law
1833	Privy Council becomes court of appeals	English law
1858	Governance of India transferred to Foreign Office	English law
1861	Unification of company and crown courts	English law
1872	English Contract Act	English law
1882	Negotiable Instruments Act	English law
1911	Indian Patents Act	English law
1914	Indian Copyrights Act	English law
1925	Bombay Securities and Control Act	English law
1935	Government of India Act establishes federal court	English law
	Development of a national legal system	
Independence (1947)	Constitution, land reform, labor law, etc.	Indigenous

Source: India team report; Hooker (1988).

Table 3A.2   Law Reception in Malaysia before 1960

Period	Legal change	Source of law
Precolonial	Trade, commerce, family, and inheritance matters	Customary and Islamic (Sharia) law
British control (1874–1957)	Gradual reception of Western law	
1874-1989	Court system established	Courts use English precedents; they do not recognize Sharia
1896	Federated Malay States established following enactment of laws governing contracts, property, commercial law	English law and local customs
1906	Supreme court of the federation established	English law
1937	Civil law enactment	English law
1940–1946	Various companies ordinances	English law
1948	Bills of Exchange Act	English law
1949	Contract Act	English law
1950	Bills of Sale Act	English law
1956	Civil Law Act	English law
Independent (1957)	Development of a national legal system	
	Constitution, land laws, etc.	English law; element of Islamic law

Source: Malaysia team report; Hooker (1988).

Table 3A.3   Law Reception in Japan before 1960

Period	Legal change	Source of law
Tokugawa shogunate (1600–1867)		
1742	Codification of various acts and precedents, including criminal and civil law (*kujikata osadamegaki*) Commercial law develops (mostly uncodified) during eighteenth century, including rules for trading in futures and use of limited companies	Chinese and indigenous customary law
	Modernization of law and reception of Western law	
Meiji restoration (1868)		
1890	Civil procedure code, law on court organization	German law
1896–1998	Civil code	French/German
1906	Commercial code	German
	Infusion of US law	
US occupation (1945–1947)	Law on court organization (administrative courts abolished)	US law
	Amendments to civil code (family and inheritance) and commercial code (company law)	German/US law
	New labor laws	German/US law
	Antitrust law	US law
	Reestablishing legal sovereignty	
Post-war period (1947–1960)	Adaptation of US laws	US law, indigenous sources

Source: Oda (1992).

Table 3A.4   Law Reception in the Island of Taiwan before 1946

Period	Legal change	Source of law
	Ch'ing dynasty	
Ch'ing dynasty (1644–1895)	Criminal law, legal procedures; administrative law; limited provisions on commercial law	Earlier Chinese codes
	Period of colonial westernized Japanese law	
Japanese occupation (1895–1945)	Traditional institutions sustained to the extent they benefited colonial power	Indigenous and Japanese law
1898	Law adopted providing that all civil, commercial, and criminal matters in Taiwan shall conform to the Japanese civil, commercial, criminal codes, and the codes of civil and criminal procedure	Japanese/ German law
1923	Japanese company law and other commercial legislation enacted	Japanese/ German law
	Nationalist government	
(Since 1945)	Most Japanese laws are rescinded and law that existed on mainland applied	Chinese with Japanese/ German influence

Note: The island of Taiwan came under Japanese occupation in 1895. The Ch'ing dynasty lasted until 1911 on mainland China.
Source: Wang (1992).

Table 3A.5   Law Reception in Korea before 1960

Period	Legal change	Source of law
	Traditional legal system	
Yi dynasty (1392–1910)		
1485	Codification of criminal, tax, administrative law; military organization	Chinese law
	Trade and commerce	Customary law
	First westernization of law	
1895–96	Law on the constitution and the courts	Japanese/ German
Japanese protectorate (1905–1910)	New law on constitution and the courts	Japanese/
	Civil and criminal procedure codes	German law
	Imposition of Japanese law	
Japanese colonial rule (1910–45)	Japanese law, including the civil code and civil and criminal procedure laws, applicable unless otherwise provided by the law of the government general	Japanese/ German law
	Civil disputes among Koreans governed by Korean law, including customary law	Korean law
	Banking laws and financial institutions law	English commercial banking doctrine
	Infusion of US law	
US military government (1945–1948)	Judicial procedure laws	Japanese/
	Labor laws (safety, health, and rights protection)	German/ US law
	Patent and trademark acts	International conventions

Sources: Shaw (1996); Hahm (1996a and b).

Table 3A.6   Law Reception in China before 1949

Period	Legal change	Source of law
	Law of the great Ch'ing dynasty	
Ch'ing dynasty (1644–1911)		
1646	Criminal law, legal procedures; administrative law; limited provisions on commercial law	Earlier Chinese codes
	Incorporating western law	
1904	Company law	Germany/Japan
	Modernization of law	
China (1912–1949)		
1929–1930	Civil Code Commercial law, including contract and property law Civil and criminal procedural law	German/ Japanese law, indigenous law

Source: Chiu, Dobinson, and Findlay (1991).

Chapter 4

ECONOMIC POLICY PERIODS AND CHANGES IN LEGAL SYSTEMS

Over the 35 years after 1960, each of the six economies of our survey made fundamental shifts in government policies toward the economy. The shifts followed broadly similar patterns of movement from periods of mainly state-led policies to periods when they were more market-led although the vehicles for movement varied from economy to economy. A set of economic, social, and political policies might, for example, promote what came to be called a period of import substitution or export promotion; or they might lead to a decade devoted to doubling income per capita, or to an open door policy. Some countries instituted a "new economic policy" to guide much of government action. The evolution of the legal systems in these economies closely tracks the policy periods and the changes appear to have supported the prevailing economic strategy. The causal links were not uniform, however, and were not restricted to the interaction between law and economic development. We find the strength and direction of that interaction determined by the third variable—economic policy. These multilevel, multistrand relationships are portrayed in figure 4.1. Their interaction will be analyzed at the end of the chapter after we have discussed their performance in the different economies.

Figure 4.1   Causal Links between the Legal System, Economic Policy, and Economic Development

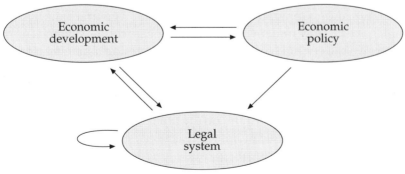

Source: Authors' compilation.

POLICY PERIODS AND LEGAL CHANGE
IN THE SIX ASIAN ECONOMIES

We are interested in the economic policy regimes insofar as they provide a context for the evolution of the legal system and its relation to the economy. As an economy switches from an economic strategy of import substitution to export-led growth, for example, the legal system may adjust to support the new strategy. As an economy opens to the rest of the world, the content, or substance, of laws in such areas as property rights and cross-border transactions could change to fit international standards. Overall, we found that broad patterns in economic policy periods and economic growth during these periods related to the broad pattern identified for the legal system. Major legal changes adopted during a policy period were generally appropriate to that period. When the policy was to promote growth in certain sectors, such as high-technology industries or financial services, the economy often enacted a law oriented toward intellectual property or banks and stock exchanges.

This chapter describes the extent to which law evolved as policy periods changed in each economy. Though we use the labels provided by each team to describe the periods, the reader will notice similarities across many of the economies. The various economic policy periods are well described in the literature, so we give only very brief descriptions with a few outcome indicators based on economic performance to indicate the success of the policies and structural changes that are taking place in the economy. These policy periods are presented for each economy in the following sections, which include reports on the changes in substantive laws and legal process that occurred during each period. We characterize these changes in terms of the allocative and procedural dimensions explained in chapter 3. Often a new law will create allocative rights and also procedures to implement them, so the text does not always separate the two dimensions. A central bank act may, for example, give the government the power to allocate certain financial resources and also give the central bank considerable discretion as a regulator.

Note that in most cases, our 1960 starting date and 1995 ending date may fall in the middle of a policy period. Overall, in one economy after the other, there is a remarkable congruence between law and the policy periods in the changes that occurred. A constant, on the other hand, is that the substance of the laws governing private economic transactions, such as contracts and bankruptcy, did not change during the periods. Their enforcement, however, was more flexible.

The basic point that emerges is that in different periods, state or market-oriented allocative law combines with rule-based or discretionary procedures to create a legal system that generally supports the prevailing economic strategy during that policy period. Four combinations are possible. In general, however, in periods of increased government intervention in the economy, through command and direct ownership of production, one sees an increasing role of state-allocative law (compared with market-allocative law) and of discretionary procedures (compared with rule-based ones). The reverse occurs when the economic strategy promotes markets. This is true in economy after economy, despite the idiosyncrasies of each. In almost all cases, however, discretionary and rule-based legal procedures overlap, and the periods are defined by whichever characteristics are dominant.

The sketches that follow are based on the reports prepared by the country teams with considerable loss of richness and complexity in the condensation. We begin with Taipei,China because it provides a good introduction to our approach. We end with the PRC as the only economy in our sample that had to build a legal framework from scratch at the time it embarked on fast-track economic development. The following table (table 4.1) summarizes the economic policy periods and the type of law during each period for each of the economies.

TAIPEI,CHINA

From 1960 to 1995, Taipei,China passed through three major policy periods, the first two based on external trade in goods and the third on opening to domestic and world markets. So the policy periods consist initially of export promotion, from 1960 to 1972, followed by import substitution and export-led growth from 1973 to 1985, and globalization and liberalization from 1985 to 1995.

Taipei,China's Policy Period 1, 1960–1972

During the first economic policy period, the laws supported a strategy of export promotion.

Economic Policy in Period 1, 1960–1972

Beginning in 1958, an increasingly active government mobilized internal and external resources to promote export industries, mainly labor intensive light industries in the private sector. Export incentives included tax and customs relief, limited exchange control exemptions, cheap credit, export zones, and foreign investment promotion. The strategy succeeded. From 1960 to 1972, manufactures grew from 19 percent of exports to 34 percent, and as a

Table 4.1   Economic Policy Periods and Type of Law and Legal Processes, by Economy, 1960–1995

Economy	1960	1965	1970	1975	1980	1985	1990	1995
Taipei,China Economic	1960–72: export led growth			1973–85: import substitution, export led growth		Liberalization and globalization		
Korea, Republic of Economic	1961–73: export led growth			1973–79: heavy and chemical industry drive	Consolidation, stabilization, and export led growth	Technology-driven industrialization		
India Economic	1948–65: closed high-growth economy	1957–80: closed stagnant socialist economy				Reform and liberalization		

(table continues on following page)

(Table 4.1 Continued)

Economy	1960	1965	1970	1975	1980	1985	1990	1995
Malaysia								
Economic	1960–69: postcolonial conservatism		1969–85: increased state intervention			Deregulation and reregulation		
Legal	Market-allocative law and rule-based processes begin to decline		Influence of state/discretionary system increases			Law becomes more market-allocative and processes more discretionary		
Japan								
Economic	High targeted growth		Balancing growth, social stability, and environmental protection			Fostering demand led growth		
Legal	Pervasive state-allocative law and discretionary processes, but market/rule-based for basic economic transactions		State/discretionary system tempered by environmental and consumer rights		State/discretionary system gradually reduced in scope, and market-allocative laws with rule-based processes grow			
PRC								
Economic	Until 1978: economic policy uses central planning system				Since 1978: market reform creates open door policy and rural reforms, promotes nonstate sector and government decentralizes			
Legal	Legal system is state allocative with discretionary procedures; no formal market-allocative law				State/discretionary system tempered by market-allocative law and from 1982 some rule-based processes			

Note: Italics indicate dimensions of legal system: either state allocation or market allocation and either rule-based processes or discretionary processes.
Source: Team reports.

share of GNP, agriculture fell from 29 percent to 12 percent, gross capital formation (most of it private) grew from 20 percent to 26 percent, and savings rose from 18 percent to 32 percent.

The Law in Period 1, 1960–1972

Substantive laws and procedures in place in 1960 or added by 1972 supported this period's economic strategy of promoting exports by giving a basic but unsophisticated framework for private business and significant power to the executive.

Laws supported allocative decisions by the market but were weak. Property rights were well established, but the land use system was inefficient and frequently changed, laws governing corporate governance were weak, and intellectual property laws were limited and unimportant. Laws governing private economic activity were in place with three exceptions: no special laws governed trusts, competition, or secured transactions. The first two were not seen as important to economic policy. A law for secured transactions was enacted in 1963, though it and the bankruptcy law were incomplete by Western standards. Laws were used to regulate or control access to foreign exchange and finance. Backed by law, the government controlled labor, limited land use in many ways, and regulated capital. Although it enacted the stock exchange law in 1968 and forced big companies to go public, the government did not need efficient capital markets and the stock market remained small for almost 20 years.

Discretionary procedures deepened during this period. Law and legal processes supported an increasingly authoritarian government, in which the executive dominated at the national level and the central government dominated provincial ones. Laws controlling government activity left much discretion to the executive, since martial law was in force from 1970 to 1986, the administrative law was not effective, and judicial review was very limited, with the courts subject to the justice ministry. Executive policy and bureaucratic rules took precedence over legislation. The courts' role was small. In 1970, the administrative court reversed only 3.9 percent of appeals to it from bureaucrats' actions, a low for the 35 years and down from the 10.3 percent reversals in 1960. The powers of the government were not completely unrestrained, however. Broad anticorruption laws limited the willingness of officials to take risk. The government made rules for certain activities without invoking formal law. These activities included external trade, manufacturing, and water purification. Government monopolies imported energy, for example, without a basis in the law to do so.

As has been true for much of the region's history the public, during this period, saw law as an instrument of the state and distrusted lawyers. The military dominated the private bar, though many people practiced law without a license, since only 2 percent of applicants received one.

Taipei,China's Policy Period 2,1973–1985

The law during the second period supported the interventionist government's strategy of import substitution and export-led growth by continuing to give the executive substantial power and discretion.

Economic Policy in Period 2, 1973–1985

The first oil shock coupled with the advent of a new leader and Taipei,China's forced withdrawal from the United Nations, prompted the government—still very active—to shift to promoting heavy industries such as petrochemicals, steel, shipbuilding, and machinery. Massive government funding supported public sector entities, which along with a conglomerate owned by the dominant political party, supplanted private firms. The government managed pricing, particularly to deal with the new monopolies. It adopted protectionist policies for infant industries while continuing to give export incentives with the goal of creating strong home-based industries upstream to support the export drive and reduce the economy's vulnerability to imports.

The Law in Period 2, 1973–1985

In this period state-allocative law and discretionary procedures came even more to the fore, as administrative discretion played a still more important role than formal rules for the market. The laws and legal processes in place in the first period, from 1960 to 1972, provided the base. Laws were enacted to plan, guide, and develop rural and urban land use, in order to extend the shift away from agriculture. Tax laws became important: complex, formalistic, and seen as unfair, they helped to distort the economy. But in some cases the government found it easier to change policy without using legislation, a matter of increasing discretionary procedures. To end government monopolies, it simply let others enter; it could do so because it had not relied earlier on law to create the monopolies.

New laws signaled the coming shift to liberalization, as described below.

Taipei,China's Policy Period 3, 1985–1995

As Taipei,China's economic strategy became more liberal and global, the law became more market-based and the executive's discretion somewhat reduced.

Economic Policy in Period 3, 1985–1995

The government began in the mid-1980s to liberalize trade and domestic economic activities. Trade barriers fell so foreign imports could compete with inefficient domestic firms. The currency rose 40 percent against the dollar. High-tech industrial parks replaced export processing zones. Domestic firms started to make substantial overseas investments as the current account surplus grew. Huge infrastructure projects now relied on private participation. Tax incentives rewarded research and development, automation, and pollution abatement. Incentives to develop the new policies included the following: domestic industries that were weak, having played second fiddle to the exporters; declining investment rates; huge trade surpluses that alienated commercially and politically important trade partners; the end of martial law in 1986; and the emergence of a two-party system.

The Law in Period 3, 1985–1995

The legal system adjusted to accommodate the new market oriented policies and to constrain the executive. Substantive laws and legal processes changed along both allocative and procedural dimensions.

To support the market based policies and the new strategy, Taipei,China passed new substantive laws and modified existing ones, increasing market-allocative law. A competition law that had taken ten years to draft was now relevant for a domestic economy subject to market forces. An intellectual property law was important for the domestic market and high-tech growth strategy. Changes in the laws to promote the private sector's role in the huge infrastructure projects included an end to the monopoly on telecommunications and a law governing electricity supply that permitted the establishment of private utilities. Access to markets was eased for portfolio and foreign direct investors and regularized for foreign trade. Labor laws changed to give workers a bigger voice in disputes. Financial sector laws reduced government control: the government allowed the market more latitude deciding who could issue stock to the public, relaxing merit regulation somewhat for the stock exchange. More financial intermediaries were permitted in both capital markets and banking, where government banks saw their market share decline to about 50 percent. A trust law facilitated broader financial activities. Despite these improvements in the quality of the law, lawyers specializing in commercial law became aware of the need for further improvements in quality, while doubting that the legislature was capable of writing laws that were adequate to the new situation.

Legal processes and institutions affecting the economy became the object of reform to increase rule-based procedures, as the harmful impact of an inefficient bureaucracy became clear and unpopular after 1985. More lawyers entered the profession. A higher portion of applicants (10 percent rather than 2 percent in 1960) qualified for a license to practice law, though the rise in the number of lawyers per capita was only modest. Civilian lawyers took control of the bar from military lawyers. Resources allocated to the courts reached their highest share during this period: courts accounted for 2.15 percent of the national budget, compared with 1.31 percent in the second period. The courts became more assertive. Commercial arbitration grew while mediation fell. To improve court efficiency, the government set caseload targets for judges; during this period, judges exceeded their targets. Judicial corruption became an issue in public opinion polls.

The arbitrary power of the bureaucracy was reduced somewhat through changes in laws. Prosecution of corruption reached a large scale by 1994 and the government eliminated some of the laws that prompted bureaucrats to avoid risk. Laws increased local autonomy, reducing the relative power of the center. Tax laws were amended to share funds more equitably among the provinces, reducing the flow to the city of Taipei, the center. Efforts by the executive to influence judges became less acceptable to the public, forcing a minister to resign. The courts became more assertive toward, and independent of, the executive. Disputes over public construction of infrastructure exploded. Administrative courts reversed 12.5 percent of all contested bureaucratic decisions by 1995, three times the rate in 1970, and with appeals, 25 percent were reversed. Judicial review of constitutional issues involving the executive grew from the mid-1980s and in 1993 the law changed to expand the powers of review.

Government control over the economy through the legal system did not evaporate. At home, controls remained tight on the media, which is of great political significance. Privatization was slow but political factors, rather than the legal system, were the major cause of delay. Offshore investment in derivatives was regulated, which is explained at least in part by prudential concerns.

Relation between the Law and Economic Policy Periods in Taipei,China

Overall, the shift to more state-allocative law and discretionary procedures and then away toward a more market/rule-based system mirrored the changes in the political economy of Taipei,China, both at home and abroad. At the start, in 1960 laws were simple and loose: private businesses had the basic framework (a Ford, not a Cadillac) and the executive used law to legitimize its actions, sometimes even acting without it. This worked adequately for an export promotion policy based on the private sector. In the second period, as the state role in the economy grew during 1972–1985, most of the legal framework required for government policy was in place and relatively little change was needed for the even more managed economy. For the third period, beginning about 1986, the contemporaneous shift in politics toward democracy and, in economic strategy, toward a more open, market oriented economy required qualitative change in law and the legal process. Market-allocative law began to supplement state-allocative law.

Some constants exist in this story. Basic laws governing private economic activity, like contracts and corporations law, did not change. Tax laws were important throughout, though they did change a lot.

The legal system did not lead to changes in policy but laws did signal coming shifts in basic economic policy, serving as bellwethers of change. Increasingly discretionary procedures and some state-allocative laws in 1960–1972 set the stage for an even more government-dominated economic policy in 1973–1985. Changes in laws from as early as 1980 signaled the shift in economic policy that came in the mid 1980s. As a sign of less government control over finance, the 1983 trust law permitted mutual funds to operate domestically. The environmental law was enacted during this part of the first period. Trade laws began to be liberalized then as well.

The notion that Taipei,China is "inwardly Confucian, outwardly legalistic" is supported in the first two periods (1960–1985) and qualified in the third (1985–1995). In these first two periods, an authoritarian progrowth ideology, easy-to-transplant European sourced legal rules for contracts and property rights, and a Chinese tradition of using law as an instrument allowed a state/discretionary legal system with a market/rule-based facade. In the words of the team,

"Informal institutions, such as mediation, settlement, consultation, coercion, broad and flexible guidelines, unfettered discretion conferred through respect for personal leadership, and moral suasion, supplemented and, where necessary, preempted the transplanted formal legal institutions such as litigation, adversary advocacy, public hearings, specific substantive rules, and procedures."

Changes in laws during the first period were in the nature of fine tuning the existing system. Though law was available as a tool, policies could change without changes in law because of the power of the authoritarian government.

In the third period (1985–1995), changes in the legal system were qualitative, signaling a basic shift needed so that the legal system could serve a country in the process of creating both a democracy and a complex economy. The changes strengthened market-allocative law relative to state-allocative law and rule-based procedures, including more formal legal institutions, over discretionary procedures.

REPUBLIC OF KOREA

From 1960 to 1995, the Republic of Korea went from being one of Asia's poorest economies to qualifying by worldwide standards as upper middle income, according to the World Bank. This transition followed a period of stabilization after the Korean War and extended across four policy periods.

Republic of Korea's Policy Period 1, 1961–1973

In this period, an active government pursuing a strategy of export led growth benefited from changes that increased the role of state-allocative law and discretionary procedures.

Economic Policy in Period 1, 1961–1973

Period 1 in the Republic of Korea started with a coup. The new government offered multiple export incentives (through taxes, credits, and imports of essential inputs, among other things) applying uniformly to all businesses, which tended to be labor-intensive light industries like apparel, steel, electronic products, and plywood. Key industries were nationalized, imports liberalized, and access to foreign capital markets permitted. An abundant supply of low-cost educated labor supported this push. Exports grew 40 percent a year, manufacturing's share of GDP rose from 12 percent in 1960 to 34 percent in 1973, and real GDP grew 13 percent a year.

The Law in Period 1, 1961–1973

State-allocative law coupled with discretionary procedures supported this strategy. Following a military coup d'état in 1961, an emergency law displaced the Constitution, which was subsequently rewritten. As amended, it increased centralization of powers in the executive. Although the existing basic framework of property rights, contract law, and business organization was market based on the books, it was applied and enforced to support the state. Other economic laws frankly supported the state: labor laws and unions were suspended in 1961 and ensuing legislation improved labor standards without increasing labor's power or cost. Most new economic laws during the period placed allocative rights with the state. Foreign investment laws shifted from a neutral approach to investment to permitting it in a list of acceptable industries while giving regulators authority to make rules for investment in some restricted ones. Efforts to improve the stock exchange laws culminated in a government owned fund charged with stabilizing securities prices. Laws were enacted to promote key export industries, such as shipbuilding, steel, chemicals, and electronics, prefiguring the second economic period. These laws delegated to the officials the power to select key sectors of each industry and major recipients of the many incentives. Government enforcement of certain laws, such as those for intellectual property, was dormant.

Broad discretionary procedures supported the strong authoritarian government. Despite constitutional protection and administrative law, citizens during this period were limited in their ability to seek redress for official acts. In practice, government officials "were able to abuse citizens' rights with impunity," according to the team. The appointment of judges was heavily politicized. Licensed lawyers were few in number, because of strict limits on applicants, so the supply of legal services was constrained. Though courts were seen as fair in nonpolitical cases, the legal system was seen as a means for rapid political regimentation and public attitudes toward using the courts to resolve disputes were largely negative.

Republic of Korea's Policy Period 2, 1973–1979

The increasingly interventionist government of the Republic of Korea switched to import substitution in heavy and chemical industries during the second period, helped by state-allocative law and discretionary procedures, but some rule-based processes were introduced.

Economic Policy in Period 2, 1973–1979

The oil shock prompted the government to modify its strategy in order to substitute domestic production for imports in heavy and chemical industries, and to promote the export of construction services, particularly to the Middle East. The government targeted specific industries (like shipbuilding and electrical machinery) and firms to receive import protection, low-cost credit from state banks, and tax benefits. This controversial drive is seen in retrospect to have wasted substantial resources, even though shipbuilding met with some success. Inflation picked up as the government deficit rose to finance the sectors targeted for support, growth of exports and GDP slowed, and the current account deficit rose sharply. The strategy ended with the assassination in 1979 of President Park Chung Hee, the president for almost two decades.

The Law in Period 2, 1973–1979

The sectoral laws enacted in period 1 to promote key industries formed the basis for the second policy period, and were supported by the array of state-allocative laws and discretionary procedures also developed during the first period. Most new legislation reinforced this. A constitutional amendment gave economic development priority over workers' rights (an example of state-allocative law). The competition law was used mainly to control and so stabilize prices. Foreign investors became subject to sectoral preferences and standards for minimum size that left the regulators substantial discretion. A combination of emergency decrees (a form of discretionary procedure) and legislation directed private companies to reduce their debt/equity ratio, mandating some to go public (an exercise of state-allocative rights over market). Further laws and taxes were passed to dampen the resulting growth in the securities market.

Flying against this general tendency to reinforce state-allocative laws and discretionary procedures were a few indicators of market-allocative law and rule-based procedures. Among financial sector laws, the fund to stabilize securities prices was abolished during this period. For publicly listed companies, disclosure requirements were strengthened and the power of the government to select external auditors was dropped. The government's discretion became subject to some external review with the creation of tax tribunals to review decisions of the tax authorities.

Republic of Korea's Policy Period 3, 1980–1985

In this period, the government's gradual shift from active direct economic management was supported by the same system of state-allocative laws and discretionary procedures as in the previous policy period, and with the same gradual move to rule-based procedures.

Economic Policy in Period 3, 1980–1985

In the early 1980s, the government began to reduce its direct intervention in the economy and to rely more on market oriented economic policy. Economic consolidation and stabilization led to a return to export led growth. Macroeconomic policies aimed for price stability. Import substitution and the drive for heavy and chemical industries were slowed and the industries rationalized. Uniform support for research and development and technical training replaced targeted incentives. GDP picked up as inflation and the current account deficit fell. But government activism remained strong.

The Law in Period 3, 1980–1985

New laws and revisions of existing laws echoed the partial shift in economic policy, embodying features both market-and state-allocative law. This trend continued into the fourth period. The government revised the intellectual property law and began to enforce it, since manufacturers of the high-tech products at the core of the export push wanted protection. The competition laws were changed to reduce concentration, but not eliminate it, and to promote competition. The industry specific laws that formed the underpinning of the previous policy period were relaxed but not abolished, and certain powers were delegated to the private sector. The company law was amended to facilitate the exit of insolvent firms and allow joint stock companies to raise funds from the public more easily. The law constraining foreign direct investment and credit was rewritten to open the economy a bit more, but not fully, and particularly to encourage the transfer of technology. As part of a plan announced in 1981 to slowly open the Republic of Korea's capital markets, the government began to issue rules allowing limited access by foreign portfolio investors to the Republic of Korea and increased outward flows of funds by Korean savers.

Discretionary procedures continued, but were now leavened by some rule-based procedures. The power of the bureaucracy was reduced with the shift from a positive list specifying permitted industries in which foreigners could invest to a negative list that simply identified a small number of industries from which foreign investors were excluded (and that declined as the law was later amended). Though room existed for officials to grant exemptions in both cases, the burden of proof shifted from the applicant to the official, since with a positive list the assumption was that if an industry was not listed it was not available for foreign investment, while with a negative list the idea was that if the industry was not listed it was open.

Although the state retained extensive discretion over economic activity, new laws and institutions improved the capacity of private actors to fend for their own rights. This trend was reflected in the relationship between the state and its citizens. During this period, a new administrative law was passed that, more effectively than the law it replaced, could force the government to undergo judicial review and provide redress for wrongful acts. Lawyers began to act as spokesmen for the judiciary in criticizing government acts. The trend was also reflected in the growing supply of legal services. The number of newly admitted lawyers rose from 72 in 1980 to 310 in 1985. To lift the inadequate supply of judges, the annual authorized number of candidates for judicial positions was raised to exceed substantially the vacancies in the courts. Even so, average caseloads per judge grew dramatically during this period. From only 445 cases in 1978 and 553 in 1980, the caseload grew to 698 in 1985, or about 25 percent in five years despite a 33 percent increase in the number of judges. This suggests the growing demand for judicial services in the Republic of Korea during this transition period.

Republic of Korea's Policy Period 4, 1985–1995

The government's economic strategy of liberalization, globalization, and technology driven industrialization was supported by the great influence of market-allocative law and rule-based processes.

Economic Policy in Period 4, 1985–1995

Government intervention vied even more than in period 3 with market oriented policies, as external and domestic political pressure for liberalization rose. Imports were liberalized, and though protection continued, it shifted to machinery and agriculture and away from traditional light industries. Although the economic structure changed less in this period than earlier ones the strategy seemed to work. By 1995, exports and imports were both about 30 percent of GDP, manufacturing 28 percent, and agriculture 7 percent. Domestic savings and investment were high, each about 30 percent of GDP. Electronics led exports, with cars, chemical products, ships, and machinery. Heavy and chemical industries accounted for 73 percent of total manufacturing, having risen from 41 percent in 1971 and 54 percent in 1981.

The Law in Period 4, 1985–1995

To accommodate a new set of political and economic policies, the legal system continued to shift from state-allocative laws and discretionary procedures to market-allocative laws and rule-based procedures. At the most fundamental level, the 1987 Constitution, designed to eliminate all authoritarianism, was the first one to draw the full support of governing and opposition parties. It eliminated the president's emergency powers and power to dissolve the legislature, and it increased the rights of workers. It mandated minimum wage laws, for example. Labor laws were amended, removing obstacles to unions and limiting the government's ability to interfere with dispute resolution. Labor disputes increased. The increase in workers' rights is seen as perhaps reducing the Republic of Korea's international competitiveness. Rather than suggesting that law impedes economic growth, however, this demonstrates the conflicting goals of the policies of this period, which sought to increase both democracy and export strength.

Laws and procedures were changed to fit the new economic policies. In 1986, the industry specific laws were consolidated, government subsidies reduced, and procedures using the public and private sector were established to rationalize the industries. Not only were intellectual property laws expanded further, still primarily due to foreign pressure, but Koreans increasingly enforced the market-oriented allocative rights granted by the laws. Procedures for establishing firms under company law were simplified to permit easier access, reducing discretion. Cross border barriers in the law were lowered further, increasing market oriented allocative rights. Foreign portfolio investors were allowed access to the Korean stock market, subject to an overall ceiling that was raised twice. By 1994, the negative list of businesses off-limits to foreign investors was down to 47 categories out of 1,195, reducing government discretion substantially.

Legal institutions changed in ways that reduced the government's discretion. Implementation of the competition law shifted from the Ministry of Finance and Economy to a legally independent agency that became more vocal and began to contradict government ministries. Despite considerable efforts by that agency, however, concentration has not visibly reduced. A greater propensity by Koreans to challenge the state is evidenced by the big increase in cases taken to the courts. Changes in the law in 1994 and 1995 gave Koreans more direct access to the courts than they had before. By the 1990s, the courts were increasingly willing to decide against the executive on important matters.

Relation between the Law and Economic Policy Periods in the Republic of Korea

As the Republic of Korea moved through policy periods that first increased the government's direct role in the economy and then reduced it, law changed in the same way. State-allocative laws and discretionary procedures became entrenched in the first policy period and, with little formal change, supported the managed economy in the second period. During the transition to democracy and a more open economy, the laws changed to meet new needs.

The process is iterative. Laws are used or enacted to support economic policies, the effect of which is to change economic performance for better or worse. The performance leads to a demand for new laws. In some situations, changes in law prefigure a new economic policy, as happened at the end of the second policy period when market based procedures began to appear. In others, changes in the law are delayed until a major political shift has occurred; labor laws are a case in point.

The Republic of Korea does not yet have fully market-allocative laws and rule-based procedures, but it seems to be heading in that direction. Although attitudes toward resolving disputes through the legal system gradually improved since the 1960s and Koreans increasingly regard violation of the law as unacceptable, they do not yet believe that law is effective, according to polls. When asked if a person who lives successfully but violates the law is a "man of ability," 53 percent agreed in 1971, 43 percent agreed in 1981, and only 32 percent agreed in 1991. In a 1991 poll, to the question, "Do you think law is well observed in Korean society?" 82 percent answered no. Negative attitudes toward the legislature and executive and distrust of the judiciary increased over the entire 35-year period. However, people feel more empowered now than in the past to influence the content of the law, which suggests the growing legitimacy of law.

INDIA

India reported two major policy periods: first, a closed, centralized, planned economy beginning in 1948 that was high growth until 1965/66 and then became a stagnant socialist economy until about 1980; and second a period of reform and liberalization from about 1980 to 1995. We report these as three periods, since although the first two are subsets of a longer period, they differ enough to merit separate attention.

India's Policy Period 1, 1948–1965/66

In a period of closed centralized economic planning aimed at high growth, the conventional market-allocative laws and rule-based procedures started to decline, first in the allocative dimension and later the procedural.

Economic Policy in Period 1, 1948–1965/66

Working from a belief in the welfare state and a distrust of markets, India centralized economic planning and regulation in a national government headed by its charismatic leader, Jawaharlal Nehru. Planning emphasized the development of basic industries and infrastructure, reserving the production of basic and capital goods for the public sector. Major land reforms redistributed ownership to small farmers from large landholders. Major banks were nationalized. External resources came from foreign aid, as private trade and investment were restricted; import substitution took the field; and quotas became important. From 1956 to 1965, real GNP grew by 4 percent a year, led by transport and manufacturing, particularly in basic and capital goods. Agricultural growth fell behind accelerating population growth. Public and private investment outstripped GNP growth.

The Law in Period 1, 1948–1965/66

India started in 1960 with apparently market-allocative laws and rule-based procedures—the legacy of the British. The Constitution guaranteed property rights and many basic laws governed private transactions. But even in this first period one sees the beginning of state-allocative laws and discretionary procedures. The license Raj was underway: government licensing of domestic and foreign business grew, along with controls of trade and foreign exchange, creating discretionary procedures that, consistent with the policy of the period, became administrative barriers to private commerce. Company law provided a vehicle to authorize some of these controls. A new law defined those industries open to the public sector and those open to the private sector. Much economic activity was regulated, even prohibited, thereby narrowing market-oriented allocative rights. The securities laws required government consent for any company seeking to issue its stock, and the government used this opportunity to underprice substantially the securities at issue. The process for getting a license favored the large companies.

The discretion of the bureaucracy grew on the statutory authority of the Defense of India Act but unconstrained by either administrative or procurement laws, though regulations existed for procurement. Tribunals in the executive grew as a partial substitute for courts since they were not subject to the same rules as courts and could in theory act more quickly. Long established for tax matters, tribunals were also used to resolve issues concerning wages and company law in period 1.

The tug-of-war between the executive and judiciary over major land reforms proved to be the first of a long string of battles for ascendancy between state-allocative laws and discretionary procedures on the one hand and market-allocative laws and rule-based procedures on the other. The government's redistribution of holdings and the ceilings on them prompted the Supreme Court, relying on market-allocative law—property rights guaranteed by the Constitution—to challenge the government's state-allocative approach. The court at this time was reasonably strong, though perhaps unschooled about economic law. In addition, in the early years of this period, the legal profession was rationalized, streamlining the many existing types of legal service providers.

India's Policy Period 2, 1967–1980

A more explicitly socialist strategy accelerated the process of superseding market-allocative laws and rule-based procedures with state-allocative laws and discretionary procedures as the economy became increasingly stagnant.

Economic Policy in Period 2, 1967–1980

War, drought, and a passing of the old guard generated a crisis that prompted a shift in policy to much more active government involvement in the economy. For part of the period, Mrs. Gandhi led an authoritarian government. Nationalization and other forms of state control swept major industries: banking, mining, insurance, foodstuffs, and international trade. Competition was limited. Bottlenecks grew in the provision of key infrastructure—both quality and quantity. Exports, seen as important after the first oil shock, began to receive incentives and briefly flowered, only to fail in part due to the low level of private investment. The private sector was not, however, obliterated. Private investment in new varieties of grains increased agricultural yields, reducing import dependence. Fiscal policy was conservative and inflation low until 1975, then deficits and prices rose. Between 1970 and 1980, however, growth slowed and the structure of the economy remained unchanged.

The Law in Period 2, 1967–1980

India's increasingly state-allocative laws supported the interventionist government. Freedom of contract was limited. Tax laws became highly redistributive. Agricultural landownership was restricted; corporations could not own it and nonagricultural uses required state permission. Rent control became extremely restrictive for the owner, crippling the market for urban land. Land held in excess of a legislated ceiling on urban landholdings would vest in the state. These rules made it very difficult to restructure manufacturing firms later. The right to compensation for expropriation was diluted. The government even changed the Constitution by removing property rights from the list of basic rights in it. Environmental laws were first introduced largely to comply with international conventions, but enforcement was poor. The social welfare laws were interpreted in a way that created a dual labor market, one protected and unproductive, the other not protected. Exchange controls on foreign direct investors tightened. "Implicit contracts" governed employment in the organized sector, preventing dismissal for other than proven misconduct. This was seen as a tradeoff for protection employers received from the government but, as a result, organized labor fell as a share of the total workforce. Capacity ceilings limited the size of firms in industries like textiles, preventing economies of scale.

Administrative discretion grew as legal institutions other than the Supreme Court supported the new system. Most of the new rules took the form of administrative regulations rather than legislation so the executive made the rules. The executive invoked emergency powers in the Constitution frequently. The sheer size of the public sector grew with many more nationalizations. The Official Secrets Act was extended to prohibit revelation of information about the government's commercial role, making it difficult for anyone to investigate the government's role in the economy.

During this period, the executive tried to protect its asserted discretionary procedures by reducing the judiciary's power to enforce market allocative law. The executive had ample incentive to try this because it had become a litigant in 60 percent of all civil cases during this period. Most litigation concerned executive made rules about tax, credit, rent control, or the urban land ceiling, suggesting the tension between market/rule-based and state/discretionary law in India at the time. The Supreme Court continued to defend and assert rights guaranteed by the Constitution, although it recognized the socialist cast of the Constitution and tried to implement the tenets of socialism when they did not conflict with other parts of the Constitution. By neglect or design, the executive and legislature let the judiciary's budget fall relative to the government's total budget, which exacerbated sclerotic tendencies in the lower level courts and encouraged more use of tribunals to solve the problems of inefficiency as well as political incorrectness on the part of the courts. Frequent amendments to the Constitution suggested the mutability of its rules in the legal system.

India's Policy Period 3, 1980–1995

As the Government reformed and liberalized the economy, market-allocative laws and rule-based procedures reasserted themselves. However, discretionary processes persisted.

Economic Policy in Period 3, 1980–1995

An International Monetary Fund (IMF) plan in 1981 redirected macroeconomic policy and made a start at instituting fewer controls. The government pulled back from many industries. It abolished import quotas and sharply reduced tariffs, but continued to restrict consumer and agricultural goods. Bank reforms allowed new private entrants. Public sector enterprises were restructured. Foreign assistance continued as a major source of foreign exchange, although the foreign exchange regime was liberalized. The pace of liberalization picked up after a foreign exchange crisis in 1991. Throughout the period, the political power of the governing party or parties progressively weakened. Gross domestic product (GDP) grew 6.5 percent a year for the last five years of the period. As exports rose dramatically, the trade deficit fell. The economy responded to the new economic policies. The private corporate sector's share in gross value added rose from 8 percent in 1960 and 9.6 percent in 1980 to 13 percent in 1990.

The Law in Period 3, 1980–1995

In this period, changes tilted back a bit toward market-allocative law, though the entire system retained its state-allocative and discretionary cast.

Property rights were strengthened with a major change that limited the executive's ability to expropriate land. Licensing of business was abolished in all but 16 industries and industries reserved for the public sector were reduced from 17 to 6. Intellectual property laws were reformed, though they remained unclear in important ways and patent laws were not substantially amended. Controls over trade and capital relaxed. Banking law was reformed and the securities law strengthened substantially. Tax laws were streamlined. Environmental laws were improved, though often not enforced. The "implicit contract" giving organized labor job security was undermined as protection for corporations fell.

India's legal processes continued to mix discretionary and rule-based regimes, with the former still quite strong but the latter ascending slightly. The old style bureaucrats implemented the new market-allocative laws. This may help to explain the problems with the environmental laws, but weak enforcement also undercut the state-allocative laws. For example, minimum wage rules were often not well enforced. Restrictive land laws continued to be poorly administered and enforced, and registration was often defective. Lawyers in major urban centers began to specialize in commercial law, reflecting a growing demand that suggested a shift toward rule-based procedures. The courts, however, were too few in number and/or skilled staff for the huge economy that is India, despite budgetary resources that grew relative to the past. Civil cases involving, for example, credit, security interests, and bankruptcy, could take 8 to 12 years or longer to resolve through the courts. Legislation shifted bankruptcy from the courts, some of which had earlier held that loss-making was not a sufficient reason for winding up, to an administrative agency that was more willing to close insolvent firms. New tribunals were established for consumer protection and firms in sick industries, but the latter at least did not function effectively so that procedural weakness undercut new market-allocative rights. At the highest level, however, the Supreme Court stepped into the power vacuum left by the weak executive branch, ordering the executive to take steps to enforce certain rights when it otherwise was politically unable to act. Affected areas included the environment, human rights, and child labor.

Relation between the Law and Economic Policy Periods in India

The congruence of economic policy periods with changes in law and legal institutions is striking. As economic policy became increasingly authoritarian and the economy increasingly managed, the role of state-allocative law increased and the legal process became more discretionary. As economic policy liberalized, laws and processes tilted back to the market-allocative laws and rule-based procedures. Across the periods, legal institutions and particularly the judiciary tried to check the government's arbitrary use of its power or reverse its failure to carry out its duties. But the courts also recognized the political context of their actions and actually enhanced the executive's power in some cases.

As an integral tool to implement government policy, the legal system appears to have contributed to the poor performance of the economy from 1965 to 1980 and to its stronger performance later. Not changing much over the period were the laws concerning private transactions, such as agency, security interests, or contracts. But this does not mean the laws worked effectively. Numerous examples are given of the inadequacies of these laws. India even lacked some basic laws, such as for bankruptcy, throughout the 35 years.

Formal dispute resolution grew substantially and traditional informal methods declined over the 35 years and earlier, beginning immediately after independence. But it is not clear that other informal techniques to resolve disputes disappeared. The latter were particularly in evidence during the second half of the earlier period when the underground economy, or black market, flourished due to the many forms of government involvement with the economy. Estimates of the black market's share in total GDP then varied from 8 percent to over 50 percent. The inefficiency of the courts would also have contributed to the use of informal techniques.

MALAYSIA

Malaysia reported three policy periods: postcolonial conservatism (1960–69), increased state intervention (1969–1985), and deregulation and reregulation (1986–1995).

Malaysia's Policy Period 1, 1960–1969

In the postcolonial period, the initial reliance on the private sector gradually gave way to modest government intervention as the role of market-allocative law and rule-based processes began to decline.

Economic Policy in Period 1, 1960–1969

Having received independence in 1957, the government established an institutional framework to diversify the economy and to Malayanize the civil service, especially with ethnic Malay officers. The new government developed infrastructure, promoted education, adopted relatively laissez-faire policies and made some efforts to diversify the economy, particularly in agriculture and rural development. A modest but growing affirmative action in favor of ethnic Malays and other indigenous peoples (*bumiputra*) took place in the context of a commitment to defend British interests in the economy, which in turn allowed the mainly Chinese business community to consolidate. In 1965, Singapore seceded. A communist led insurgency prompted the government to declare an emergency. To check British capital flight , the government promoted import substituting industrialization largely done by subsidiaries of foreign firms selling in the protected Malaysian market. However, the small domestic market could not support continued growth based on this strategy and government policy began to shift to exports at the end of the period. As income distribution worsened, Malay resentment against ethnic Chinese overflowed into race riots in 1969.

The Law in Period 1, 1960–1969

Existing laws and legal procedures were market-allocative and rule-based, with important exceptions. New laws, many of them needed to govern a new nation, supported not only market allocation but economic diversification in a quasi laissez-faire economy. Indeed 77, or two-thirds of the 110, new laws enacted during this period concerned the economy. A central bank was established. Gaps in existing laws were filled by a banking law for a simple financial system, a copyright law (that was not much enforced), an insurance law, a bankruptcy law, a hire purchase law to provide a substitute for secured lending, and an efficient uniform land law. These would allow private business to grow. New procedures suggested a rights-based approach to internal government controls for audit, financial procedures, borrowing, statistics, and loan guarantees. Laws provided for the regulation of professions (accounting, architecture, engineering).

A mix of market and state-allocative laws supported the government's economic strategy. To encourage import substituting industrialization, a new legal framework for investment, trade, and labor was put in place. The Pioneer Industries Ordinance from the 1950s provided the investment framework. For agriculture, laws were passed governing rubber, fisheries, agricultural research, fishing, and commodity exchanges. Land tenure was reformed and rationalized, simplifying and clarifying land title and its transfer. To support infrastructure, the government passed laws providing for toll roads. For manufacturing, a factories and machinery act took effect. Private sector activity was encouraged by strengthening the laws governing companies and partnerships. Laws benefited labor while moderating its power: the Employees' Social Security Act went into effect at about the same time that the Industrial Relations Act required compulsory arbitration and the Employment Restriction Act was passed. Many of these laws supported market allocation. Some state-allocative laws promoted certain government policies. To help Malays particularly, the government passed acts for federal housing and rent control and made Malay the official language of government (though it was not used in courts until the 1980s and then not in earnest). When the government began to shift to export-oriented policies, anticipating the second period, it passed the Industrial Incentives Act of 1968 providing for labor intensive business. Investment incentives were regularized in a comprehensive foreign investment law that set up the first free trade zone for which the government again changed labor and tax laws.

Legal processes also supported the strategy, laying the base for greater discretion. To promote agricultural diversification, the government established many regulatory and development boards. It began to set up state-owned enterprises to help *bumiputra*. The government strengthened its own powers, beginning what would later become a more obvious shift to state-allocative laws and discretionary procedures. It began to exercise the vast powers given to it by the constitution even in spheres exclusive to individual states (or provinces). For example, the government claimed 45 percent of taxable income from petroleum production even though this was a prerogative of the states. The executive's emergency powers were augmented by constitutional amendment and exercised three times. Government authorities were established to spearhead or coordinate change: the Federal Industrial Development Authority and the Federal Agricultural Marketing Authority are examples.

Countervailing legal efforts to control the government's growing power took several forms, suggesting a rule-based approach. The administrative law, as interpreted by the courts, provided rudimentary controls over the government. Judicial independence seemed high; indeed, judges were career appointees and not at that time part of the political majority. But the organized bar was small, consisting of only 540 advocates and solicitors in 1966. These lawyers also were not from the political majority, since they were mainly non-Malay and predominantly expatriate in the early 1960s. It was the government lawyers that tended to be Malay, though their numbers were small at first.

Malaysia's Policy Period 2, 1969–1985

The influence of state-allocative laws and discretionary procedures increased with rising state intervention in the economy during the second period.

Economic Policy in Period 2, 1969–1985

Following a state of emergency in 1969, a "new economic policy" expanded the public sector considerably, particularly to redistribute income and wealth to the *bumiputra*. New rules increasingly deterred private investment by ethnic Chinese and foreign direct investment (FDI) in general. An initially low skill, labor intensive, export oriented industrialization policy attracted FDI that was considered acceptable, notably through government sponsored joint ventures with Japanese investors to develop heavy industry. Gradually the production processes increased in complexity and labor skills grew. State owned enterprises mushroomed in all sectors. Public expenditure rose throughout the period, and public investment offset private. The public sector's share of gross national product (GNP) doubled in 11 years, rising from 29 percent in 1970 to a peak of 58 percent in 1981. In 1982, it contributed 4.8 percent of the 6 percent GNP growth. Growing oil revenues, mainly from sales to Japan, financed much of the growth in the government budget, but capital productivity declined. Abuses of public office grew. Agricultural development was conservative, supporting existing crops by improving productivity and rural infrastructure. Only at the end of the period was more commercialization of agriculture promoted. Domestic private investment concentrated in nontradable sectors like property. Government macroeconomic policy was deflationary at the end of the period, and the Government abandoned its commitment to full employment.

The Law in Period 2, 1969–1985

The legal system came to rely increasingly on state-allocative laws and discretionary procedures to support the policies of more state economic control, continued reliance on foreign firms as investors in export industries, and promotion of those in the political majority.

To strengthen the federal government, state-allocative laws and discretionary procedures played a major role. Indeed, legislation was the vehicle by which economic policy was implemented and the body of statutory law grew considerably during this period. Consultation with the private sector was ad hoc, if at all. At the core of the new economic policy was the Industrial Coordination Act, which required every manufacturer (or at least those with 25 or more employees) to hold a license from the government (which was the basis for enforcing the rule requiring at least 30 percent *bumiputra* ownership). Like India's License Raj, this bolsters the bureaucracy's discretion. As oil became increasingly important, and since the Constitution gave the states a substantial claim on oil revenues, the government passed the Petroleum Development Act in 1974 giving it all rights to petroleum development. A new banking act—in effect state-allocative law—broadened the Central Bank's power to manage the monetary system and supervise banks. The Central Bank preferred to exercise its influence through moral suasion—discretionary procedures—rather than the use of courts. In the abstract, this preference need not indicate a shift from market-allocative laws and rule-based procedures to state-allocative laws and discretionary procedures since rationalization of financial regulation and informal Central Bank operations are common worldwide. In practice, however, the Central Bank wielded considerable power in the financial sector by virtue of law and practice granting it allocative rights and discretion. More generally, governmental administrative decisions in Malaysia were usually not transparent, even to affected parties and, during this period, the legislature made a widespread practice of curtailing or excluding judicial review of laws. Limited information and limited judicial review emerge as two hallmarks of discretionary procedures.

The courts cooperated, accepting limits on judicial review of legislation. Though they occasionally checked executive or legislative power, Malaysian courts were not as active as those in India. They did limit the power of local authorities. They held that unreasonable delay in exercising administrative discretion abused fairness. But from 1957 to 1985 courts struck down only seven statutory provisions and three of those decisions were reversed on appeal.

Laws helped to make the economy more attractive to foreign companies investing in Malaysia. Labor laws were amended to curtail the trade unions' power (restricting market-allocative rights) and permit women to work on shifts around the clock. Prohibitions against foreigners' ownership of land did not extend to industrial uses, creating an exemption to laws restricting market allocation. New trademark and patent laws were passed. And in the early 1970s, the Free Trade Zone Act gave foreign investors duty free status and other benefits that allowed them to import semifinished goods and complete them in Malaysia.

To redistribute income, and presumably economic and political power, the government took various steps to support the Malay majority and in doing so demonstrated the role of state-allocative law. A government regulation required that at least 30 percent of the shareholders of each corporation be *bumiputra* and the government established an agency to oversee ownership of corporate wealth and assets. Legislation facilitated the creation of Islamic banks that could offer interest free deposits. The land code restricted noncitizens and foreign companies from owning land.

Many other laws advanced government's hands-on policies in important sectors. To promote agriculture, the government enacted laws governing tobacco, rubber, palm oil, and forests. Other laws supported infrastructure: highways, ports, atomic energy, and telecommunication. For the financial sector, in addition to the banking act, two securities laws were passed a decade apart, supplemented by a commodities trading act. The first comprehensive environmental law was passed in 1974. The Legal Profession Act of 1976 regulated lawyers, creating the Malaysian Bar as a statutory body. We do not classify these laws because we lack data about their practice. Here the important point is that through legislation the legal system was used extensively to implement policy.

Malaysia's Policy Period 3, 1986–1995

In a period of alternating deregulation and reregulation, the law became more market-allocative, but processes became more discretionary.

Economic Policy in Period 3, 1986–1995

A recession in the mid-1980s led the government to pull back somewhat from its active role in the economy. The new policies included greater fiscal discipline, depreciation of the currency, partial economic liberalization and privatization, and greater government support for the private sector, including encouragement of private investment and faster technological development. State owned enterprises stopped growing, as their inefficiency and losses roused public opposition. Large Malay owned business groups now supported a reduced economic role for government and stood to benefit from privatization. The public sector's share of GNP fell to 25 percent by 1993, having contributed a negative growth since 1984. Oil revenues helped to bail out government owned banks swamped with bad debt and to finance prestige projects like the construction of the world's largest building. The government encouraged private, often foreign (and particularly from Japan and Taipei,China), manufacturing investment in technologically sophisticated export oriented industries. Emphasis on income redistribution may have abated somewhat and local Chinese capital allowed more scope. Average GDP growth exceeded 10 percent a year from 1988. The new policies did not, however, aim to create an open liberal economy in Malaysia and government intervention remained strong.

The Law in Period 3, 1986–1995

The government's strategy—reducing the state's direct role in production while retaining a role in decisions about the key parts of the economy— is mirrored in shifts in the legal system. One does not find a simple shift from state-allocative laws and discretionary procedures to market- allocative laws and rule-based procedures. The legal changes, while helping to reduce the government's direct involvement in the economy, did not reduce its overall political power or replace it with a system relying more on courts to check the administration.

Laws and legal processes facilitated the reduced role of the state in the economy. New law was often market-allocative. Non bumiputra were given more scope to own manufacturing firms. New laws promoted markets in various ways. A revision of the bankruptcy law assisted credit and eased exit. Reforms were designed to make the financial sector more efficient and competitive. Laws reformed banks and financial institutions, provident funds, and major stock market activities. Licensing and controls were reduced for manufacturing companies, streamlined by changes in the administrative process, and relaxed for screening foreign technology. A securities depositories act supported essential infrastructure for custody. Company Law amendments strengthened shareholders' rights and new laws permitted greater investment of Chinese capital. Greater diversity of financial instruments, designed to broaden the markets, was the goal of the Futures Trading Act and of commodity trading reform. New procedures were market-based. A securities commission centralized fragmentary regulatory authorities supervising the trading of stocks and bonds. A major undertaking, to create an offshore financial market in Labuan, required acts for offshore insurance, banking, and trusts.

Changes in the law encouraged export oriented foreign investment to continue. Some of the new laws were market-allocative. The foreign exchange regime was liberalized. Tax incentives were offered for manufacturing, agriculture, and tourism. Malaysia acceded to the convention on recognition and enforcement of foreign arbitral awards and enacted a new copyright law, both relevant to foreign investors. Others, however, were reminiscent of the earlier state-allocative laws and discretionary procedures. The extent of foreign investors' control would be a function of the degree to which the local firm exported its products and did not compete with Malaysian producers. The government exercised substantial discretion in interpreting these guidelines.

The legal changes did not signal a major reduction in the power of the executive over the economy. Privatization policy is an example. To support privatization, the pension law was changed as it affected state employees. But the focus for economic initiative did not shift from the government to the private sector. Despite policies to promote privatization of existing state enterprises and new projects using a build-operate-transfer approach rather than government ownership, the government took the initiative in identifying the project and the recipient, and relied primarily on directives and persuasion to guide the process. The framework provided by laws and legal institutions had yet to play a significant role in this process. The practice continued to be one of state-allocative powers and discretionary procedures.

In the same vein, judicial activism was put to the test and lost during this period, leaving substantial discretion with the executive. At the start of this period, superior courts decided against the executive on cases in political arenas involving sedition, internal security, the political opposition, and appointment of state officials and also in economic arena, in a case involving privatization. The executive responded by arranging the ouster of the head of the Supreme Court, effectively limiting judicial activism and the public perception of courts as equal to the executive.

Relation between the Law and Economic Policy Periods in Malaysia

At first blush, Malaysia appears to have market-allocative laws and rule-based procedures. Laws undergird major and minor government initiatives. Over time, however, the laws entrenched the executive's power, largely unchallenged by the courts (in contrast to India). The Constitution allowed emergency exceptions from its strictures, but in economic matters this liberty has expanded over time to cover increasingly state-allocative procedures. Though judicial review is available, courts seem to invoke self-restraint when presiding over cases involving alleged executive abuses of power. Coalescing even in the earliest policy period from 1960 to 1969, when emergency powers were invoked three times in 10 years, the executive's power deepened even more in the second policy period, from 1969 to 1985. Rule making in the executive expanded as its economic activism spread. The executive did so despite the significant growth of lawyers in the economy: there were almost 6,000 advocates and solicitors by the end of 1995, which would suggest that law was playing a much more important role than in 1960. This trend contrasts with other countries, where the number of lawyers was constrained in the more authoritarian phases.

In an interesting contrast to the economies reviewed above, during the third period, with its more economically liberal policies, Malaysia's legal system does not as clearly shift away from state-allocative laws and discretionary procedures and toward market-allocative laws and rule-based procedures. In Malaysia, allocative law moved from market (at the start of period 1) to state (period 2) and then a little back toward market (period 3). Procedures were rule-based (period 1), became increasingly discretionary (period 2), and stayed discretionary on balance (period 3). State-allocative law and discretionary policies permitted the executive to exercise significant influence over the economy. The thwarted drive by the judiciary for a more equal role meant that the courts could not speak for market allocative law. This trend is consistent with an economic strategy that continued to give the executive a substantial role in the third period.

JAPAN

For our purposes, Japan has three policy periods: creating high growth (mid 1950s to 1970); balancing economic growth, social stability, and environmental protection (1971–1979), and fostering domestic demand led growth (1980–1995).

Japan's Policy Period 1, 1960–1970

In the first period, the government's strategy of targeting key industries for high growth was supported by state-allocative law and discretionary processes. Market-allocative laws and rule-based procedures governed basic economic transactions.

Economic Policy in Period 1, 1960–1970

By the mid-1950s, with Japan's industry at prewar production levels, the country sought fast growth. The government targeted basic manufacturing industries, using tax incentives and allocating funds, including credit and, by helping to relocate labor, reduced supply in declining industries. It protected domestic markets, let the real value of the yen depreciate against the dollar, and managed cross border capital flows. By the late 1960s, some of these controls were lifted. Manufactures dominated output. They fluctuated around 35 percent of GDP, real estate and construction rose from 13 percent in 1960 to 16 percent in 1970, services rose from 8 percent to 10 percent, and agriculture fell. Private investment averaged almost 25 percent of GDP each year, financed by very high domestic savings. Exports fluctuated at around 10 percent of GDP during the period, and a trade surplus existed after 1960 and grew for most years from the mid-1960s. Japan was a consistent net exporter of capital from 1964 on, and outflows reached 3 percent of GDP in 1971. Despite its policy role, the government's direct contribution to output was low, about 15 percent of GDP throughout. The policies, as implemented, exceeded their targets: real GDP per capita grew at almost 10 percent a year and real wages per capita doubled during the 10 years between 1960 and 1970.

The Law in Period 1, 1960–1970

Although laws governing basic economic transactions were market-allocative, and procedures were rule-based, Japanese law was predominantly state-allocative and processes were discretionary during this first period, despite a constitutional requirement that administrative action be based on legislation.

Bureaucratic discretion and state-allocative power was substantial but bounded during the period. Actively driving industrial policy at the time was the Ministry of International Trade and Industry (MITI). To avoid excess competition, its allocative powers allowed it to restrict entry, control investments, and even manage the types of products chosen for output at the level of each firm. In industries depending on foreign technology, notably petrochemicals, it relied on the law regulating foreign capital to justify its rules. But practice and politics set procedural bounds on its discretion. Where it lacked statutory authority, as with machine tools, MITI had less success. It attempted to apply its criteria through selfregulation by industry associations, but firms only stopped producing half the number of products MITI listed as restricted. MITI's attempt to increase its authority through legislation was unsuccessful. It continued to seek to apply administrative guidance (a special term describing broad discretion in the bureaucracy to make, interpret, and enforce detailed rules of economic behavior). But MITI was forced to leave more discretion to businesses than would have been allowed by the draft legislation. For our study, this suggests that legislation was seen as an important source of authority for state/discretionary action both by the executive and by market participants.

This dependence on general law is consistent with the constitutional requirement that administrative action be based on legislation. The legislation set general guidelines and authorized the bureaucracy to flesh out the rules, giving them substantial discretion in practice. Laws existed by 1960 to support an industrial policy elaborated and enforced by administrative action and allowing policy change by ordinance. Sectoral laws allowed strong regulation of energy, telecommunications, and transportation, generating intense debate within Japan about whether such laws promoted or impeded development during this period. Legislation also provided for tax incentives and subsidies. Financial regulation and control of foreign exchange and cross border financial flows were authorized by interwar laws predating World War II, which gave the Ministry of Finance (MOF) wide administrative discretion. The MOF frequently changed policy by ordinance. The exchange control law enabled the government to protect domestic firms from internal competition by firms subsidized by direct foreign investors. In the arena of government finance, a law was enacted to authorize government bond issues. Legislation provided for the establishment of state owned agencies to build infrastructure, including housing, highways, railways, airports, bridges, and sewers, and to promote forestation and agricultural land. Legislation allowed MITI to protect smaller firms from the competition of larger ones in such areas as retail merchandising. MITI managed the process in a way that generally gave smaller retailers a veto over plans to open larger stores nearby. This was seen as a device to redistribute income.

The legal process gave these laws legitimacy and kept the bureaucrats honest. The process of making law required that all ministries and agencies and major groups that were affected agree to proposals submitted to the Diet. Here is consensus building that reduced ex post legal control through litigation. Laws on budgetary control imposed strict procedural requirements on government expenditures such as procurement, subsidies, and the operations of state owned enterprise. Laws set procedural requirements for ministerial decisions, of which one was that they reflect the views of deliberation councils. The councils were to consist of people from the academy, press, labor, consumer groups, and business. In practice, however, the councils were controlled by the bureaucracy and tended to justify the government's decisions.

Japan's Policy Period 2, 1971–1979

As economic policies shifted to balanced growth, social stability, and environmental protection, state-allocative laws and discretionary procedures were tempered by growing environmental and consumer rights in period 2.

Economic Policy in Period 2, 1971–1979

During this period, Japan accepted more moderate growth in the face of adverse external shocks. The public became vocal about environmental and welfare issues. MITI continued to apply industrial policy, though to a lesser extent, emphasizing electronics, transportation, and general machinery. Trade friction with the US heated up, as Japan's exports grew as a share of GDP to almost 14 percent by 1974 and returned to that level in 1979. But trade was in deficit in 1975 immediately after the oil shock and again in 1979 with the world recession. Trade surpluses were smaller than at the end of the first period, but few economies as dependent on external trade as Japan reported surpluses so quickly. Even so, the economy was reminded of its vulnerability to external events. Japan sought to diversify export markets from the US and Europe to Asia and to rely more on Asia for imports. It reduced its dependence on oil, and secured sources to cover its reduced needs. Over the period, it let the yen revalue substantially. Japan was a net exporter of capital every year except 1974 and 1979/80. The structure of the economy changed, as manufactures fell from 36 percent to just under 30 percent of GDP, while real estate and construction rose from 16 percent to 19 percent and services rose from 10 percent to 12 percent. The government became a bigger direct player in the markets. It borrowed much more to support the economy after the 1973/74 oil shock and let money grow more easily except during the contractionary period immediately after the oil shock. Its expenditures rose to about 20 percent of GDP in the middle to late1970s, as its investment rose to offset declining private investment. Real per capita GDP grew 3.67 percent a year over the period, which included over 2 percent negative growth in 1974. Real wages per capita increased about 60 percent during these nine years, a much slower rate than in the first period.

The Law in Period 2, 1971–79

In a system of state-allocative laws and discretionary procedures, one would not expect to see as many publicized initiatives in law or legal processes as in a system of market-allocative laws and rule-based procedures. In Japan, indeed, much of the rule making took place within the bureaucracy and administrative guidance continued to play an important role. New legislation, however, permitted some of the initiatives taken during this period.

State-allocative laws enabled the government to reduce the harmful effects of the first oil shock. The government relied on existing laws that permitted it to control directly the prices of several oil products, as well as to monitor and intervene in certain types of commodity transactions to prevent speculation. These controls continued into the early 1990s. Discretionary procedures helped the government restructure manufacturing and respond to external pressure. To reduce pollution, a law was enacted in 1972 to regulate the hazardous activities of private enterprise and authorize incentives for them to reduce pollution. To decentralize industrial operations, laws authorized infrastructure projects in local areas and incentives for private investment in those areas. Control over the incentives would give the executive leverage. Administrative guidance made industry associations adopt voluntary solutions to trade friction with the US. Legislation was seen as inadequate.

Japan's Policy Period 3, 1980–1995

As the government fostered growth led by domestic demand, state-allocative laws and discretionary procedures gradually declined and market-allocative laws with rule-based processes grew.

Economic Policy in Period 3, 1980–1995

Acknowledging the risks inherent in relying on export led growth, Japan sought growth in its domestic economy in the third period. As trade surpluses mounted, Japan continued to open and deregulate its economy but the appreciating yen forced the government to seek a low interest rate in order to dampen the effect of revaluation. This stimulated asset prices such as land and stock. Banks flocked to finance trade in these assets since their traditional customer base was eroding in the face of easy money with low interest rates. Simultaneously, this was compounded by a long term decline in corporate demand for bank services as customers bypassed them when the financial system deregulated and barriers to offshore markets fell. Then in 1991, the asset bubble burst. The party that had governed since before the first period lost its mandate, breaking the political leg of Japan's policies. Although the government's contribution to output had fallen by 1989 to about 15 percent of GDP, it recovered by 1995 to about 18 percent, or the same level as at the start of our first period. The real story of the government's changed direct role in the economy over the three periods was the increase in its transfer payments, as the government redistributed funds among groups; the amounts rose from 1 percent of GDP in 1955 to 14.5 percent in 1995. Government borrowing to fund transfer payments led to growing budget deficits. This and the acknowledged inefficiency of large state owned firms led the government to privatize them.

Despite the policies to promote domestic growth, export trade played a significant role during this period. Exports averaged 14 to 15 percent of GDP from 1980 to 1985, higher than at any other time in the 35 years, then fell to about 10 percent, their level in the first period. Trade was in surplus every year except 1980, sometimes significantly. Japan was a huge net exporter of capital, with amounts reaching 3.5 percent of GDP in 1986 and smaller net outflows continuing in the 1990s. The domestic economy languished, particularly after the asset price bubble burst. Real GDP per capita grew about 2.5 percent a year throughout, but the growth was concentrated in the years 1985-1991 and barely reached 1 percent thereafter. Real wages per capita grew more slowly than in the past—about 25 percent over 15 years. Manufactures fell from 30 percent of GDP to 25 percent. Any growth during this period was in real estate and construction—from 19 percent to 24 percent of GDP—and in services, which rose from 12 percent to 17 percent. In other words, the government had not realized its goals for this period.

The Law in Period 3, 1980–1995

For domestic markets to flourish—the stated goal of policy—deregulation was necessary but, despite acceptance over the course of the third policy period by an ever wider group of people in Japan, this essential tenet of demand led growth was not fully articulated by government policy. Although state-allocative laws and discretionary procedures diminished significantly during this period, they did not give way fully to market-allocative laws and rule-based procedures. Deregulation was being pursued, but mainly to reverse the hollowing out of Japan's economy as manufacturers moved offshore.

To promote deregulation, state-allocative laws were reduced in scope, decreasing the government's role in the economy. Exchange control legislation in 1980 substantially reduced barriers to capital flows in and out of Japan, though important limits (on individuals, for example) persisted well into this third period (this change also reduced government discretion). Laws were passed to enable the privatization in telecommunications, tobacco, and railways but ensured that the government could continue to regulate them consistent with market-allocative law. The corporate law was amended in 1990, to remove the waiting period for takeovers, which had given the government both allocative authority and discretion. Until then, Japan had seen only three takeovers. After the change, takeovers increased. Nine occurred in 1993 alone. Shareholder derivative suits in public corporations increased dramatically.

However, other allocative laws, new or existing, continued to be used to justify government intervention in the economy. Legislation permitted the government to tighten control on transactions in land during the asset bubble. The government could monitor prices and discourage speculation. Legislation passed in the post-World War II period was revived to support the government's infrastructure projects (housing, sewers, parks) in the third period. Laws to protect consumers tended to be enacted product by product, leaving it to the bureaucracy to coordinate them.

Nevertheless, discretionary procedures were modified at the very end of this period in a way that could shift the system toward market-allocative laws and rule-based procedures and away from state-allocative laws and discretionary procedures. In 1993, the administrative procedure law was enacted to increase the transparency of government activities that affected the private sector. It set formal standards for decisionmaking and gave affected parties the right to clear explanations for those decisions plus ways to challenge them. Not only foreigners but also academics and even government officials accepted the need for such a law, but it is too early to evaluate its effectiveness. Recent cases alleging corruption involving the budget raised the possibility that the laws on budgetary control were not as effective by the end of the 35 years as they had been at its start.

Overall, during this period, piecemeal adjustments in substantive law and legal processes responded to different policy needs, but often hesitantly. Despite a reduction in some state-allocative laws and discretionary procedures, a substantial body of procedures remained discretionary in key sectors (like finance), and some laws even remained state-allocative.

Relation between the Law and Economic Policy Periods in Japan

Formal law in Japan throughout the 35 years was sufficiently important that even very discretionary activity was grounded in legislation. The laws were, however, so very general that the executive branch had to determine how they applied. In a key part of the economy, for example, the MOF based its substantial control over the financial sector on two laws, the Banking Act of 1928 and the Foreign Exchange Control Act of 1933. The latter act set out only principles, delegating their interpretation and enforcement to the administration.

The team summarized the relation between law and economic policy in Japan as follows: (a) the government has in principle tried to base its actions on law; however (b), the many ambiguities in the laws give government ample room for discretion; (c) in carrying out policy actions that are not specified in law, the government has used explicit or implicit administrative guidelines and moral persuasion by industry associations; (d) in most cases new laws or policies have been discussed in deliberative councils in advance so that people concerned all agreed with the implementation; and (e) most notably, some of the laws have worked against the free play of the market mechanism. We would add that the executive operated without substantial judicial review.

The link between economic policy and the legal system is clearest in the early periods. The government's interventionist policies then were supported by state-allocative laws and discretionary procedures. Indeed, many of the laws conferring substantial discretion on the bureaucracy seem justified by the recovery after World War II. In the third period, both policies and law share a fuzziness. The government pulled back, then reasserted its role, then adjusted again. The laws and procedures, though modified, continued to support substantial discretion. By 1995, these laws gave the bureaucracy excessive authority to intervene in private activities, contributing to economic inefficiency. Opinion in Japan at the end of the third period supports this proposition.

PEOPLE'S REPUBLIC OF CHINA

From 1960 to 1995, the PRC team reported two policy periods: the first, to 1978, was a period of state dominance over the economy; the second period was one of growing nonstate activity (from 1978).

PRC's Policy Period 1, 1960–1978

The first period is not pertinent to this study, because much of the formal legal system had been dismantled by 1960. This does not mean that there were no laws in the PRC. A large number of rules, guidelines, and policy directives were issued by the Communist Party of China (CPC) and various state agencies under the guidance of the CPC. However, these rules and regulations lacked the longer term stability that legislation usually confers.

PRC's Policy Period 2, 1979–1995

Our analysis therefore begins in 1978, when the PRC embarked on establishing a new legal system virtually from scratch. Note that the "nonstate" sector includes all entities other than the central and local governments. The main policies pursued in the second period are sketched in the following subparagraphs.

Economic Policy in Period 2, 1979–1995

Rural reform led economic policy change when, in 1978, farmers were permitted to sell products exceeding their quotas on the market.

In the nonstate sector, for the four years that followed, farmers began to acquire power to decide what to do on their land and how to use surplus labor. In the process they became less public and, of all major groups, least subject to state control. Many of the rural businesses that developed in this way supplied urban producers that were still state owned, and by 1995 grew to compete with them. As a result, nonstate sector producers grew to be a major force in the economy. Their share of total output value rose from 24 percent in 1980 to 69 percent in 1995. However, although they accounted for around 83 percent of all jobs throughout the period, their share of urban jobs rose from 21 percent in 1978 to only 38 percent in 1995. Their share of total fixed investment in the PRC rose from 34 percent in 1985 to 43 percent in 1994, an indicator of their smaller size and labor intensity compared with the state sector.

Markets were slowly liberalized. State controls of production were gradually reduced (to 5 percent of all production by 1994) and competition permitted in many, though not all, industries. Price liberalization followed a dual track system. For a product, the government set the price of the portion of the supply rationed by it and allowed the market to set the price for the rest. In theory, the rationed price would converge with the market price over time, often more than a decade. Practice was sometimes different, but by the end of 1994 only 40 kinds of goods were subject to state pricing.

The financial system remained tightly controlled by the state. Although foreign banks have been allowed to set up branch offices, by 1995, there were still no nonstate domestic banks. State owned banks have been encouraged to become more profitable in recent years and have begun to extend more credits to the nonstate sector. However, they remained subject to state controls and obliged to give priority credits to the state owned sector.

The state sector reformed and decentralized. While retaining ownership, the PRC government allowed state enterprise to decentralize. The government did, however, continue to provide policy loans to the state owned sector at low cost through state banks and allowed delays in servicing them. As competition forced down monopoly returns and wages and benefits did not fall commensurately, the state enterprises' losses rose and the banks' bad debts grew.

Provincial and local governments became increasingly autonomous and encouraged economic development. They began to retain funds they would previously have remitted to the Central Government. Regional and local governments have also often used their leverage over banks to encourage them to lend to enterprises they controlled, including township and village enterprises.

External trade and capital slowly opened. A key element of the PRC's reform efforts after 1978 was the opening of the economy to foreign investment. However, many controls over foreign trade and investment are still in place. The PRC used two currencies, one for external trade and the other for the domestic economy from 1979 to 1986, when it began to unify them and reduce exchange controls. Tariff rates gradually fell in real terms, and import barriers were low compared with other developing economies; however, only state trading companies had licenses to import, so smuggling was rife. Foreign trade was crucial for economic growth; it grew at an average annual rate of 16.6 percent over 17 years after 1978 and produced a surplus in the 1990s. Exports, mainly labor intensive, accounted for almost 22 percent of GDP in 1994. Foreign direct investment was gradually allowed to contribute an increasing share of domestic investment, rising from 1 percent in 1984 to 3 percent in 1991 and then shooting up to almost 16 percent in 1994 despite a very high domestic savings rate (40 percent of GDP in 1994).

Between 1978 and 1995, the PRC grew on average 9 percent a year. Nonfarming employment rose from 29 percent of all employment in 1978 to 50 percent in 1995.

The Law in Period 2, 1979–1995

Law in the PRC was primarily state-allocative throughout this period, consistent with the economic strategy, but elements of market-allocative laws were put in place. In contrast to the other countries in this study, the PRC did not have laws to fall back on in 1978. It had to enact the full panoply. New substantive laws were promulgated in every sphere. They reflected the evolving economic policies. Some existing restrictions were repealed without creating a firm legal basis for market activities. An important example is the reversal of earlier policies that favored collectivization in agriculture. Changes in land policies allowed first rural households and increasingly urban households and firms to acquire land use rights. Although the distribution of land use rights and their transfer is still closely monitored by the state, an active market for land use rights has developed.

Given the central role of the PRC's open door policies toward external trade and capital in the economic reform strategy, it is not surprising that one of the first laws that was enacted after 1978 was the Sino-Foreign Joint Venture Law (1979). A law on wholly foreign owned enterprises followed a few years later. The PRC enacted a general law for foreign economic contracts in 1985. In the special economic zones that were established in some coastal regions' state controls were substantially reduced. Tax holidays and somewhat faster licensing and approval procedures created an environment favorable to foreign investment and promoted an export led growth strategy.

When the PRC embarked on its reform course, it decided that to liberalize markets and develop the nonstate sector it needed laws that would support the growth of markets. These included laws governing urban housing and property rights (patent, trademarks, copyright, the general principles of the civil law). Most of these laws were enacted within the first decade after the introduction of economic reform. Laws for nonstate economic activity including insurance, technology transfer, farm sales, transportation, warehouses, private enterprise, and bankruptcy appeared for the most part in the second half of the 1980s. An important legal change was the acknowledgment of private enterprises by a constitutional amendment in 1988. Since then the number of firms registered as private entities increased substantially. Laws for companies, competition, consumer rights, and secured transactions appeared in the 1990s. Many of these laws conferred allocative power on market players, but those made at the national level frequently imposed more constraints on nonstate activities than regulations at the provincial level. This suggests an attempt by the national government to regain its overall governance function over nonstate activities at a time when the actual development had often already gone beyond the original policy expectations.

Procedures for the nonstate sector remained discretionary and often informal, in the absence of legal framework. The nonstate enterprise sector developed without elaborate company or partnership laws in place. Though many nonstate entities were subject to government control, firms run de facto as privately owned entities were organized and registered as collectives. A new corporate law, adopted in 1993, was rather late and it is still too early to assess its effect. However, several provinces began to enact local legislation on joint stock companies in the late 1980s. Similarly, rules governing the newly emerging stock markets were first enacted at the provincial level before national regulations were issued in 1992.

Attempts to reform the state owned sector, made near the end of the period, used law as a tool. The laws were allocative to the extent that they defined or made more regular the relative powers of state entities and market players. A number of SOEs were corporatized. Their shares were distributed among different state agencies and employees, and fractions of their shares were floated on stock markets in the PRC and abroad. A legal framework for enterprise reform was put in place. A bankruptcy law for state enterprises was adopted in 1986. Indeed, limited implementation of these laws suggests the government retained substantial discretion in practice. The state stopped short of ownership reform or closing down major SOEs. Much of the legal framework for enterprise remains unenforced. Although the number of bankruptcy cases filed has increased, state-owned enterprises have so far escaped the fate of liquidation.

Laws to control the government were adopted, but the overall effect has been limited, keeping their implementation consistent with economic policy. These procedural laws appeared in two phases; the first, to provide for basic institutions (a new constitution in 1982, organic laws for the National Peoples' Congress (NPC), autonomous regions, local government, the courts, and procurators) appeared within the first few years after the introduction of economic reforms. Later, laws were enacted for administrative litigation and tax. Despite these substantial improvements and the growing practice of suing government officials for corruption or malfeasance, state and party officials are still subject to few legal constraints.

The lawmaking process suggests the relatively less important role of formal law, enhancing even more the executive's discretion. The sequence of law adoption was generally three-fold. First came the policy change, second a behavioral change, and only third a formal rule. Policy changes were often implemented at the provincial level. The first laws governing, for example, corporations and stock exchanges were enacted at the provincial level. Only after extensive trial periods and the review of different models across the economy were national laws adopted. The role of the NPC in promulgating laws increased substantially over the years, but most national rules were promulgated by the executive (often the state council), which thus acquired substantial discretion.

Although nonstate parties received the right to challenge the legality of state acts in the courts, the relative weakness of the courts enhanced the government's discretion. Parties that filed a case with the courts were obliged until 1991 to submit to mediation by the courts and only after mediation had failed were they allowed to pursue litigation. Judges were few in numbers and not well trained as many law schools had been closed in the late 1950s. As a result, they were not in a position to enforce laws in a regime of market-allocative laws and rule-based procedures. They lacked social status as well as financial and state/discretionary independence, which distorted perceptions of their fairness. Still, important efforts have been made to improve the situation of courts. The number of court officials, including judges, has been increased substantially. Legal training has been improved, and chambers for economic cases have been established to deal with their growing numbers.

The number of legal service providers grew but remained small in proportion to the size of the economy, population, and land, and they could not create or staff a profession that was independent of the government. From a small base, the numbers rose quickly in the early years, from 1979 to 1984. Law schools began to train lawyers again, and the number of lawyers increased to over 9,000; court personnel roughly tripled in number. Over the next five years, the numbers continued to rise but at a slower rate. However, law like economics, was a very popular course of study and law graduates increased until by 1995, the PRC had over 100,000 lawyers, still a small number for a population of over 1 billion. Notaries increased from 6,859 (1983) to 16,925 (1994).

Relation between the Law and Economic Policy Periods in the PRC

In the PRC, the reform process presents a picture in which economic policies and bottom up economic development led and law followed. The government felt the need to put in place a panoply of laws that would support the economic policies in the period from 1978 to 1995. In part this was done in an attempt to regain control over the rapidly developing economy. Discretionary procedures remained strong, allowing the government to play an important direct role in the economy. However, legal change also responded to demands by entrepreneurs, including foreign and domestic investors. They increasingly called for a general and reliable framework that would reduce the need to negotiate the details of each new project with state officials and that would provide them with a set of default rules. They gradually got much substantive law, but the legal process remained discretionary rather than rule based. Although the legal system is still incomplete in many ways and many of the rules put in place in earlier years urgently require reform, the history of new law in the PRC over the 17 years is impressive. As the PRC is the only economy in our sample that lacked a legal framework at the time it embarked on fast-track economic development, its legal development, thus far, provides us with at least a glimpse of evidence about the importance of a basic set of rules for economic development.

RELATIONSHIP BETWEEN ECONOMIC POLICY PERIODS AND LEGAL SYSTEMS, COMPARED ACROSS ECONOMIES

Common patterns of change among five of the six economies examined above suggest common forces at work on the policy side, as economic policy periods followed similar paths. Four economies— India, Republic of Korea, Malaysia, and Taipei,China—started with at least quasi market based policies that soon shifted to more active direct intervention by government; then in the early or mid 1980s, they began to wind down the state's role and let markets reassert themselves. Japan differed more in the timing of its economic policies than in the relative changes in the role of the state. Japan's era of very active government began before 1960, unlike the other four, and began to unwind a bit earlier. All five faced the same or similar pressures. Policymakers in each economy had to react to such external events as the floating of the US dollar and the oil shock. Certainly each country's leaders watched their neighbors' policies. Suppliers of foreign assistance may have played a role in making policies similar across recipient economies—the US early in our 35-year study, multilateral institutions later. Domestic concerns about national status, consumer well-being or economic inefficiency may have extended across some or all of the six economies

Unlike the other five economies, the PRC pursued a very different set of economic policies throughout the 35 years. Its shift from a command economy with no formal private sector to a market oriented economy was not simply a more extreme case of the other five. When the PRC decided to switch policy, it had to build from scratch basic economic institutions and relationships that existed throughout the 35 years in each of the other five economies. Although one sees for the PRC the same labels on the elements of its economic policy (market liberalization, decentralization and reform of the state sector, opening external trade and capital) that one sees for the other economies, the content of these policies is quite different. The PRC's evolutionary policies addressed the need for much more fundamental change.

The difference between the PRC and the other five economies persists when one examines the composition and functioning of their legal systems. This leads us, in our comparisons, to distinguish between the PRC and the other five economies. The PRC came close to a purely state/discretionary and highly politicized system in the period before 1978, having abolished market/rule-based laws and institutions earlier. The story for the PRC concerns the process by which it builds a legal system from scratch as it also builds the institutions for a more market-based economy. For the PRC, we do not compare the role of law in different periods, since there is only one period.

In the five economies, one sees overall a similarity in the relation between the type of legal system and the economic policy period. State-allocative law dominates in periods of state economic control, and market-allocative law increases in more market-oriented periods. None of the five had, at any point, a legal system that was entirely market-allocative and rule-based or state-allocative and discretionary; each economy and period mixed the two. But, as policies increasingly promoted markets, the legal system shifted along the other dimension from discretionary to rule-based procedures. This is an important finding because it says the general function of law is not unique to an economy. Does the shift toward market/rule-based law suggest convergence? In a later chapter, we address this question.

Legal Systems During Policy Periods of Direct State Intervention

During periods in which the state intervened directly and actively in the economies, legal systems were composed largely of state-allocative laws and discretionary procedures. The following paragraphs illustrate critical elements in each of the five economies during its period when the state was active. The periods are as follows:

- Taipei,China, 1973–1985, the period of import substitution and export promotion;
- Republic of Korea, 1973–1979, the period of heavy and chemical industry development;
- India, 1967–1980, the period of closed stagnant socialist economy;
- Malaysia, 1969–1985, the period of increased state intervention; and
- Japan, 1960–1970, the high growth period.

The laws used below as illustrations were either enacted during the period of active state intervention or held over from the previous period; each is economic law.

In each of the five economies, the purpose of law was to implement state policy and control and direct economic behavior. Taipei,China enacted laws enabling the government to play a direct role in planning, guiding, and developing rural and urban land use in order to extend the shift away from agriculture. In the Republic of Korea, a constitutional amendment gave economic development priority over workers' rights. The Republic of Korea used an early competition law mainly to control and stabilize prices. In India, land-use laws directed economic behavior in many ways; for example, urban rent control became extremely restrictive for owners. Malaysia amended its labor laws to curtail the power of unions. Japan's MITI used very general legislation to restrict entry of goods, control investments, and manage product types at the company level in industries that depended on foreign technology. Many examples are possible in each economy, but this generalization does not hold in all cases, since even in this period, market-allocative laws remained in place and we even found evidence of rule-based legal processes. During this period, some market-allocative laws signaled a coming transition to a more market/rule-based legal system. Taipei,China, for example, liberalized existing trade laws and enacted new laws supporting domestic mutual funds several years before its more open policy period began in 1985.

The governments often adopted laws that set policy goals and delegated substantial discretion to bureaucrats with few procedural constraints. In Taipei,China, laws gave the executive power to control labor, limit land use, and regulate capital. Martial law left the executive largely unconstrained, despite some limited scope for judicial review of administrative law. In the Republic of Korea, laws promoting key export industries delegated to officials power to select key sectors of each industry and major recipients of incentives. Judicial review was minimal. The government of India invoked emergency powers during this period and reduced the resources of the courts, but judicial review was a normal part of India's legal system and the court continued to try to protect constitutional rights. Malaysian law required every manufacturer with at least 25 employees to hold a license from the government, which exercised substantial discretion. Malaysian courts' activism was qualified by restraint and in only a few cases did they strike down a government action. Many laws during this period curtailed or excluded judicial review, and the Malaysian courts accepted this practice. Indeed, as noted in the section on Malaysia, the Malaysian courts, throughout the period, only struck down seven statutory provisions, and three of these decisions were reversed on appeal. For Japan, the example of MITI in the previous paragraph illustrates substantial administrative discretion, which was subject to internal review but not to judicial review.

Many of the rules were made by administrative regulation and decree—an example of discretionary procedures—in several, but not all, of the countries. In the Republic of Korea, emergency decrees and other regulations were the vehicle for important rules. In Taipei,China, the government went a step further by simply ignoring the antimonopoly law when it changed competition policy. Most of the new rules in India during this period took the form of administrative regulations rather than legislation. In Japan, very general legislation permitted the bureaucrats to provide detailed administrative guidance. The MOF, for example, frequently changed its policy by ordinance. Malaysia, however, used legislation, so that the body of statutory law grew substantially during the period of the survey.

Limited dissemination of rules facilitated the government's discretion. The administrative secrets acts in India prohibited revelation of the government's commercial role. In Malaysia, administrative decisions were generally not transparent, even to affected parties. In Japan, the lack of transparency of law has been a major problem for decades, at least for foreigners doing business there. The Republic of Korea shares Japan's problems of lack of transparency and the unpredictability of administrative decisions, but does not restrict publication of rules and provides them on request.

As these examples illustrate, laws and legal processes in the five economies had significant elements of state-allocative laws and discretionary procedures during the economic policy period of high government control. During this period, each economy also had market-allocative laws governing at least basic transactions, such as contract law. These did not change, nor was there any need for them to change. Some economies even enacted new market-allocative laws. The important point is that, in periods when the state actively controlled the economy, a legal system based on state-allocative law and discretionary procedures supported activities key to economic policy.

The Legal System During Market Oriented Policy Periods

The same picture of convergence between the economic policy and the type of law supporting it emerges from a comparison of the shift toward market-allocative law as the economic policies in each economy become more market-oriented. The policy periods are as follows:

- Taipei,China, 1985–1995, liberalization and globalization;
- Republic of Korea, 1985–1995, technology-driven industrialization;
- India, 1980–1995, reform and liberalization;
- Malaysia, 1986–1995, deregulation and reregulation; and
- Japan, 1980–1995, domestic-led growth.

In this more market-oriented period, the five economies adopted or adapted laws that supported market transactions. Several adopted or amended intellectual property laws (India, Republic of Korea, Malaysia, Taipei,China) or simplified or strengthened their company law (Japan, Republic of Korea, Malaysia). Malaysia amended its bankruptcy law to ease exit and adopted a new copyright law. Most of these neutral laws providing off-the-shelf rules for private transactions were already in place, but were revised to meet the needs of market oriented economic policies.

Important changes took place in implementation of rule-based procedures, giving private parties procedural rights to mobilize the law on their behalf and limiting the government in its ability to enforce its interests.

Although not all laws that reduce government power include procedural rights for private parties, the laws we describe seem to have done both. Changes in laws reduced the government's role in finance in Japan, Malaysia, and Taipei,China. For example, laws reducing merit regulation of securities gave issuers procedural rights in the form of time limits and procedures for regulatory action. The government's role was reduced in the licensing and controlling of business (Malaysia and India). Laws for these purposes typically give the applicant the right to a license if it meets certain objective tests. Governmental control of foreign exchange and external trade was lessened in all economies, giving private parties the right to exchange currency if they followed certain procedures. Important changes reduced governmental power in labor matters in Taipei,China and the Republic of Korea (by constitution as well as by statute). A revised competition law in the Republic of Korea made the enforcement agency somewhat independent of the executive. The Government's role was reduced in infrastructure projects (Taipei,China) and in land management (India).

Formal procedural checks on executive power increased or held steady in three economies. Judicial review of executive acts and constitutional matters became more common in the Republic of Korea and Taipei,China, and continued in India even to the point of having the supreme court direct the executive to enforce affirmative rights granted by law or the constitution (e.g., child labor rules or human rights).

Despite these changes in implementation, many state-allocative laws and discretionary procedures continued to support the role of the executive branch. In India, the executive continued to play an important role. To the extent that the executive was called on to implement new or amended laws, the system of state-allocative laws and discretionary procedures prevailing in earlier policy periods asserted itself (minimum wage rules are an example). In Malaysia, the government continued to exercise substantial discretion by interpreting guidelines for foreign investors, kept close control of privatization, and eviscerated judicial review. In Japan, judicial review continued to be insignificant and new legislation allowed the government to intervene in transactions in land to dampen speculation, in consumer protection, and in infrastructure projects. Broad and often vague laws that left ample discretion with the executive were still seen by much of the public as a source of trouble for the economy in 1995.

The main point here is that the relative weight of market-allocative laws and rule-based procedures compared to state-allocative laws and discretionary procedures changed from one economic policy period to the next. In the period of direct government involvement in the economy, state-allocative law increased and so, by and large, did discretionary procedures. In the period of more market-oriented policies, allocative laws and rule-based procedures grew.

THE MULTICAUSAL RELATION BETWEEN ECONOMIC POLICIES, LEGAL SYSTEMS, AND ECONOMIC DEVELOPMENT

The evolution of legal systems in Asia offers important insights into the causal relations between legal development and economic development. This is not a simple unidirectional causality, nor are the legal system and economic development the only variables. Economic policies need to be factored in. The relationship between these three variables is multicausal.

We find the strongest evidence for causal links that go from changes in economic policy both to economic development and to the legal system which then further affects economic development. This is seen in the broad shifts in periods of economic policy and legal systems, described above. It means that for rule-based law to play an effective role in economic development, economic policies must be in place that reduce direct state management of economic activities.

Economic development has a direct impact on the legal system. For example, wealthier consumers (made so by economic development) increasingly demand rule-based laws governing security interests (collateral for loans) to protect their interests. This in turn affects the economy, because it permits substantial increases in consumer lending, fueling demand for consumer goods. This reciprocal activity expresses the notion of demand-led legal change.

Chains of Causality

Economic policies and development also affect one another and in so doing, affect the legal system. The links in these chains of causality can arrange themselves in two different ways, and examples are given below. One goes from economic policy to economic development to legal system to economic development; the other goes from economic development to economic policy to legal system to economic development. Figure 4.2 illustrates both chains.

Chain 1. Economic policies ⟶ *economic development* ⟶ *legal system* ⟶ *economic development:* New economic policies that allow unhindered cross-border capital flows (economic development, since it implies structural change) will undermine the ability of state/discretionary laws (such as merit regulation) to control the flow of issuers in domestic capital markets (since issuers denied access at home can go abroad and repatriate the funds), which would broaden access to domestic corporate finance (economic development).

Figure 4.2   Chains of Causality between Legal System, Economic Policy, and Economic Development

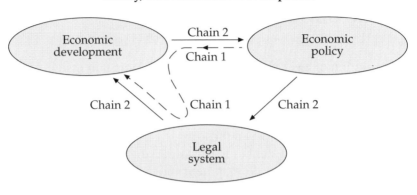

Source: Authors' compilation.

Chain 2. *Economic development* ⟶ *economic policies* ⟶ *legal system* ⟶ *economic development:* When development generates demand for new sources of financing, including stronger capital markets, policy changes to promote capital markets may lead to market development as well as serious abuse of investors by financial intermediaries, which induces the state to improve market oversight and provide more investor protection (rule-based law), which would affect corporate finance (development). A more general example is provided by the costs created by state led development strategies that undermine the executive's ability to make a state-allocative legal system work effectively, reducing its credibility and its impact on economic actors.

Thus, predictions of the impact of legal change on development must consider very complex interactions between economic policy and performance. Such interactions also make it very difficult to quantify the effect of law on the economy.

Within the context of economic law and policy, legal systems in the five economies affected development. Inefficient state-allocative laws and discretionary procedures hurt economic growth. In India, for example, the legal system helped to paralyze markets in urban real estate. Harder to determine is whether market-allocative laws and rule-based procedures promote economic growth independently of economic policies. Our analysis of security interests in chapter 6 reveals important ways in which a variety of laws facilitated either credit and security interests or substitutes that allowed secured lending to take place, promoting development. Analysis of other areas of commercial law may well reveal that rule-based laws promote economic development. But we cannot answer this definitively. The shift we have observed towards more market-allocative law and rule-based procedures took place only after 1980, so the period during which market/rule-based law had a greater impact on development in most economies in our sample is relatively short. It may also be true that market/rule-based law can have a measurable effect on future economic development only after economies have reached a certain threshold of development. Japan, as the most developed economy in our sample, provides the best test case for the importance of market-allocative laws and rule-based procedures for economic development. By contrast, the PRC and India may still have not yet reached this threshold. These differences among the economies in our relatively small sample make it difficult to reach conclusive results. Our interpretation of the legal system as a tool of the broader economic strategy, however, suggests that it may not be appropriate to evaluate law independently of economic policy. Indeed, one could even see the inefficient effect of the legal system in India as part of a broader policy of income redistribution, supported by other economic policies.

The active use of market-allocative laws and rule-based procedures has a self-reinforcing effect for the further use of market-allocative law. The successful enforcement of legal rights against the state stimulates further administrative disputes. Market-based economic development and the use of market/rule-based law create a demand for the expansion of market-allocative laws and rule-based procedures, as economic agents discover the costs and benefits for their transactions of rules already in existence.

We found little empirical evidence of a causal link running from market-allocative laws and rule-based procedures to economic policy in the six Asian economies. The impetus almost always seemed to go the other way, and economic policies generally prevailed over market-allocative laws and rule-based procedures. Even where courts enforced existing market-allocative law and pointed out the boundaries of bureaucratic controls in a system with basic elements of market/rule-based law, this tended to have only minor implications for economic policies. The oil cartel cases in Japan in the early 1970s provide an example of the weak effect of law on economic policy. Courts explicitly challenged the legality of administrative guidance, which circumvented existing antitrust regulations. Although the state became more cautious with respect to violating explicit rules thereafter, the decision did little to moderate the use of administrative guidance. A stronger impact was made by Supreme Court decisions in India that forced a weak executive to implement social welfare rights created by the Constitution.

The next three chapters will explore these chains of causality through the three areas of law we have selected for our microanalysis of the role of law in the economic development of Asian economies. They are business governance, security interests, and dispute settlement.

Chapter 5

BUSINESS GOVERNANCE AND CAPITAL FORMATION

In this chapter we analyze the role of corporate law for the governance of firms and the process of capital formation. The corporate form, as we know it today, has several important characteristics. It endows a firm with independent legal personality so that it can act, sue, and be sued under its own name. It provides investors with limited liability and thereby enables companies to raise capital from a pool of investors. Lastly, it defines the rights and responsibilities of the key participants in the firm, including its owners, managers, and creditors. These features have made the corporate form an important vehicle for the process of capital formation in Western economic development. This chapter addresses the question of whether the corporate form has played an equally important role for economic development in Asia. If it has, this would suggest convergence of legal institutions between the two regions; if alternative institutional arrangements have proved to be more viable in Asia, this would suggest divergence of legal institutions.[1] To answer these questions, we review the development of corporate law in Asia and in the West.

The importance of the corporate form in economic development can be gauged by measuring the contribution of the corporate sector to capital formation. Capital formation refers to the process of constructing physical assets for productive use; such assets include machinery, equipment, buildings, and other physical goods. Capital formation can be financed primarily by the state or by the private sector. It may take place both in the private corporate sector that uses the corporate form (incorporated sector), and in the part of the private sector dominated by firms that are neither independent legal personalities nor confer limited liability to their investors (unincorporated sector). To the extent permitted by available data we therefore present data on capital formation in the state sector, the incorporated private, and the unincorporated private sectors. As the quality of corporate law, in particular the extent of shareholder protection it confers, is also thought to be crucial for capital market development, we provide an analysis of the law governing shareholder protection and securities market development. The results of this research lead us to the following conclusions:

---

[1] For a comprehensive definition of our Convergence and Divergence Hypotheses, see chapter 2.

- Corporate law in Asia had converged with Western style corporate law already prior to 1960. However, the contribution of the corporate form to the process of capital formation depended on the development strategies pursued in different economies and during different policy periods. State-owned enterprises outperformed the private corporate sector in the PRC and India for the entire period after 1960, and in Republic of Korea, Malaysia, and Taipei,China during policy periods that relied heavily on state led economic development. The only economy where the state-owned sector has been significantly smaller than the private sector for the entire period from 1960 and 1995 is Japan.
- Policies favoring the growth of the state-owned sector marginalized the development of the private sector. This had further implications for the relative importance of the incorporated versus unincorporated private sectors. Where an extensive state-owned sector existed, the incorporated private sector was less important for capital formation than the unincorporated sector. Once these policies were reversed and private sector development was encouraged, the incorporated sector outperformed the unincorporated sector.
- When the corporate form was applied to state owned enterprises, this by and large did not prevent state agents from using their discretionary power to interfere in the affairs of the company. This suggests that procedural controls are weak when the state's allocative control functions are strong.
- We find evidence that limited liability has been important for the growth of the private sector. However, we cannot show that differences in the rules on shareholder protection had a measurable impact on the process of capital formation, and thus on economic development. An important reason appears to be that the prevailing sources of corporate finance—which were largely determined by economic policies—promoted patterns of business governance that paid less attention to corporate shareholders and more attention to state bureaucrats and family owners.
- There are signs that the importance of state guidance and family control in the governance of firms is diminishing. The cause of this change is the development of domestic and international capital markets that provide new sources of finance.

CORPORATE LAW AND CAPITAL FORMATION IN HISTORICAL PERSPECTIVE

Firms are key economic institutions. It is possible to imagine an economy which functions without firms and instead relies exclusively on contractual relationships among the different parties who provide labor, capital, and supplies and who purchase the finished goods. In reality, however, organizations that internalize the production process—and are therefore structured like firms—exist in virtually all economies. These organizations are governed by an elaborate set of norms that define the relations among its participants. We refer to this set of norms as business governance.

Firms existed long before general norms or laws on partnerships and corporations existed. Thus, law is evidently not a precondition for the existence of firms. However, law may have facilitated the emergence and dominance of firms with a particular governance structure—the investor owned firm. The investor owned firm is the prototype of enterprises in capitalism as it has evolved in the West. This does not exclude the existence of other forms of ownership. Indeed, to this date one can find a wide variety of ownership patterns even in the most developed Western market economies. They include worker owned firms (such as law firms), firms owned by suppliers of raw material (such as agricultural cooperatives), or firms owned by their customers (such as consumer cooperatives and rural electric cooperatives). Still, the dominant type of firm in these economies is the investor owned firm. The reason for this is the high cost of contracting for financial capital in market economies relative to the cost of contracting for other inputs, including labor and supplies. These costs typically exceed the costs associated with ownership, such as agency costs in large corporations (Hansmann 1996). Available data from economic development in the West suggest that the law, including corporate law and the legal framework for equity financing, has facilitated the growth of the investor owned firm by reducing the cost, including the risk, of investor ownership (Forbes 1986). In this chapter we analyze this proposition in the context of Asian economic development. In particular, we investigate the history of corporate law in Asia, the use of the corporate form in capital formation, the sources of finance used by firms for new investment projects, and the development of capital markets.

The rise of the investor owned firm in Europe and the US is closely associated with the rise of the corporate form (Blumberg 1993, Forbes 1986). The origins of the corporate form go back to the establishment of the large trading, colonization, and shipping companies. These companies, including the East India Company of England, which was chartered in 1600, received their rights as independent legal entities by a special decree granted by the monarch of whichever country the company originated in. They had independent legal personality and their directors and investors enjoyed limited liability. The expansion of trade led to a growing demand for companies that could raise capital from a large pool of investors, and to the development of the modern *joint stock company* in the seventeenth century. These companies raised capital from a large number of investors, but they did not confer limited liability on them. However, shares were freely transferable and the management of companies was delegated to a committee elected by shareholders. In England, joint stock companies were temporarily prohibited following a series of scandals and the collapse of the market for shares. Still, the famous Bubble Act of 1719 did not succeed in preventing a major scandal from occurring only a year after its enactment—the scandal has later become known as the South Sea Bubble (Blumberg 1993). In light of the economic demands for capital formation, the prohibition of companies that could raise capital from a broad base proved to be unsustainable. During the eighteenth century companies began to stipulate limited liability in their charters and courts recognized pro rata liability of shareholders. In 1844, joint stock companies, i.e. companies with large numbers of stockholders and a centralized management, were permitted to register freely in England. In comparison with the prevailing laws of continental Europe, which still required a special concession to be granted by the state bureaucracy for each company to be registered, this was a major liberalization. Finally, in 1856 joint stock companies were permitted to register as companies with limited liability as long as they complied with the stipulated legal requirements. The corporate form in the US developed along similar lines. Indeed, much of the original law was transplanted from the English common law. By 1787, several companies that had been chartered in England were pursuing colonial and commercial activities in the US. After independence, most states ruled that private companies could be established only in accordance with state law. As in England, joint stock companies developed as private companies without state controls or registration. They did not confer limited liability or enjoy independent legal personality. However, over the years courts acknowledged the limitation of shareholder liability by charter and invoked only pro rata liability. By the middle of the nineteenth century most states' corporate laws provided pro rata liability for shareholders in joint stock companies.

The French *Code de Commerce* (1807) was the first comprehensive regulation of the law on joint stock companies. The Code moved away from the traditional *octroi* system, which endowed individual companies with sovereign rights and introduced the concession system. However, this still meant that each company required special approval from the state bureaucracy to establish itself as a company with limited liability. By contrast, the registration system, which allows companies that meet the requirements stipulated by law to register freely, was introduced only 60 years later. In the meantime, private entrepreneurs made extensive use of another legal form—a hybrid between limited and unlimited companies. This *société en commandite*, roughly equivalent to a limited partnership, confers limited liability to the majority of investors. However, at least one partner must accept full liability with all his personal assets. This arrangement still allowed companies to raise funds from a large pool of investors and helped to circumvent the restrictions that applied for companies with full limited liability. Following the Napoleonic wars, the French *Code de Commerce* applied in many parts of Europe. The first German law on joint stock companies was adopted in 1843. It followed the French example in adhering to the concession system.

Table 5.1 below gives a chronology of the development of the corporate form.

Table 5.1   Limited Liability and Registration in the West

County	Pro rata liability or limited liability for most shareholders	Limited liability for all shareholders	Registration system for corporations
England	18th century	1856	1844
France	1807	1807	1867
Germany	1843	1843	1870
United States	Early 19th century by statute	Mid-19th century	Mid-19th century
New York	1811		
New Jersey	1816		
Connecticut	1823		

Source: Beckerath (1956); Blumberg (1993).

The development of a corporate law with the combined features of limited liability, independent legal personality, and the ability to raise capital from a large pool of investors proved to be an important invention. The historical overview has shown that it was not a necessary condition for the emergence of fairly large companies, as many large companies evolved originally as joint stock companies without full limited liability for their investors. However, the trend towards reducing the liability of stockholders in company statutes in England and the US during the late eighteenth and early nineteenth centuries provides evidence that investors became increasingly concerned about the extent of their liability and that courts recognized these concerns. The subsequent enactment of statutory laws offering limited liability and free registration was only the last step in the evolution of corporate law. Even after these laws were enacted, the economic value of the joint stock companies took some time to unfold. In England it was well into the twentieth century before the majority of large companies were reorganized as companies with limited liability. The established traditional joint stock companies were reluctant to associate themselves with the corporate form, which had provided a vehicle for many new entries to the market and therefore increased competition for them. In addition, many of the newly created companies with limited liability misused investors' rights and ended up as business failures, which increased incentives for other companies to disassociate themselves from the corporate form (Smart 1996). Evidence from continental Europe also demonstrates the relatively slow advance of the corporate form. In Germany, for example, the share of joint stock company capital in total capital stock was still less than 20 percent in 1913, on the eve of World War I (Edwards and Ogilvie 1996).

In the long term, the availability of the corporate form benefited the process of capital formation in Western economies (Forbes 1986). Figure 1 below shows that the corporate sector's share in total capital formation exceeded 50 percent for most of the period between 1960 and 1995 in Canada, Germany, and the US.[2] In the UK, capital formation in the corporate sector was considerably lower until the end of the 1970s when the new economic policies led to the privatization of many state-owned enterprises and deregulation measures provided a basis for extensive private sector, including corporate sector, growth.

Basic corporate statutes were enacted in Asia not long after the "invention" of the corporate form and its codification in the West. Prior to this event several Asian economies had already developed partial limited liability. An important example is the Hindu joint family firm, which provided that only the head of the family is personally liable while all other members enjoy

Figure 5.1   Corporate Fixed Investment as a Share of Capital Formation in Canada, Germany, UK and US
(percentage of GDI)

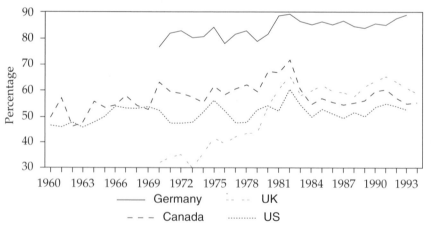

Note: Corporate capital formation is measured as a share
of gross domestic investment (GDI).
Source: World Bank (1997).

---

[2] The reason for Germany's corporate sector contribution being so much higher seems to be that publicly owned companies are typically organized as corporations and included in these data.

limited liability (Rosen 1979). The Western type corporation with its major attributes of full limited liability for all shareholders, free tradability of shares, and independent legal personality was transplanted in the nineteenth century during colonization or as part of a modernization strategy that resulted in the reception of law, including corporate law, from the West.

Over time, economies began to copy elements of corporate law from other sources and added new features to their corporate laws that were essentially homegrown. In Japan, the originally German corporate law was changed and adapted to domestic needs after the enactment of the commercial code. Under US occupation, the part of the commercial code dealing with company law was substantially amended to incorporate elements from the US corporate law. Subsequent changes to the law made further use of foreign models, but they also included provisions reflecting domestic interests that did not borrow from foreign models. As a Japanese colony (1910–1945) Korea received its first commercial code from Japan. The revision of the commercial code in 1962 borrowed from the new Japanese company law and as a result also included some elements of US corporate law. Malaysia inherited British company law, but subsequently borrowed increasingly from Australian law. The new Malaysian company law of 1965 was based on the 1961 company law of New South Wales. Multisourcing for corporate law has been particularly important for the development of corporate law and securities markets in Asia after 1960.

The fact that extensive corporate codes were already on the books prior to the onset of fast economic growth makes it difficult to draw simple conclusions about the causality between legal change and economic development. Causality is also difficult to establish for the West, as many large companies emerged prior to the development of the corporate form. Asia differs from the West in that the corporate form was available prior to the onset of economic growth and development. The transplant of the corporate form provided an important tool for capital formation. However, the introduction of this tool in itself did not trigger growth. For most economies it took until well after World War II to utilize whatever tools were available to launch economic development. This leads us to conclude that the availability of the corporate form may have facilitated economic growth after other factors were put in place, but it was not a primary cause for the economic takeoff.

CAPITAL FORMATION IN ASIAN ECONOMIES, 1960–1995

In most economies both the state and the private sector contribute to capital formation. The relative share in capital formation of the state and private sectors differs considerably across economies. In most the share of the

Table 5.2   Development and Sources of Corporate Law in Asia

Economy	Enactment of first corporate law	Corporate law in force as of 1960	Source of law in force as of 1960	Corporate law in force as of 1995	Source of law in force as of 1995
PRC	1904	n.a.	n.a.	1994	various
India	1850	1956	England	1956–96	England
Japan	1899	1950	Germany/ Japan/ United States	1981–93	Germany/ Japan/ United States
Korea, Republic of	1910	1962	Germany/ Japan/ United States	1984	Germany/ Japan/ United States
Malaysia	1940	1940–46	England	1965–97	England/ Australia
Taipei,China	1904	1929	Germany/ Japan	1988	Germany/ United States

n.a. = not applicable
Note: The PRC did not have corporate law between 1949 and 1994.
Source: Team reports.

private sector in the economy exceeds the share of the state. In developed market economies in particular, the share of state owned enterprises in the economy has been relatively small. By comparison, in many developing economies, including Asian economies, the share of the state owned sector has been much larger (see table 5.3).

Table 5.3   Average Share of State-Owned Enterprises in Economic Activities, 1978–1991

Region	Share of state-owned enterprises in the economy (percentage of GDP)	Share of state-owned enterprises in gross domestic investment (percentage of GDP)
Industrial economies	4.9	7.7
	(7.8)	(13.2)
Developing economies	10.7	24.1
	(10.9)	(21.1)
Latin America and	9.1	20.4
Caribbean	(9.6)	(16.1)
Africa	18.4	27.8
	(13.9)	(27.1)
Asia	10.5	27.6
	(8.3)	(24.6)

Note: Data are for weighted and unweighted average. Unweighted averages are given in parentheses.
Source: World Bank (1995).

If the corporate form has unique attributes that facilitate the process of capital formation, we would expect to see it play an important role in Asian economic development as well. What we do find is that the importance of the corporate form for the process of capital formation has depended largely on prevailing economic policies. Although it has served to limit investors' liability, its role for raising capital from a large pool of investors increased only after economic policies that gave the state substantial control over the financial sector were relaxed. In the sections that follow we analyze the contribution of the corporation to capital formation in the economies of the survey. In order to do this we will compare capital formation in the state and in the private—or nonstate—sector. For capital formation we use fixed investment as a percentage of gross domestic product (GDP). For some economies, the only data available were on gross domestic investment (GDI), which include fixed investment plus inventory. However, inventory accounts for only a fraction of total GDI so that the data are roughly comparable with those for capital formation. Where data availability permitted, we have broken down the state sector into state enterprises and other government investments, and the private sector into corporate and unincorporated sectors.

Capital Formation in the People's Republic of China

In the PRC, total fixed capital formation as a share of GDP was 20 percent in 1981. The share of the state sector amounted to over 70 percent of total fixed investment. The remaining 30 percent can be attributed to the nonstate sector, in particular collective firms. The latter do not belong to the state owned sector, although their creation and scope of activities was determined by state and party policies. Since the introduction of economic reforms, fixed investment has increased to over 30 percent of GDP. Interestingly, the share of the state sector has declined, and the share of the nonstate sector has increased. In terms of total fixed investments, the state owned sector still accounted for over 50 percent of total fixed investment in 1995, but the nonstate sector has taken an increasing share in capital formation (see figure 5.2).

Figure 5.2   Capital Formation in the PRC
(percentage of GDP)

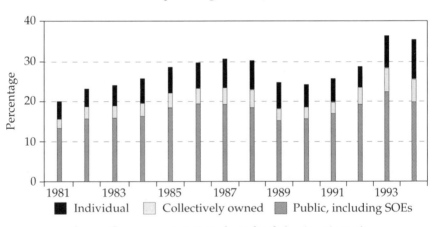

Source: Government statistical yearbook (various issues).

In addition, the nonstate sector has become increasingly diversified. This is difficult to show by relying only on data that break down the nonstate sector into individuals and collectives. An increasing number of firms registered as collectives are in fact managed by individuals. In addition, many township and village enterprises are organized as collectives. The actual control structure of township and village enterprises is much debated. Recent empirical data suggest that local and regional governments play an important role in establishing township and village enterprises and benefit substantially from the revenue created by them (Jin and Qian 1997). At the same time, the number of firms that are controlled by individuals and nonstate entities is rising. Since the legalization of the privately owned firm in 1988, many firms have registered as partnerships or as limited liability companies. Since 1989, the increase in the latter has been dramatic both in terms of number of companies and volume of registered capital. In 1989, companies with limited liability accounted for only 4.23 percent of all registered nonstate companies and 18.2 percent of total registered capital. By 1995, their share in the total number of nonstate companies had increased to 35.9 percent. More important, companies with limited liability now account for almost 70 percent of registered capital outside the state sector.

Although it is too early to draw conclusions for the PRC's further development process, this data nevertheless suggests that the nonstate sector is contributing a growing share to capital formation. Within the nonstate sector, companies that offer investors limited liability are likely to come to dominate the nonstate sector.

Capital Formation in India

State led capital formation has also played an important role in India. Unlike the PRC, India permitted privately owned companies, including large corporations, even during periods of heavy state involvement in the economy. However, private activities were severely restricted by legislation enacted in the 1960s that defined the respective spheres of influence for public and private industries. Numerous companies were nationalized especially in the early 1970s. Nationalization policies continued well into the 1980s with the nationalization of major banks. The combined effect of restrictions for private sector capital formation and nationalization of key industries was that the private corporate sector showed virtually no growth in the period from 1965 to 1975 (see figure 5.3).

A comparison of capital formation in India before and after the introduction of reforms that relaxed the system of state controls and opened more sectors of the economy to private investors reveals the extent to which capital formation was driven by economic policies. The first policy shift occurred around 1980, which is reflected in the significant improvement in private corporate capital formation starting in 1981. Since then, private corporate capital formation as a percentage of GDP has almost caught up with the state sector. With respect to employment and capital stock, the private corporate sector also shows higher growth rates since the mid 1980s, but remains smaller than the public sector. The second policy shift was introduced in 1990 with an even stronger commitment to market based economic growth. This is reflected in a decline of capital formation in the state sector. Within the private sector, the corporate sector has grown significantly since 1989 and even surpassed the household sector. In 1988, the corporate sector contributed less than 30 percent

Figure 5.3   Capital Formation in India
(percentage of GDP)

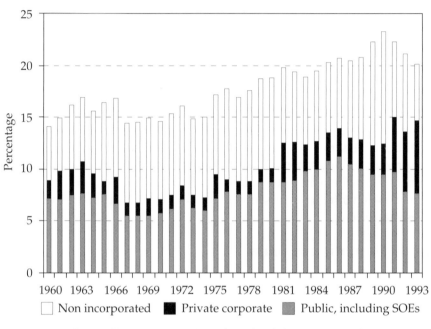

Source: Government statistical yearbook (various issues).

to total capital formation in the private sector. By 1993, its share had doubled to almost 60 percent of private investment, and its share of total fixed investment was more than 30 percent.

An interesting phenomenon in India's economic development over the past 35 years is that the size of the informal sector, which comprises unincorporated proprietorships, partnerships, and family organizations, has remained almost constant despite the decline of the primary, or agricultural, sector. The former accounted for 74.4 percent of GNP in 1960 and 64.9 percent in 1990. During the same period, the primary sector declined from 52.2 percent to 34.1 percent. An important explanation for this trend is the rise of the service sector. However, the large share of the informal sector in India may also be the result of the entry barriers to the formal sector created by state regulations. In fact, empirical studies in Latin America as well as in transition economies have shown that the size of the informal (often non-tax-paying) sector correlates with the cost imposed by state regulations, law enforcement, and official corruption, which forces many entrepreneurs into the informal sector (de Soto 1990; Kaufmann and Kaliberda 1997).

Capital Formation in Japan

In stark contrast to the PRC and India, the state owned enterprise sector has played only a marginal role in capital formation in Japan. Between 1960 and 1984 the share of state-owned enterprises in fixed investment was roughly 10 percent. With the privatization of Japan Railways and other large public sector enterprises in the 1980s, the share of the state enterprise sector has further declined. The private corporate sector dominated capital formation throughout the 35-year period. However, its contribution has fluctuated considerably over time. In 1960, its share by far exceeded 50 percent of total capital formation. Between 1969 and 1979, it declined. The subsequent increase is only partly the result of the privatization of state owned companies, but it reflects the ability of the corporate sector to bounce back after changes in policies increased the scope of private sector activities.

Figure 5.4   Capital Formation in Japan
(percentage of GDP)

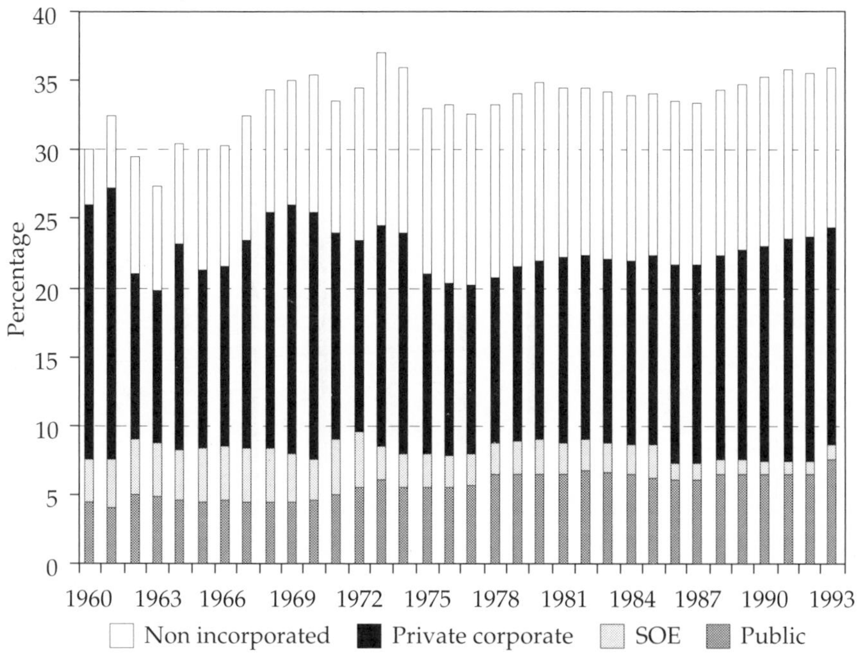

Source: Government statistical yearbook (various issues).

Capital Formation in the Republic of Korea

The share of the private and state sector in capital formation in the Republic of Korea is difficult to determine. In part this is the result of statistical data that do not clearly separate private and state-owned firms in the corporate sector. Although wholly state-owned enterprises have not been as numerous as in India or the PRC, "government invested enterprises" (in which the state holds at least 50 percent of total stock) or their subsidiaries have greatly contributed to the process of capital formation. The share of these enterprises in total capital formation has declined over time, but in the first half of the 1980s it was still as high as the average for state-owned holdings in developing economies.

A closer analysis of companies with different ownership structure and organizational form in mining and manufacturing, one of the most important sectors of the economy,[3] using total fixed assets as opposed to gross domestic

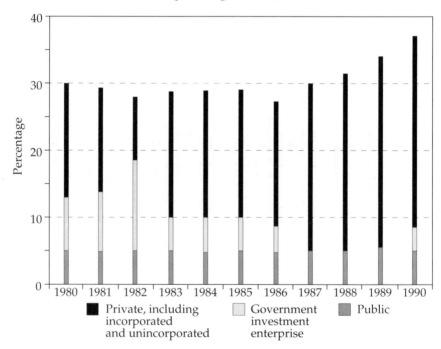

Figure 5.5   Capital Formation in the Republic of Korea
(percentage of GDP)

Private, including incorporated and unincorporated   Government investment enterprise   Public

Source: Government statistical yearbook (various issues).

---

[3] The value added to GDP of the mining and manufacturing sector was over 15 percent in 1960 and more than 30 percent in 1995.

investment shows that government invested enterprises and the private corporate sector together have dominated the economy. Initially the government invested sector was larger in terms of total fixed assets, although the private corporate sector always took a larger share in total employment. The private corporate sector has grown at a higher rate throughout the 1980s. As a result, the fixed assets of all corporations with limited liability today almost rival fixed assets of the government invested sector. In 1994, total fixed assets of the sector amounted to 146,582,122 million won. Total fixed assets of the corporate sector was at 129,200,267 million won, up from 19,636,161 million won in 1980.

Family owned business conglomerates, the *chaebol*, dominate the private corporate sector in the Republic of Korea. In 1983, the total sales of the 50 largest chaebol equaled 94 percent of GNP (Fields 1995). The chaebol were established after the war. The impressive growth of these highly diversified business conglomerates is closely related to state policies, which actively promoted investments in selected industries and encouraged chaebol to pursue these investments.

Capital Formation in Malaysia

Data on capital formation in Malaysia clearly reflect changes in economic policies. The first policy shift occurred in the early 1970s. After a period of economic growth that relied heavily on the private sector, the introduction of the "new economic policy" favored heavier involvement of the state in the economy. Total investment as a share of GDP was around 15 percent in 1960. The relative share of the private sector in total investment amounted to almost 80 percent. Throughout the 1960s it fluctuated between 55 and 70 percent of total investment, but declined relative to the state owned sector in the late 1970s and early 1980s. A reversal of the new economic policy after 1985 has provided the basis for private sector investments to pick up again. As of 1992, private sector investments accounted once more for roughly 70 percent of total fixed investments, which had risen to over 40 percent of GDP (see figure 5.6).

Data has not been available to permit breakdown of the private sector into the corporate and the unincorporated sector.

Capital Formation in Taipei,China

In Taipei,China, the private sector has accounted for the largest share of total fixed investment for most of the period between 1960 and 1995, although total government investment including state owned enterprises at times outperformed the private sector. The increase in the share of the public sector in the early 1970s was largely driven by fixed investments by public enterprises.

Figure 5.6   Capital Formation in Malaysia
(percentage of GDP)

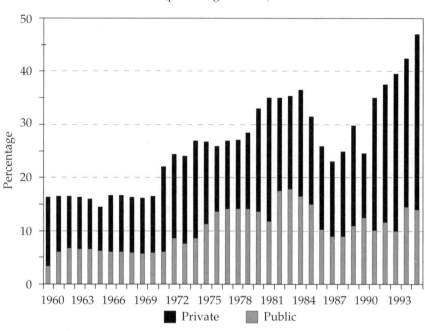

Source: Government statistical yearbook (various issues).

This is reflected in the different growth rates in fixed investment of the general public sector on the one hand and the state owned enterprise sector on the other hand. By contrast, in the late 1980s, government investments in infrastructure and utilities projects appear to be mostly responsible for the share of public sector in capital formation, as the share of the public enterprise sector continued to decline.

Unfortunately, we do not have a breakdown of the private sector into the corporate and the unincorporated sectors. However, other data sources suggest that until the mid 1980s, small and medium sized companies, which more often than not were unincorporated, were the more dynamic sector of the economy, although data on their contribution to capital formation are not available. A large proportion of private sector enterprise in Taipei,China is conducted by small and medium sized companies.[4] Given the size and scope of these firms, which were concentrated in labor rather than capital intensive industries, it seems fair to assume that their share has been relatively low. However, small and medium sized enterprises contributed 70 percent of total

---

[4]   Small and medium sized companies are defined here as companies with not more than 100 employees.

Figure 5.7   Capital Formation in Taipei,China
(percentage of GDP)

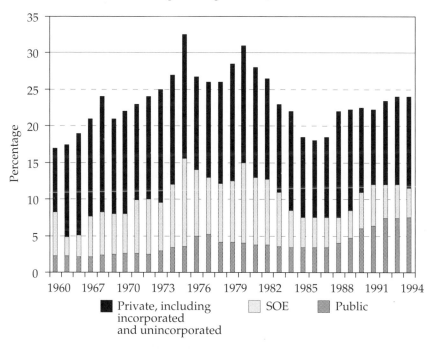

Source: Government statistical yearbook (various issues).

exports during the export peak in the late 1970s and early 1980s (Hu and Chi 1996). Small and medium sized enterprises today still account for the largest number of companies in the economy of Taipei,China. Over the last decade, however, incorporated companies, including limited liability companies and joint stock companies, have experienced accelerated growth. In 1982 there were 199,750 corporate entities registered in Taipei,China with an average registered capital of NT$7.2 million. By 1995, the number of corporations had doubled, and the amount of registered capital multiplied by five. In comparison, there were over 500,000 unincorporated companies registered in 1982 with an average registered capital of NT$0.16 million. Between 1982 and 1995 the number of unincorporated registered companies increased by 27 percent. The average amount of registered capital increased as well, but was still at only NT$0.61 million in 1995.

The growth of the corporate sector after 1980 is also reflected in empirical data measuring the value added by industry sectors. Data from the 1970s suggest that sectors with strong presence of small and medium sized enterprises had a higher value-added ratio. By contrast, data from 1986 signal a reversal of this trend. A possible explanation is that in the more mature economy of Taipei,China in the mid 1980s, vertical integration offers higher returns (Hu and Chi 1996). The findings of the same study also reveal that sectors with less foreign investment tended to have a lower share of small and medium sized enterprises. This suggests that the large incorporated enterprise sector benefited most from of the capital inflow subsequent to the liberalization measures introduced in the early 1980s.

The discussion of capital formation in the six Asian economies clearly shows the changes in the relative importance of the state versus the nonstate sector. In all the economies with the exception of Japan the state sector made an important contribution to capital formation at least during some period between 1960 and 1995. The PRC and India are clearly the front runners in terms of state led capital formation. In both economies the relative share of the state sector in capital formation did not decline following the introduction of economic reforms that provided the basis for a more market based development strategy. However, capital formation in the nonstate sector accelerated with the introduction of economic reforms. As a result, total capital formation increased. The data on India also reveal that after the policy shift, the incorporated private sector outperformed the nonincorporated private sector for the first time since 1960. In Japan, the incorporated sector has been more important for capital formation than either the household sector or the state owned enterprise (SOE) sector. For Republic of Korea, Malaysia, and Taipei,China we lack data that would break down the private sector into the incorporated and the unincorporated sectors. Nevertheless, other data sources suggest that at least after 1980, the corporate sector has taken up a larger share in the process of capital formation.

BUSINESS GOVERNANCE IN ASIAN ECONOMIC DEVELOPMENT

The existence of a corporate law does not necessarily imply that the governance of firms is determined primarily by the norms set forth in this law. The governance of businesses takes different forms across nations and in different policy settings. The relationships between participants in a business undertaking are embedded in both cultural and social, as well as legal norms. Differences in culture therefore affect the governance of businesses (Granovetter 1985). The organization of firms is frequently cited as an example of Asia's difference from the West. Family ownership and networks of trust relations appear to dominate over the more formalistic patterns based on property rights and corporate law we can observe in the West (Jones 1994; Kirby 1995). This comparison of the "Western" and "Asian" prototypes of business does not reflect the variance and richness in norms, including legal norms, which affect businesses governance in Asia and which have shaped the organization of firms even prior to the transplantation of Western type formal law. Although the family based firm has been dominant in most Asian economies, this has not precluded the development of norms that protect the members of these family firms against unlimited liability. An example is the Indian Hindu joint family firm, mentioned above, which provided limited liability for most, though not all, owners.

Four main patterns of business governance can be distinguished for the economies in our sample for the period from 1960 to 1995: governance of state-owned firms; governance of private firms under state guidance; governance of family owned firms; and governance of firms that are owned by (nonfamily) investors. These governance structures have different implications for a firm's sources of financing, its business objectives, and the contents of the norms that determine the governance of firms. By the same token, they render the legal framework for corporate law more or less important in determining a firm's business conduct. Our findings show that this general normative framework for a corporation becomes less important where factors other than the economic interests of shareholders, managers, and creditors determine the sources of financing and business strategies of a firm. Conversely, where these other factors cease to play an important role for the governance of firms, the role of corporate law increases.

In discussing capital formation in the six Asian economies we have shown changes in the relative importance of the state versus the nonstate sector. More subtle changes, such as the transition from family to nonfamily ownership, or the level of state guidance over private firms, are difficult to quantify. A qualitative assessment of the changes that have taken place suggests that patterns of business governance have changed in all economies after 1980. During the first 20 years after 1960, the most important change was the increasing importance of state-owned and state guided firms. After 1980, a reversal of this trend took place. Family ownership has survived most of these changes so far, although there are some indications that family owned firms are facing limits to expansion and have begun to seek additional external financing. This may induce further change in the governance structure of these firms.

The Governance of State Owned Firms

The SOE sector played a major role in the process of capital formation in the PRC and India after 1960. It has also been important for part of this period in the Republic of Korea, Malaysia, and Taipei,China. The economy with relatively the smallest contribution of the SOE sector to capital formation is Japan. The role of SOEs has decreased in all economies over the last decade.

This was the result of a decisive policy change from state led capital formation to market based economic development. The policy change was largely induced by the increasing cost of state led capital formation, most importantly, by the burden on the state budget and the failure of SOEs to meet their set performance targets. The growth of the state-owned sector and the capital accumulation it can achieve over relatively short periods of time is impressive. However, in the long term, these growth rates have proved to be unsustainable. Moreover, misinvestments by SOEs and their inefficiencies have not only slowed the growth of the state-owned sector. They have created significant costs for the state budget and have decreased the ability of economies to adjust to economic and technological change. These inherent limits of extensive state ownership have led economies to shift away from state led economic growth. In some, the change was relatively easy to accomplish, because the state sector had been small, and political and ideological barriers to privatization were weak. In other economies, privatization has proceeded at a slower pace. The PRC and India are still hesitating to transfer SOEs to the nonstate sector. In the PRC, first steps towards privatization were made by permitting the transfer of shares in state owned companies to employees and the trading of small fractions of shares on the stock exchange. In late 1997, the PRC announced plans to implement comprehensive privatization measures. India has made efforts to restore some of the ailing state owned companies with the passage of legislation on sick industries.

A separate question is whether corporate law is relevant to the functioning of the state owned sector—in particular, whether the state makes use of the corporate form for SOEs. There are different ways of setting up SOEs. They can be established as joint stock companies using the general corporate law or they may be created as subdivisions of branch or sectoral ministries. Special laws on state enterprises, internal administrative guidelines, or individual company statutes may provide governance structures. Finally, SOEs may be governed on an ad hoc basis subject to changing administrative decisions.

The experience of the six Asian economies in our sample precludes defining a clear pattern of governance structure for state owned companies. It may be said that the incorporation of state owned companies prior to their privatization is a partial exception, because there is evidence that management improves after incorporation occurs. However, in these cases the changes may reflect a response to the pending change in ownership, not to the formal reorganization of the firm. Moreover, incorporation does not necessarily imply that a company will be privatized. Some economies have incorporated SOEs because the corporate form appeared to provide them more transparent governance structure. In the PRC, for example, the objective of incorporating SOEs following the enactment of the 1994 company law was to streamline the governance of these firms; the idea was not to change their ownership structure, although there are signs that this may now be happening. In India, many of the nationalized companies have retained their corporate form. Newly created SOEs were set up either as departmental enterprises or as corporations. Whenever companies received international aid the corporate form was typically preferred. Several companies that were originally established as departmental enterprises were later corporatized. However, they have remained subject to the same administrative control structure and the same political constraints. In the Republic of Korea the majority of the so-called government invested enterprises are departmental enterprises. In Malaysia, only a minority of SOEs are governed by separate administrative statutes. The majority are organized as corporations. In Taipei,China the companies that were nationalized in 1946 typically retained their corporate form. A number of companies were recently corporatized to prepare them for privatization. However, for the remaining SOEs that were set up as corporations from the beginning, the reason for the choice of the corporate form is less apparent.

In light of the economic function of corporate law, the finding that the corporate law does not appear to have been crucial for the growth of the SOE sector is not surprising. The function of corporate law is to provide investor-owners with a legal framework to exercise property rights and to ensure their limited liability. The state as an owner has other means to enforce its property rights. It exercises broad discretion over the allocation of financial resources in the economy and may therefore also define the extent of its own liability. For these reasons, the corporate form has only limited use for the state as an owner.

The experience with incorporated SOEs has been mixed. Managers often prefer corporatization, as it enhances their independence. But empirical studies in transition economies using performance measures do not suggest dramatic improvements in governance after incorporation (Pinto 1993). Evidence from the experience of SOEs in the six Asian economies in our sample is also ambiguous. Incorporation does not always result in greater autonomy of managers or in improved business governance. In Malaysia, however, there is evidence that the incorporation of firms, especially prior to their privatization, improved financial discipline (Bennett 1995). Still, where the state is inclined to use SOEs as a means to implement public policies, the corporate form has proved to be an ineffective constraint against state actions.

Recent trends suggest that the clear demarcation of SOEs that rely primarily on financial resources provided by the state on the one hand and nonstate companies that contract for financial resources on the market on the other hand is becoming increasingly blurred. In several economies, SOEs are among some of the largest publicly traded companies although so far, private equity finance has made up only a relatively small share of their new investment capital. However, its share may be growing as SOEs are accessing not only domestic, but also foreign and international capital markets. In the long term, this trend may dilute the stake of the state and lead to a creeping privatization of companies that are currently owned by the state. It is also conceivable that these forms of mixed ownership with diversified sources of finance may persist for some time.

The Governance of Private Firms under State Guidance

For the governance of firms in practice, corporate law appears to be not very important even for firms in private ownership as long as state intervention changes the costs of contracting for financial resources, and economic policies determine business strategies and investment patterns. The presence of administrative guidance or state controls over the flow of financial resources limits the relevance of corporate law. Corporate law defines the respective rights and responsibility of private economic actors. It assumes that these relations are decisive in determining the governance of firms. This assumption does not hold, if the governance of firms is determined by other factors, including state policies. As one Japanese expert put it, "bureaucratic involvement in industry overrides management responsibility for corporate conduct" (quoted in Milhaupt 1996). The prevalence of bureaucratic law also helps explain the common notion that Japanese firms have been run for the interest of employees, and not for shareholders. This does not necessarily imply that shareholders were victimized, but their interests were relatively less important than other interests, including those of state bureaucrats and company insiders (especially permanent employees), or a coalition of both.

Bureaucratic involvement in otherwise private industry has been most prevalent in Japan, Republic of Korea, and Taipei,China. State guidance has taken various forms. In Japan the state represented by the MITI chose to guide industries in their investment decisions and marketing practices through formal and informal directives, a practice known as administrative guidance. This included the creation of cartels and price controls for selected sectors (Upham 1987). The actual effect of administrative guidance on economic outcome variables is disputed (Weinstein 1995). However, state guidance has had a decisive effect on the governance of Japanese firms. Company management has been more likely to turn to state bureaucrats for advice than to seek approval from shareholders for important business transactions. As a result, the lines of responsibility of corporate managers on the one hand and bureaucrats on the other hand have become blurred. Courts have hesitated to allocate responsibilities to private parties that rely on either explicit or implicit administrative guidance (Milhaupt 1996). This has created a vacuum where corporate managers are frequently neither accountable to the state—which uses its discretion not to intervene—nor to their shareholders, as the legality of corporate action is difficult to establish in light of implicit government backing.

In the Republic of Korea, bureaucratic involvement has taken a different path. The state has been more directly involved in the economy than in Japan. Most importantly, by controlling the financial sector—the state owned the major banks until the early 1980s—it has directed the flow of funds to state and private firms. The state's control over the flow of funds has continued even after the privatization of banks. In 1985, more than 50 percent of total domestic credits were still policy credits (Stern 1995). Policy credits as a means of financing the Republic of Korea's heavy and chemical industry drive has not come without costs. Many companies that invested in shipbuilding and chemicals in response to these policies have experienced heavy losses. Banks have frequently been asked to bail out companies. As a result, losses were shifted to the financial sector. Some of the negative effects of the role of debt financing induced by government policies in the economy were recognized early on by policy advisers. Excessive reliance on the banking sector to finance the Korean economic development strategy would expose this sector to serious risks in the long term. By the end of the 1970, the debt/equity ratio of Korean companies was sufficiently high to lead the government to adopt plans for the development of capital markets in order to reduce the costs of equity financing. However, changes in the pattern of business governance, including a more decisive retreat of the state, have been slow. Little effort has been made to change the legal framework for business governance, and to improve the rights of investors who could provide new forms of financing. The amendments to the commercial code in 1984 only barely addressed shareholder issues (Kim, K.S. 1996).

In Taipei,China the state has used a variety of means to govern the emerging economy (Wade 1990). Only one of them was the direct control over SOEs. As we have seen, the role of SOEs in the economy declined in the 1980s. Other more indirect governance mechanisms included fiscal investment incentives, controlling entry into business, state support for investment choices, and industrial reorganizations. In general, these policy devices did not direct economic development, but rather supported and accompanied major trends (Wade 1990). Only in exceptional cases were they used to counteract economic strategies by nonstate agents. Moreover, the use of these mechanisms has declined over the years.

State guidance continues to be an important factor in business governance in Asia. However, there are signs that this is changing. We do not have conclusive data, but the following factors suggest important changes. First, the withdrawal of the state from controlling the allocation of financial resources changed their relative prices. Second, policy measures that opened the economies to foreign capital inflows decreased the costs of equity finance. Third, as a result of these measures, outside investors are gaining influence in corporations. Fourth, competition on domestic and world markets has increased.

For much of the period after 1960 state guidance provided much needed certainty for investors and firms through a predictable and stable business environment. However, in the rapidly changing business environment of recent years, state guidance has changed from being a major source of stability and reliance into a constraint that stifles the development of business. Negotiations and consultations between state officials and entrepreneurs were mutually beneficial as long as other factors did not constrain economic actors. With growing competition, however, state tutelage has developed from a source of stability to a burden that deprives companies of the flexibility to respond to market forces.

The Governance of Family Controlled Firms

The dichotomy of family ownership and trust relations on the one hand, and formal law, including corporate law, on the other hand, are often used to describe differences in the governance of firms in Asia and in the West. Our findings suggest that this dichotomy might be misleading. It supposes that the two governance patterns are mutually exclusive. By contrast, the Asian experience demonstrates that they can be highly complementary, as many of the large family controlled businesses in Asia have found the corporate form to be beneficial for their interests and have therefore organized many firms as corporations.

In theory, capital formation based on trust and kin is limited by the size of the extended family and the resources the family members can mobilize. However, family owned businesses have found ways to circumvent these inherent limits by mixing formal legal tools with traditional governance patterns. The large nonstate business groups we can find in India, Republic of Korea, Malaysia, and Taipei,China have grown around family owned businesses. The same was true for the zaibatsu in Japan during the first decades of this century. The zaibatsu were dissolved following World War II, but the roots of three of the six largest keiretsu in Japan can still be traced to former zaibatsu.

The size of these business conglomerates and their importance in the six Asian economies vary. Data on the extent of family control are difficult to come by. The clearest evidence for extensive family control is to be found in the Republic of Korea's large business conglomerates, the chaebol, which evolved around family controlled firms. In Malaysia, a 1992 survey revealed that over one-third of the companies listed under the industrial counter of the Kuala Lumpur stock exchange were controlled by Malaysian Chinese families. Bumiputra families also own several large business groups, but we lack data to assess their importance in the economy. Several of the largest businesses in Taipei,China are also family controlled. By contrast, the Indian Tata and other large business conglomerates are based on communities that are linked by kinship rather than families in the narrower sense. They often control firms that have adopted the corporate form. In Japan, the role of family ownership declined after the zaibatsu were destroyed. Finally, in the PRC the period of economic reform has been too short to witness the growth of new family owned empires.

The persistence of family ownership throughout the economic development process reflects the mutual benefits of family control and the corporate form, which provides family members with limited liability. Family controlled conglomerates have relied extensively on retained earnings as a source of finance. In some economies, notably the Republic of Korea, family controlled firms have benefited from subsidized credits provided by the state for targeted industries and have also benefited from interest rate controls imposed by the state. By contrast, the public issuance of shares in family controlled businesses and their public trading is a more recent phenomenon.

Over the past 10-15 years family owned firms have increasingly made use of the equity market as a source of finance, but they have tried to find ways to raise funds without giving up control, although in the long run this has not always been successful. An example is the experience with the "new preferred stock" in the Republic of Korea between 1986 and 1989 (Kim 1996). After lobbying unsuccessfully for a change in the law in order to allow the issue of nonvoting common stock, companies issued preferred stock that yielded a dividend only marginally higher than for common stock ("common stock plus 1 percent"). This new type of share was a remarkable success. In 1986, only one single issuance of preferred stock had been reported raising 2 billion won or 0.3 percent of the total equity that was raised in that year. In 1989, there were 102 issuances raising 3,982.2 billion won. This amounted to 35.7 percent of total equity capital raised. In 1990, however, the new stock frenzy subsided when the price of this type of stock collapsed. A major reason appears to have been an oversupply of equity to the market. The price of the new stock was further depressed by the tendency of controlling shareholders to sell their preferred stock in order to finance the acquisition of shares assigned to them in a rights offering (Kim 1996). In 1994, preferred stock further declined to a discounted price of between 32.3 and 53.8 percent below that of the common stock. In response to a public outcry against this development, the Korean securities and exchange commission encouraged firms to repurchase the preferred stock. This latest development is a first sign that controlling shareholders may face a more serious tradeoff between raising equity capital and sharing control and/or profits with new outside owners in the future.

To summarize, as long as family controlled firms were financially self-sufficient, or as long as they benefited from state credit policies reducing the

costs of contracting for financial capital, the governance of these firms was determined by norms that often differed from the textbook corporate law. Rights
and responsibilities of the participants in the family enterprise were allocated
not according to the size of equity holdings, but to the status of family members
and their relationship vis-a-vis each other. This did not exclude the
professionalization of firm management, which has been a common feature of
many family controlled firms in Asia. However, the need for additional external
funds may alter this pattern of governance, at least, if the raising of new capital
goes hand in hand with a share of control rights. So far, most family controlled
business conglomerates have avoided the dilution of family control. The case
of the preferred stock in the Republic of Korea documents their ingenuity in
doing so. However, it also demonstrates that investors are not powerless. Though
they may lack "voice" and actual control rights, they can vote with their feet
and "exit" from nonrewarding investment opportunities. The combination of
family control and corporate financing patterns that increasingly rely on modern securities markets poses important challenges for the governance of these
firms. Families intend to retain control, but in order to raise additional capital,
they are pressed to respect the rights and interests of outside investors. The
history of the preferred stock in the Republic of Korea is only one of many
examples of the renegotiation of control rights in family conglomerates (and
also in state owned firms that have floated parts of their stock) that are currently
under way. It is too early to assess the viability of alternative contractual arrangements that are being tested. Moreover, much more detailed data on ownership structure, different types of stock issues, and changes in the control structure of firms are needed for such an analysis.

A comparison of these developments with the history of family ownership in the West or the use of preferred stock and similar instruments to ensure control by company insiders suggests that Asia is developing along a
path that does not differ significantly from the West. The variance between
family controlled firms and the pace of change between Asia and the West are
not considerably larger than the variance we can observe within the two regions themselves. To date, the incidence of family control in the UK is higher
than in the US (Chandler 1990). However, even in the US we find widespread
family ownership not only among medium sized companies, but also among
the largest firms. In fact, one-third of the Fortune 500 companies are family
controlled (Jordan 1997).[5] The same is true for many of the largest firms in
Germany. This is changing, but change has been slow. In 1963, 26.7 percent of
the listed joint stock companies in Germany, for example, had a family as a

---

[5]   According to data presented by Jordan, 99 percent of Italian businesses, 70 percent of Portuguese, 75 percent
of British, 80 percent of Spanish, 85-90 percent of Swiss, 90 percent of Swedish, 80 percent of Canadian, and
80-95 percent of businesses in the US are family controlled (Jordan 1997).

majority shareholder. By 1983, the number had decreased to 22.6 percent. In terms of the market value of equity capital, family control in 1963 accounted for 10.2 percent of all listed companies, and 6.4 percent in 1983 (Edwards and Fischer 1994, p. 185). Thus, variations in the patterns of business governance are not confined to one economy or one region. Although there are signs of convergence towards the model of investor owned firms, the process of change in the ownership structure and governance of firms has been slow both in Asia and in the West.

The Governance of Investor-owned Firms

In the previous sections we analyzed patterns of business governance that provide alternatives to the pattern typically laid out in company law, which assigns specific rights and responsibilities to shareholders, managers, and creditors. These alternative patterns of business governance developed in the six Asian economies in our sample after a corporate law had been put in place. This is the case for most state owned companies, and for the practice of state guidance. It is also true for many of the family owned business conglomerates. Although family owned firms have a long tradition in all economies, today's chaebol in the Republic of Korea and large business groups in Taipei,China are more recent foundations. This sequence of events raises an important question about shareholder protection and the effect of the content and the quality of corporate law on the evolving patterns of business governance in investor owned firms.

Empirical studies using data from 40 economies around the world have found that the quality of shareholder protection has influenced the concentration of ownership in large corporations. They claim that it has also influenced the ability of firms to raise funds from external sources (La Porta et al. 1997a and b). According to La Porta et al. (1997a), common law countries on average provide better shareholder protection than civil law countries. Among civil law countries those with a legacy of German law do better overall than the countries with a French legacy.

A major drawback of the analysis is that countries are classified according to the origin of their legal systems without recognizing that investor protection developed in most countries only after the period of transplanting major legal systems. The US has taken a leading role in the refinement of investor protection. Many countries, including civil law countries, have subsequently copied from Anglo-American law. This is the case for Japan, Republic of Korea, and Taipei,China, which had originally borrowed from civil law countries (see table 5.2 above). This sequence of events defies a simple categorization of countries according to the origin of their legal systems for laws governing investor protection.

An analysis of the type of investor protection offered in the corporate laws of the six economies in our sample provides further evidence that the scope and type of shareholder protection is independent of the origin of a country's legal system. We distinguish between two types of shareholder protection: substantive protection and procedural protection (Black and Kraakman 1996). Substantive protection creates entry barriers (such as minimum capitalization requirements) and/or defines the limits of permissible corporate activities. For the most part, these provisions are enforced by the state. The company registrar ensures compliance at the time of incorporation and when changes in corporate statutes that require registration take place. In some instances, shareholders may have the right to challenge actions taken in violation of these provisions. Procedural protection offers a different mechanism for enforcing shareholder protection. It does not rely on state oversight, but offers shareholders devices to defend their own interests through voting, appraisal rights, and more extensive recourse to judicial review.

The evidence provided in table 5.4 shows that different economies use different combinations of substantive and procedural protection in their laws. These combinations are the result of repeated legal change that can hardly be traced to the origins of an economy's legal system. Moreover, they do not necessarily offer clues to the importance of bureaucratic controls. The PRC, for example, has an impressive range of measures for procedural protection on the books. Nevertheless, the new corporate law is primarily designed to serve the state in implementing policies for SOEs and to enforce bureaucratic controls. By contrast, the improvement of the rights of nonstate shareholders was not intended.

This leaves us with the question of whether the existence or absence of effective shareholder protection has influenced the patterns of business governance we have observed and ultimately the performance of companies. In theory, we would expect higher share concentration in privately owned companies in economies with less shareholder protection. This is based on the assumption that shareholders who cannot rely on the law to provide them with adequate protection of their rights are likely to revert to direct control. In addition, economies with better shareholder protection should have better developed markets for equity financing as investors are more likely to invest in minority positions, giving firms a larger pool of investors from which to raise capital. The studies on shareholder protection and finance mentioned above suggest that countries with legal systems offering less shareholder protection indeed have a higher concentration of ownership stakes in their largest companies (La Porta et al. 1997a and b). Such economies also tend to have less developed capital markets than economies that are associated with legal systems offering better shareholder protection. These results show a positive correlation, not causation, but the authors of the La Porta study have con-

Table 5.4   Shareholder Protection (economy; year of enactment and year of last major revision of corporate law)

Type of protection	PRC 1994	India 1956/1996	Japan 1899/1997	Republic of Korea 1962/1984	Malaysia 1965/997	Taipei,China 1988
Substantive Protection						
Bans authorized but unissued shares[a]	X	0	0	0	0	0
Requires shares to be issued at par[b] or nominal value	0	0	0	0	X	0
Requires minimum capitalization	X	0	X	X	0	X
Limits debt or preferred stock	0	X	0	X	X	X
Bans or strictly limits share repurchase	X	X	X	X	0	X
Bans self-dealing with directors or officers	X	0	0	0	X	X
Bans or strictly limits subsidiary ownership of parent shares	X	X	X	X	X	0
Total	5	3	3	4	4	4
Procedural protections						
Mandates one share, one vote rule	X	X	X	X	X	X
Mandates proportional board representation	0	0	0	0	0	X
Permits shareholder removal of directors without cause	0	X	X	X	X	X
Requires shareholder approval of director/officer self dealing	X	X	0	0	X	X

(table continues on following page)

(Table 5.4 continued)

Type of protection	PRC 1994	India 1956/1996	Japan 1899/1997	Republic of Korea 1962/1984	Malaysia 1965/1997	Taipei,China 1988
Requires meaningful shareholder vote on fundamental transactions	X	0	X	X	X	X
Mandates appraisal rights in mergers or sales of all assets	X	X	X	0	0	X
Requires shareholder vote on large acquisitions	X	X	X	X	X	0
Requires shareholder vote on large new stock issues	X	0	0	0	X	0
Grants preemption rights	X	X	0	X	X	X
Mandates minority put rights upon changes of control	X	0	0	0	X	X
Requires confidential voting	X	0	0	0	0	0
Proxies may be issued by mail	X	X	X	X	X	X
Total[c]	10	7	6	6	9	9

Note: "X" denotes that the law includes the relevant provisions, "0" that it does not. Some data are difficult to decide because legal provisions include qualifications and exceptions, as in (a) and (b) below.

a. X if the law itself prohibits authorized but unissued shares; 0 if the law allows it or provides that the company statutes may prohibit it.

b. X denotes that issuance must be done at par value; 0 includes cases where the law stipulates that issuance must be done at least at par value, but allows issuance over and above par value.

c. Totals indicate number of substantive or procedural protections found in the law.

Source: Black and Kraakman (1996); team reports. Where team reports deviated from the assessment by Black and Kraakman, the team results were used for this table.

structed a causal link between shareholder protection and economic out-come variables. They have done this by suggesting that the effectiveness of shareholder protection was determined by the legal system economies adopted in the process of law reception in the nineteenth and early twentieth centuries. However, we have shown that certainly for the economies included in this study, this assumption is not founded on historical evidence. Economies borrowed from different legal systems to improve investor protection over time. The original source of law for legal transplants therefore did not determine the scope of investor protection. Moreover, shareholder protection did not change for most of the period before 1980. Since then the process of change has accelerated. India introduced two important procedural protections in 1992, including shareholder approval for self-dealing by directors and officers, and shareholder votes on large acquisitions. Japan introduced minimum capital requirements in 1991. Malaysia included provisions that ban self-dealing by directors or officers in 1986 and further strengthened these protections in amendments of the corporate law in 1989 and 1992. Taipei,China added several procedural protections copied from US company law in 1988. The timing of the legal change in Taipei,China is important. It occurred during a policy period when greater emphasis was placed on market based economic development, and after capital market development had taken off in most economies. This suggests that legal change responded to economic change rather than preceding it. This would refute the proposition that law is a determinant for patterns of external finance.

BUSINESS GOVERNANCE AND THE CHANGING PATTERN OF CORPORATE FINANCE

Whatever the causes for the prevailing patterns of business governance in Asia in the past, there are signs that these patterns are in the process of change. Changes in economic policies fostered by economic development resulted in the diversification of sources of corporate finance. In particular the surge in capital market development in recent years has raised the significance of equity finance. Law played an important role in facilitating this change. Moreover, once policy changes had been introduced, legal fine tuning played a crucial role in making economic change sustainable.

A corporation can raise external financing through equity or debt. Equity finance can primarily come from contributions of core shareholders or it can be raised from a large pool of small investors, each holding only a fraction of shares in a company. The US and UK are among the economies with the most developed equity markets and the most extensive reliance on stock markets for corporate finance. However, over time the role of equity as a means of financing new investments in these economies has declined. Recent data show that in developed market economies only a fraction of new investments, which rarely exceeds 5 percent, is financed with equity (Corbett and Jenkinson 1994). An important reason is the life cycle of firms. Mature firms tend to rely heavily on internal sources of financing, such as retained earnings in contrast to external sources of finance (Rajan and Zingales 1997). Moreover, different industries have different preferences for internal versus external finance. Finally, the takeover wave in the UK and US in the 1980s has resulted in highly leveraged firms.

By contrast, equity financing has become an important source of financing in emerging markets. An empirical study of the hundred largest listed companies in nine emerging markets concludes that throughout the 1980s, these companies have financed on average 39 percent of their new investments by issuing equity (Singh 1995).

We lack time series data for most of the economies in our sample to demonstrate changes in the use of different sources of financing over time. Available data on Malaysia for 1988–90 show a surprisingly high share of internal financing (77 percent), and a high proportion of credit financing (18 percent) for an economy with a well developed capital market (see table 5.5 below). However, the privatization of SOEs in the late 1980s raised substantial funds through equity. Data for the Republic of Korea reveal that the relative share of external over internal sources of funds has increased since 1963 from 52.3 percent to over 73 percent in 1991 (Fields 1995). Bank credits have risen and subsequently declined as a share of total external finance. Since the late 1980s debt and equity securities have become more important as sources for external financing, with a preference for debt rather than equity securities. For Taipei,China, data are available only for 1967 and 1980. During this period,

Table 5.5   Stock Market Index, 1980–1995

Economy	1980	1985	1990	1995
PRC	n.a.	n.a.	3.4	4.8
India	3.4	4.0	5.2	5.4
Japan	7.8	8.6	9.2	8.8
Korea, Republic of	4.8	5.2	8.2	8.2
Malaysia	7.2	7.2	8.4	9.4
Taipei,China	5.6	6.4	8.6	8.8

n.a. = not applicable
Source: Authors' calculations based on International Finance Corporation data (1996).

the share of external finance has not changed much. However, these data do not reflect the changes that took place after 1980.

The changes in corporate finance have gone hand in hand with the development of capital markets in Asia. These changes are reflected in the cumulative stock market index we present in table 5.5. The index is based on several stock market indicators, including market capitalization as a percentage of GDP, the value traded as a share of market capitalization (turnover ratio), the number of companies per million people, and the average size of companies in terms of market capitalization. The cumulative index is based on a worldwide comparison. The ranking of the six Asian economies on the worldwide scale for each of the indicators in 1980, 1985, 1990, and 1995 is shown in the appendix. Market capitalization is given double weight, all other indicators have equal weight. The scale is from zero to ten.

The cumulative index shows that on an international scale, Japan and Malaysia had well developed markets already in 1980. By 1990, Taipei,China and the Republic of Korea had caught up with these markets. By contrast, India's stock market was much less developed in 1980 and has been left behind by the development of markets in other economies. Although India's ranking in the cumulative index has increased since, it is still barely above the median on our scale. The PRC's stock markets were established only in 1990. The rapid development over the past years is quite impressive. However, the comparative index shows that the PRC is still at the lower end of stock market development in Asia.

IMPLICATIONS FOR LEGAL DEVELOPMENT

Regression analysis across economies provides important evidence that policy changes have played a key role in promoting the development of capital markets. In particular, the liberalization of capital controls is positively correlated with stock market development (Levine and Zervos 1996). Subsequent to these policy changes and in response to the rapid development of capital markets, all six economies have enacted new laws that affect the state's role in overseeing capital markets, investor protection, and access to the markets by companies and investors. The general trend of these changes has been to reduce direct state controls and improve the transparency of the markets so that investors are able to make informed investment decisions. However, these changes were introduced only recently and have remained only halfway measures so far. Most economies still rely on extensive merit requirements, which specify criteria companies must meet to be able to issue securities to the public or to be listed on the market. However, merit requirements

have become more flexible and the increasing importance of disclosure requirements suggests that economies in Asia may also shift towards disclosure
as opposed to merit systems for regulating securities markets as is the case in
most economies in the West.

It is difficult to link to stock market indicators changes that affect, for
example, only the oversight function of the state. The reason is that most
economies, in introducing legal changes that affected different aspects of local securities market regulations, enacted them all at the same time. It is therefore difficult to identify the type of legal change that has most contributed to
the development of markets. Moreover, the areas of the law that received
most attention differ across countries, because the existing legal framework
and actual market development demanded different legal responses. To illustrate the complexity of legal change that accompanied the development of
securities markets, we provide below a brief overview of key legal developments for each of the six economies.

Legal Developments in the PRC

Trading in securities in China began in 1914, when the Shanghai govern-
ment became the first city to permit it. In 1920s, Shanghai also became the first
city in China to open a securities exchange (Dipchand 1994). Seventy years
later, in 1990, it was again Shanghai, which first opened a stock exchange.
Shenzhen followed in 1991. Until 1992 local branches of the Central Bank of
China (CBC) exercised market oversight. They were then replaced by the State
Council Securities Policy Committee and the China Securities Regulatory
Commission. Stock markets in the PRC are tightly regulated. Only companies
that meet a long list of conditions obtain access to the market for equity. The
companies that are listed on the PRC's stock exchange are state owned enterprises that have been reorganized into joint stock companies. Company shares
are divided into different groups. State shares and legal person shares cannot
be floated. "A" shares are earmarked for domestic investors and "B" shares for
foreign investors only. A provisional national securities law was adopted in
1993. It stipulates the requirements for initial public offerings and for listings
on stock exchanges. A company law with basic provisions on shareholder
rights was adopted in 1993 and went into force in 1994.

Legal Developments in India

Among the economies in our sample, India has the longest history of
stock markets. Trading in loan securities of the East India Company began in
the late eighteenth century. By the 1830s, corporate securities were trading
regularly. The first securities market regulation was enacted in Bombay in

1865. The market has been volatile since its inception as a result of external market shocks and weaknesses in the legal framework. When India became independent, the central government sought to establish tighter controls over the market. The 1956 Securities Contract Regulations Acts gave the government control over the recognition and administration of stock exchanges as well as extensive power to intervene in markets. These powers were distributed among different state agencies, including the Company Registrar and the Comptroller of Capital Issues. In line with the general policies that favored state controls, additional administrative bodies were established to ensure compliance with the law. An amendment to the Companies Act in 1963 established a company law board within the Ministry of Justice, which exercised extensive powers to investigate misuse of shareholder rights. The powers of the board were strengthened further in 1974. In 1988, the right to appeal to the board was extended to minority shareholders.

The stock market remained stagnant until the mid-1980s. With the relaxation of state controls over economic activities, market capitalization and the number of listed companies increased substantially—although on a per capita basis the total number of listed companies has remained low. Fraud and misuse of investors' rights have been rampant. In an attempt to strengthen capital market oversight, the Securities and Exchange Board of India was established in 1988 and converted into an independent statutory body in 1992. It has jurisdiction over initial offerings, trading, and licensing market participants. In 1992, the securities and exchange board replaced earlier regulations concerning public offerings. The new guidelines stipulate free access to the capital market and abolition of pricing controls. The market was opened to foreign investments, but a ceiling for aggregate foreign investment per company remains in place.

Legal Developments in Japan

Japan had a basic framework for capital markets in place prior to World War II. In 1948 these laws were replaced by a securities and exchange law that borrowed heavily from the 1933/34 securities and exchange legislation in the United States. It created a securities and exchange commission and stipulated rules on public offering, disclosure, and secondary distribution of shares. In 1952, this law was amended to abolish the securities and exchange commission and transfer the responsibility of overseeing capital markets to the Ministry of Finance (MOF). Between the mid-1960s and 1980, major legal changes concerned the improvement of investor protection, including stricter accounting and disclosure rules and the liberalization of entry requirements for foreign investors. In 1971 foreign securities firms were permitted to open branch offices and engage in securities trading subject to obtaining a license from the MOF. In the late 1970s, use of the stock market accelerated considerably. There was no major legal change in relevant laws that could have triggered these events. Companies began to make more public offerings as opposed to rights issues but the rapid development of the market coincided with the deregulation of financial business. This led to several scandals, and in response, the government tightened securities and exchange regulations. A comprehensive revision of existing financial sector legislation in 1992 expanded legal controls and clarified their scope. To improve capital market oversight, an exchange surveillance commission within the MOF was established in 1993. Its responsibility is to ensure the enforcement of laws and to initiate indictments where appropriate. Further, changes in the company law in 1994 strengthened the legal rules against insider trading.

Legal Developments in the Republic of Korea

In the Republic of Korea, the infrastructure for a securities market was established already in the late 1950s and early 1960s, although a comprehensive legal framework was not put into place until the second half of the 1970s. The Korean Stock Exchange was established as a government owned entity controlled by the MOF in 1956. Attempts to promote the development of capital markets were not very successful until the implementation of the Going Public Encouragement Act (1972). This forced companies beyond a specified size to offer some of their shares to the public and produced a first blip in market development. A securities and exchange law, modeled closely after the Japanese law, was enacted in 1976. The law governs initial public offerings and trading of securities. Two state agencies responsible for enforcing the law and overseeing securities markets, a securities and exchange commission and the Securities Supervisory Board, were established in 1977 following enactment of the securities and exchange law. Until 1980, the Korean market had been virtually closed to foreign investors. In 1981, special trust funds for indirect foreign portfolio investments were created. However, ceilings were imposed for the investment volume, and strict qualifying requirements enforced. Moreover, direct foreign investment was prohibited until 1995. The negative side effects of the developing securities markets were met with the adoption of a general antifraud provision in 1982. Insider trading rules were adopted in 1987 and strengthened in 1991.

Legal Developments in Malaysia

In Malaysia, the institutions for a stock exchange were established in the early 1960s. A comprehensive securities and industry act followed in 1973 together with detailed listing requirements issued by the Kuala Lumpur Stock

Exchange. Malaysia's legal framework governing securities markets was inherited from Britain. The traditional English model favored a self-regulatory approach to securities market regulations. Laws adopted after independence strengthened control and oversight by the state. Several state agencies, including the Ministry of Finance, the Registrar of Companies, and the Capital Issues Committee exercised control functions. A securities commission was established only in 1993 in an attempt to streamline market oversight.

By 1980, Malaysia had already a fairly well developed stock market (Scully 1984). The acceleration of market development in the subsequent years resulted in several important legal changes that strengthened shareholder and investor protection and streamlined market oversight. In 1983, securities fraud provisions and insider trading rules were enacted. In 1986, the disclosure requirements of the 1965 Companies Act were expanded. In addition, Malaysia progressively relaxed merit requirements for initial public offerings and stock exchange listings. In 1995, the price/earning multiples which previously had been used to assess the viability of a company were abolished together with other detailed merit criteria, including the quality and capability of management and the suitability of a company for listing. These reforms fell short of a shift from a merit system to a system based entirely on disclosure, but there are plans to have a full disclosure system in place by the year 2000.

Legal Developments in Taipei,China

The origins of the securities market in Taipei,China go back to the land reform in 1953, when several state owned enterprises were privatized and former landowners compensated with stocks and bonds. A securities and exchange commission was established under the Ministry of Economics in 1956 and the Taipei Stock Exchange was established in 1961. A comprehensive securities and exchange commission law was adopted in 1968. Despite the existence of a comprehensive legal framework and several measures to encourage the development of an active stock market, including tax incentives, a more vibrant market developed only after 1980. In the early 1980s, the government announced plans for a sequenced liberalization of capital markets to foreign investments. In the first stage, special trust funds were established that offered foreign investors offshore investment opportunities. The first funds began to operate in 1983. Entry requirements were relaxed in 1988, and direct investments permitted in 1991. Foreign investments remained subject to cumulative ceilings, set initially at 2 percent but subsequently relaxed. In response to the rapid development of the stock market, as well as problems concerning the misuse of shareholders' rights, a comprehensive law reform package was enacted in 1988. The Securities and Exchange Law Amendment combines state controls with the strengthening of investor rights and disclosure requirements. The law mandates offerings to the public and includes provisions that allow the state to appropriate shares in order to offer them to the public. At the same time the new law introduces insider trading rules and provides for more extensive disclosure requirements. Several amendments to the company law further strengthened shareholder protection.

CONCLUSION

A comparison of the history of legal change governing stock markets with the actual development of these markets shows that it is difficult to identify cause and effect between legal and economic change in respect of corporate governance. In some economies, such as India, trading began long before the institutional and legal infrastructure for stock markets had been established. In others, like Republic of Korea and Taipei,China, the legal and institutional infrastructure was put in place prematurely as markets developed only much later. For markets to take off, as they did in Asia in the 1980s, a combination of policies and legal infrastructure needed to be in place. Even this is not a safeguard against market crashes, which most countries experienced repeatedly. After the initial takeoff of capital markets, legal change has been primarily responsive. Most changes have addressed the need to make markets more transparent, to counter fraud, and to streamline market oversight. In addition, changes in the company law have sought to strengthen shareholder rights, at least in some countries. The importance of these improvements in the legal infrastructure for market development has been recognized by policymakers in light of the financial crisis in 1997/98. In the Republic of Korea, for example, the improvement of minority shareholder rights is high on the agenda of current reforms. The hope is to improve the existing corporate governance system and create incentives for a more extensive use of equity finance.

Our findings suggest that the role of corporate law in the process of capital formation has changed over time. The pace and scope of these changes differ considerably across economies, but they have one thing in common. These differences can be attributed largely to government policies that favored state ownership as well as debt financing through a banking sector that could be controlled and directed by the state. These alternative patterns of business governance—including state ownership, state guidance, and family ownership—often made use of elements of the corporate form—most important, of limited liability. But corporate law provided only a formal shell. It was of little importance in determining the governance of firms. This is most evident with respect to state owned enterprises. Although an increasing number of state owned enterprises is now being incorporated, for the greater part of the period after 1960, most did not make use of the corporate form. The case of private firms under state guidance and of family owned firms is less clear cut. In both cases, the corporate form provides investors with limited liability. This greatly reduces the risk of pursuing business strategies, including strategies that may be in the interest of family owners or policymakers, but may not be economically sound.

In pursuing financing, the use of the corporate form has enabled state owned enterprises as well as family owned firms to expand their sources of capital beyond the use of debt. In most cases, only minority stakes have been floated to outside shareholders, and attempts have been made to curtail their voting rights. In addition, in some economies, family controlled firms have chosen to issue preferred stock or corporate bonds that do not confer voting rights, rather than common shares. Whether this strategy will be sustainable in the long run remains to be seen. There are already signs that the demand for more funds is driving more firms to the market, although in many cases, companies have sought debt rather than equity finance. Should equity finance become more important over time, the corporate function that has remained dormant for many companies despite their form, may turn out to be an important mechanism for changing the control structure of businesses in Asia. This would be not unlike what happened in many Western market economies where family ownership declined through a process of mergers, new sources of financing, and the need to professionalize enterprise management. Still, as of 1995, this process had not been completed either in Asia or in the West. We therefore conclude that with respect to business governance, we see only partial convergence between the two regions.

APPENDIX 5A: STOCK MARKET INDICATORS

Appendix 5A: Stock Market Indicators

Table 5A   Comparative Stock Market Indicators in Six Asian Economies

Economy	Market capitalization as percentage of GDP				Value traded as a percentage of market capitalization				Number of listed companies per million people				Average size (average market capitalization)			
	1980	1985	1990	1995	1980	1985	1990	1995	1980	1985	1990	1995	1980	1985	1990	1995
PRC	n.a.	n.a.	0	3	n.a.	n.a.	9	10	n.a.	n.a.	0	0	n.a.	n.a.	8	8
India	3	4	5	8	9	9	10	4	2	3	4	3	0	0	2	4
Japan	7	9	10	9	10	9	10	9	5	6	6	6	3	4	9	9
Korea, Republic of	3	4	8	8	10	10	10	10	5	4	6	6	3	4	9	9
Malaysia	9	9	10	10	6	5	7	9	6	6	6	8	6	7	9	10
Taipei,China	5	6	9	9	10	10	10	10	3	3	5	6	5	7	10	10

n.a. = not applicable
Note: Higher scores mean more developed markets. The index is based on stock market data for 1985 and reflects relative change over time. Scale 0-10.
Source: Data: IFC (1996); the index is based on Authors' calculation.

Chapter 6

THE RELATION BETWEEN CREDIT AND LAWS GOVERNING SECURITY INTERESTS

The "invention of credit" has been hailed as a precondition for capitalism. Credit is an essential link between savings and investment. It helps allocate resources to productive use. Substantial evidence justifies our assumption that the level of lending is important for development.

This chapter asks two questions. The first is whether law plays an important role in lending in Asia. The major tools of law typically available to a creditor are the ability to levy on collateral, enforce the terms of the loan agreement, and draw on a guarantee of the debtor's obligation, in court if necessary with the police power of the state in reserve. Here we examine the role of legal interests in collateral that secures credit and ask whether legally enforceable security interests to protect the investor have been an important ingredient for credit transactions in the six Asian economies. The use of security interests is a good indicator of the relevance of formal law to lenders and borrowers.[1]

Our answer to this first question is that security interest regimes are of much greater importance to lenders seeking to reduce risk when the government's development strategy is market oriented and much less important when it is not. To the extent that the policies allow markets to work and creditors to bear risk, security interest regimes become relevant to lending decisions. For much of the 35 years reviewed in this book, governments in most of our economies intervened actively. The nature of their intervention and the tools they needed to accomplish their plans determined whether lenders would find collateral useful to reduce risk.

The second question is whether practice in Asia differs significantly from the West in the use of regimes for security interests. As described in chapter 2, practice in Asia could be converging with that in the West, could vary by

---

[1] Legal terminology in this field differs dramatically across the economies, overlapping, contradicting, and sometimes even leaving important gaps. The same word may have different meanings in two economies. For this chapter, "collateral" refers to an asset, owned or possessed by a debtor or a third party, which the creditor may take possession of or sell in order to satisfy the obligation if the debtor fails to perform. A "secured transaction" is an obligation secured by collateral and "secured credit" or a "secured loan" is a loan secured by collateral. The legal interests in the collateral are known as "security interests." The "security interest regime" defines how one creates, perfects, and enforces security interests and is not to be confused with the term "securities" as applied to stocks and shares.

economy, could be largely irrelevant, or a mix. We find a mix in which, as markets are allowed to work, one sees evidence of convergence between the regions. This and the answer to our first question are explored in the comparative analysis that follows an initial discussion of the importance of security interests and the role of credit in the economies of our survey.

Comparisons among the six economies are very difficult even at our relatively detailed level of analysis with a small sample. The six economies differ profoundly in many important substantive ways and in the data they generate for ostensibly the same activity, such as private sector credit. These differences qualify our findings.

The following sections present first background, then comparative material. As background, we review the debate about the importance of security interests, with an overview of our findings, and describe the role of credit to private borrowers in the GNP of each of the economies. The comparative analysis that follows is designed to explore the questions posed in chapter 2: does law matter and is Asia different from the West? It sketches, first, the security interest regimes in each economy, then compares the regimes' evolution and effect in lending.

THE DEBATE ABOUT SECURITY INTERESTS AND LENDING, AND A SUMMARY OF OUR FINDINGS

Our first question is whether security interests played an important role in lending in Asia. In the traditional view, good collateral promotes lending for productive purposes, which in turn fuels economic growth. The World Development Report for 1989 (World Bank 1989, pp. 87–88) explained the economic function of security and its different forms:

> The assignment and transferability of property rights promote economic efficiency directly by creating new incentives, but also indirectly by making financial intermediation possible. They do this by allowing borrowers to offer security in the form of mortgages over real estate or other collateral. Some assets are better collateral than others...
>
> When taking collateral, the lender is mainly interested in the efficient transfer of property rights, because the security is invoked only in case of default... Mortgages over land and other real estate are therefore one of the best forms of collateral. . . . If the entrepreneur has no suitable collateral, the risks to the lender increase dramatically. The lender will then need far more in-

formation and perhaps a share in the proceeds if the venture
proves a success. . . .

In some countries other assets can serve as collateral. Inventories and other movable goods are inherently poor collateral
because they have comparatively little value, are destructible,
and can be sold privately and informally. They are difficult to use
as collateral when left in the possession of the borrower. . . .

Similarly, Hernando de Soto (1990) made a compelling argument that
poorly functioning laws cripple the use of collateral and impose high transaction costs on potential borrowers. Inefficiency is rife, increasing costs to the
economy, misallocating resources, and hindering growth.

Many studies show that security interests promote efficiency in the West.
One review of the literature identified two mechanisms (Bebchuk and Fried
1996, pp. 23–25).

•   One is the right of a secured creditor to seize and apply collateral to its
debt faster than an unsecured creditor can be repaid from the debtor's general
assets. This is called a "property right." This mechanism has been shown to:

(1) reduce overinvestment by preventing the borrower from sell-
     ing or pledging the collateral to raise funds for an inefficient
     project;

(2) reduce inefficient asset dilution by preventing the borrower
     from transferring the collateral to its shareholders, or sell-
     ing or pledging the collateral to raise funds to transfer to its
     shareholders;

(3) reduce the costs associated with default by allowing the se-
     cured creditor to avoid judicial process;

(4) indirectly reduce inefficient behavior by increasing the ex-
     pected cost to the borrower of violating covenants in the
     loan contract with the secured creditor; and

(5) reduce socially excessive "monitoring" of the borrower when
     it is suffering financial difficulties.

In Asia, we found the opposite of these effects at work, since often the
regimes for security interests prevented lenders from achieving these effi-
ciencies. Japan's lending binge and asset bubble in the late 1980s is a contrary
example of (1); real property supposedly secured much of the lending. In

examples for (3) and (4), India's lenders face enforcement delays lasting beyond a decade. A contrary example for (5) is Taipei,China's use of criminal sanctions as a substitute for security interests. We encountered no explicit examples of (2).

• The second mechanism is priority—the right of a secured creditor to a prior claim on the proceeds of collateral even if it is "sold, transferred, or pledged to other properties." This mechanism, called a "priority right," has been shown to enhance efficiency in theWest because it can:

(1) reduce the cost to secured creditors of acquiring information about the borrower since they need data only about the collateral, not the entire firm;

(2) reduce socially excessive monitoring of borrowers that have more than one sophisticated creditor; and

(3) increase socially insufficient monitoring of borrowers that have more than one creditor.

In each of these ways, secured lending reduces costs to the economy and contributes to growth. In most of the six Asian economies, however, the secured creditor's priority was not paramount. In one economy, the Republic of Korea, reducing priority for secured creditors preceded a reduction in the growth of lending, though other factors may explain the decline.[2]

The summary above identifies many ways in which laws governing security interests are said to work. But they may not always work in the same way. The basic point is that law can either promote or impede use of security, which in turn can promote or impede lending. The final link, that levels of lending can augment or slow an economy's economic growth, is supported by a broad literature. Figure 6.1 tracks the causal links asserted by this literature. The simple links in the figure are supplemented in the discussion later in the paper.

The nature of the link from the use of security interests to lending is subject to an intense debate. One school shows that, in certain circumstances at least, if secured lending to a firm is increased, that increase may be offset by a reduction in unsecured lending to the same firm on the part of unsecured creditors who would be less protected. This could create a zero sum effect or worse, since the transaction costs of giving security may actually leave the debtor in a worse net position than if it could have relied entirely on unsecured lending (Schwartz and Scott 1982). Economywide, a reduction in unse-

---

[2] Bebchuk and Fried (1996) question one element of the dogma about security interests in theWest, and particularly in the US, that the law promotes efficiency by paying secured claims in full before any unsecured claims are paid.

Figure 6.1   Theoretical Links of Laws for Security Interests to Lending and Economic Development

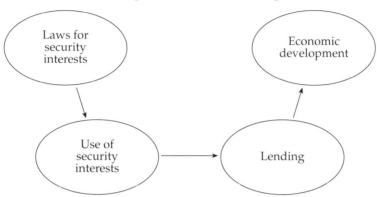

Source: Authors' compilation .

cured lending would harm business in several ways. Prime borrowers, that would otherwise have received unsecured loans because of their creditworthiness, would bear the costs of giving security to protect the lender, thereby increasing transaction costs and reducing operational efficiency. A second category, borrowers with good prospects but limited security, would find their access to credit limited. The common example is the young high-tech firm without assets for collateral but with strong prospects. If secured lending reduced aggregate unsecured lending, this firm could lose access to credit, which is arguably allocationally inefficient.

A variety of other explanations for the use and benefits of security interests have been advanced. Some look to the cost of monitoring debtors, but their implications for the lender point in different directions depending on whether the lender is informed or uninformed about the borrower. A leading article posits a complex relationship between the debtor and creditor that cannot be captured at the start of their relationship by contract. In such circumstances, security interests ameliorate possible conflicts by allowing the holder to influence the borrower's decisions during the life of their relationship (Scott 1986). We note the debate but do not attempt to resolve it here. Our research suggests that the discussion should be broadened to take into account several other factors.

We find evidence in the six economies that the simple causal relationships described in figure 6.1 do not, in Asia at least, capture the complex factors that influence the effect of laws governing security interests on the way they are used and on lending. These factors include the economic development strategy of the government, the existence of substitutes for security interests, and the performance of the macroeconomy. These factors and their effect on each other as well as lending can determine the relevance of security interests.

- *Economic Development Strategy*. Government economic strategy was significant for secured lending primarily because a regime of directed credit prevailed in many of the economies we examined for some time during the period under review. This was particularly the case during eras of fast growth. The point is that when banks must follow government directives about volume and cost of loans that are supported by official refinancing and other funding schemes, they expect the government to make good any losses they bear as a result. This can be done by supporting the borrower or lender directly or indirectly. Under these circumstances, even if the banks take security they do not rely on it to reduce risk as much as they would in market conditions. To a large extent, this seems to have been true of the economies in our study. At the end of the period, however, governments were less able or inclined to provide that essential support, and markets increasingly controlled credit allocation and pricing. It is only in such circumstances that market oriented mechanisms like security interests become important.

- *Substitutes for Security Interests*. Substitutes became important when they rendered security interests unnecessary or relatively more costly. Substitutes were provided by law, relationships that promoted trust, or illegal activity like the use of enforcers. We found evidence that the loss of substitutes (like criminal sanctions for default) drove lenders to greater use of secured loans. Personal or business relationships did not necessarily reduce the use of security interests; indeed, in the context of certain government strategies, relationships increased the use of security. Illegal activity seemed to be associated with an ineffective security interest regime.

- *Performance of the Macroeconomy*. Events in the macroeconomy affected supply and demand conditions for loans, hence the capacity of lenders to insist on secured lending.

Is Asia different? Most of the statutes governing security interests would be familiar to Western lawyers, particularly since they were drawn from Western models. Although case law in some economies modified these statutes, one does not find a uniquely Asian set of substantive laws. The differences lie more in their use. To the extent that security interests are largely irrelevant in regimes of directed or managed credit, and these Asian economies relied more on such regimes, Asia is different. But one would find similar policies of managed credit in many other regions of the world. Relationships in Asia are said to have been crucial for much business there. In several economies, however, creditors in relationships with borrowers still required security interests. We lack systematic data to show whether these creditors were less likely to enforce those interests than they were when they had no relationship with the borrower.

Is there convergence with the West? Not in one sense: essentially the same laws derived from the West were on the books in each economy in 1960 and 1995. Nor were the laws merely on the books but not observed at first, then observed later. We have no evidence that the laws governing security interests were ignored, just that secured lending was less important in the periods of direct government control of the economy. But there is convergence in use to the extent that lenders in both Asian and Western economies distinguish in the same way among types of borrowers. In the US, big borrowers need relatively much less collateral than small- and medium-sized borrowers. In some of the Asian economies, the same is true (Japan, Republic of Korea, and Taipei,China). It is not true where prudential rules require full security or are believed by loan officers to require it.

Are security interest laws from one "family" of law more appropriate than those from another? At our grassroots level, we cannot see this. Malaysia had effective laws, India did not. Both were common law jurisdictions. Malaysia borrowed some of its laws in this field from Australia. Japan and Republic of Korea had similar laws governing security interests, and shared with Taipei,China a civil law tradition, in part because Japan had occupied both and imported its law. But Taipei,China supplemented these laws with US techniques to permit broader security interests in personal property. Profound differences between India and Malaysia and the intermarriage of some civil law regimes cast doubt on efforts to generalize about families of law (see Levine 1997, La Porta et al. 1997a).

The basic story seems to be that Asian lenders used security interests as one of several ways to reduce the risk of default and loan losses and that, as noted earlier, they shifted to greater reliance on security interests as alternatives become *relatively* less effective and as markets replaced government management of the economy. Market oriented mechanisms such as security interests do appear to become important when markets are allowed to work. Indeed, as the Republic of Korea adopted market oriented policies, and a banking crisis developed, Korean banks with higher secured loans tended to have lower nonperforming loans than others. The others were not in a position to use collateral and looked to other means to deal with their bad debts. For much of the time, governments in the six economies intervened actively. Even in these periods security interests were used somewhat. The nature of the governments' intervention and the tools they needed to accomplish their plans determined whether lenders would find collateral useful to reduce risk. As we explain, government intervention in Malaysia made security interests relevant to banks lending to companies that led the economy's growth. Government intervention in the Republic of Korea made banks less interested in security interests.

A brief note on methodology is appropriate here. Useful quantitative data are rare in each of the six economies and comparable statistics for all six economies are simply unavailable. The ideal would allow one to identify secured and unsecured lending by private and public creditors to borrowers of different sizes. Three economies had data showing banks' secured and unsecured lending to all borrowers. Of these, one combined lending secured by guarantees with lending secured by personal property, while the others did not. Governments unfortunately do not collect data in a form well suited for this sort of research. The ideal would also have included a time series from 1960 to 1995. One economy had this and another had data from 1966. Interviews in each economy allowed the research teams to supplement the limited statistics, but the interviews tended to elicit practice in the 1990s rather than for the entire period. This suggests the need to gather data at the company level.

GROWTH OF GNP: THE ROLE OF CREDIT TO PRIVATE BORROWERS

Credit is an important intermediate growth variable. Maxwell Fry (1995), in his review of the literature about growth and the financial sector, reported financial deepening as economies developed. Among the measures of depth is lending as a share of GNP. The stock of outstanding loans grew relative to GNP as GNP per capita increased. Rather than all lending, however, we are interested in lending by financial intermediaries to private borrowers, for whom security interest should be particularly important since borrowers in the public sector have the state's implicit or explicit guarantee.

In the Asian economies in this study, lending to private borrowers grew relative to GNP over the period (see table 6.1). In 1966, lending by banks that take deposits ranged from 10 to 14 percent of GNP in India, Republic of Korea, Malaysia, and Taipei,China, and about twice that (31 percent) in Japan. By 1994, the ratio increased 2.5 times in India, 4 times in Japan and Taipei,China, 5 times in the Republic of Korea, and almost 6 times in Malaysia. The PRC reports different data for a shorter period. Loans to borrowers other than the central government almost doubled as a share of GNP from 1978 to 1994. But the size of the ratio misleads, because very little of this lending is to private borrowers, since most of the borrowers are quasi-public. Table 6.1 shows the debt/GNP ratio in 1966 and 1994. While one must be cautious comparing the economies, it is not surprising that the ratios for Japan are significantly higher than those of the other economies, considering Japan's much higher living standard. At the other extreme, India's low ratio should be qualified by the existence of a large informal or black market in lending that might, if its size were known, substantially raise the level of lending in relation to GNP.

To classify the six economies as Asian glosses over very big differences in their law and practice toward security interests. They vary along important dimensions of substantive law, legal processes, and use. We use several dimensions to determine whether an economy's regime support for security is strong or weak. The following identifies the dimensions (Wood 1995, p. 7):

- *The legal regime.* The laws governing security interests may provide a single source, which promotes internal consistency among the rules, or multiple sources.
- *The lenders.* The type of lenders—public or private, formal or informal, and their structure (concentrated, diverse)—affect the relationship between creditor and debtor, which can affect the use of security.
- *Range of collateral.* The broader the range of collateral, the more assets debtors can offer to secure credit. A broader range allows borrowers without the conventional forms of collateral, such as land, access to credit if they can provide other assets. The broadest range includes types of assets that the debtor may not own when it gives the security interest, such as equipment it buys later (sometimes called future assets), rights to intangibles (like copyrights), rights to future payments (accounts receivable), and rights to goods in process (inventory). The broader the range, the stronger is the regime.
- *Possession.* Although one of the surest ways a creditor can assure that collateral continues to protect against the risk of loss is to hold the collateral, this limits the ability of the debtor to use the collateral in the course of business. That a debtor can more easily misapply collateral in its possession creates a major challenge for security regimes. The stronger regimes solve it in ways that protect the creditor's interests while allowing the debtor to hold and use the collateral. The weaker ones push the creditor toward possession.
- *Registration/Publicity.* A creditor needs to be able to confirm that the collateral in which it seeks a security interest is not already subject to a prior creditor's interest. This is difficult if notice does not exist in a central location. A secured creditor generally needs to inform others of its interest in the collateral for that interest to be effective against them. The others include other creditors that want a security interest in the same asset and purchasers of the asset from the debtor. A stronger regime provides the necessary publicity through central registries for security interests and requires their use in order to perfect the interest against others. Weaker regimes lack simple methods of notification.
- *Self-enforcement.* A secured creditor prefers to avoid the cost in time and money of using courts to enforce its interest in the collateral if a borrower defaults. The stronger regimes provide fair techniques of self-enforcement.
- *Enforcement and execution.* When formal enforcement techniques must be pursued, a strong regime provides a minimal number of steps to prove the

Table 6.1   Lending by Financial Intermediaries to Borrowers in the Private Sector as a Share of GNP in Six Asian Economies, 1966 and 1994
(percentage)

Institution	PRC	India[b]	Japan	Republic of Korea[b]	Malaysia[b]	Taipei,China
Deposit taking banks						
1966	n.a.(1978)	10	31	11	14	12[c]
1994	93	26	118	58	81	51(1993)
Banks and nonbank financial institutions						
1966	52(1978)	13	113	16	18 (1969)	21
1994	95	30	211	80	121	76(1993)

n.a. = not applicable
Note: Year noted in parenthesis against date is year if other than that in the heading.
a. Nonstate (noncentral) government borrowers.
b. "Private borrowers" may include state-owned enterprises.
c. In Taipei,China, the first category includes all formal intermediaries. The second category includes both formal and informal intermediaries. The latter includes lending by business, households, employee deposit, and mutual credit clubs and use of postdated checks.
Source: Government statistical yearbooks (various issues).

creditor's rights as expeditiously as possible. The same may be said for *execution*, the process by which the creditor collects its stake in the collateral. The stronger regimes provide closure quickly, the weakest may take years.

   • *Clarity of Law*. The stronger regimes have straightforward rules, while the weaker ones have overlapping, conflicting rules that generate confusion about the rights of creditors and debtors and lead to lengthy court disputes.

   • *Costs*. Transaction costs play an important role when decisions about the use of security interests follow market-based criteria. The cost of registering and enforcing interests in stronger regimes is a low portion of the loan and in weaker regimes is high.

   • *Priority*. When a debtor is bankrupt, the secured lender wants the highest possible claim on the collateral, one superior to any other possible claimant, including later secured creditors, unsecured lenders, the government for taxes the debtor may owe, and employees for wages and benefits owed to them. For the secured creditor, the higher its priority the stronger the regime, though absolute priority is rare.

   • *Use of Secured Lending*. In few economies are all loans secured. Generally, the most creditworthy borrowers can borrow from banks without security. We know of no way to determine optimal ratios for secured and unsecured lending.

   The following sections sketch the evolution of the security interest regimes along these dimensions in each economy during the 35-year period. In some cases, we lack complete data.

   The overall effect is to identify those with stronger or weaker regimes. The strengths of the regimes in the economies vary, making overall comparisons hard. Measured by both substantive law and legal process, Malaysia emerges with the regime that is strongest among the six, but even its regime has significant gaps. Close together are Japan, Republic of Korea, and Taipei,China with Taipei,China edging ahead because of its active use of a close substitute. The weakest regimes appear in the PRC and India. This general finding is partially consistent with a similar ranking of many more economies. Wood (1995) groups countries according to their support for security. He identifies four groups: very sympathetic to security (in which he places most common law countries), quite sympathetic (including Germany and Japan), quite hostile, and very hostile (including France). Our observation of close similarities between Japan, Republic of Korea, and Taipei,China fits Wood's analysis; Malaysia, based on the UK common law system, is indeed friendly to security. But Indian law is also based on English common law and it provides one of the weakest regimes. This encourages us to question the usefulness for analysis of legal system family roots.

We therefore begin with Malaysia, then present Japan which was in part a prototype for both Taipei,China and Republic of Korea. India, with the most Byzantine regime, and the PRC, with the newest, appear last.

Security Interests in Malaysia

The law in Malaysia is creditor friendly, giving a perfected security interest the highest possible priority.

The Legal Regime. The regime governing security interests in Malaysia consisted of common law rules well established by 1960, the provisions of the Contracts Act of 1950, and two laws passed in 1965, the National Land Code and the Companies Act. The National Land Code borrowed a land registration system from Australia, and provided that only land registered according to that system could serve as collateral for loans. Once established, both the laws and institutions remained unchanged in substance throughout the period of this study. The Bill of Sale of Goods Act of 1957 and the Hire Purchase Act of 1967, as described below, regulated close substitutes to security. The regime was conservative, favoring lenders' security interests in land and corporate property. A financial crisis in the mid 1980s prompted the financial supervisors to tighten prudential regulation. The Banking and Financial Institutions Act of 1989 rationalized the industry, coordinated supervision, and granted the Central Bank the authority to limit the ability of licensed financial intermediaries to lend without security.

The Lenders. The chief lenders in Malaysia were commercial banks, 22 domestic and 16 foreign owned near the end of our period. Two large government owned banks dominated, with over one third of the assets of all banks. Another 9 medium sized banks were privately owned. The nonmonetary financial institutions included merchant banks (12), finance companies which loaned medium term (47), an Islamic bank, discount houses (7), and a credit guarantee corporation. Nonbank financial institutions, such as pension and insurance funds or development finance institutions, made up the rest of the system. From 1960 to 1988, the commercial banks' share of the assets of the financial system rose from 35 percent to 42 percent and the finance companies' share rose from less than 1 percent to 11 percent.

Range of Collateral. In Malaysia, creditors could take as collateral land, personal property in the form of securities and goods, and monetary claims in the form of accounts receivable, life insurance policies, and guarantees. The substantive law governing the use of land varied according to whether the land was peninsular Malaysia, where most of the economic growth took place, or in Sabah and Sarawak. Our analysis is of the law in peninsular Malaysia. Security interests in property that the debtor did not yet own, such as inventory or accounts receivable, could be held only when the debtor was a corporation. No such floating interest could be taken in the personal property of noncorporate entities. To secure their interest in personal property bought on credit and in the debtor's possession, lenders used a substitute called hire-purchase: the borrower was analogous to a lessee of the property, such as a car, until the loan was fully paid, at which point title transferred to the borrower as buyer. Because the creditor retained title, the debtor could not sell the property and the borrower could repossess it if the borrower defaulted.

Possession. Creditors commonly took possession of collateral, though the law had no special rules for this. A creditor also had the right to apply property in its possession and owned by the debtor against any amount in default. The common users of this right were banks, which also had a contractual right of set-off against deposits placed with them by borrowers. In the case of land, possession of the title and registration of the interest gave a lender a security interest against others. Personal property in the debtor's possession was less effective as security and avoided by banks, though not finance companies lending against equipment and consumer durables (like cars).

Registration/Publicity. Registration of a security interest in land gave the holder priority over a subsequent purchaser, transferee, or secured creditor. All dealings in land had to be registered. Interests in corporate property could be registered with the Registrar of Companies. Yet another registry was also kept for hire purchase, a substitute for security interests. The registries' staff size and skills grew substantially over the 35 years. The time between submission and entry varied with the registry and could take up to three months, but a secured creditor's interest was perfected on submission. A registry at the Road Transport Office recorded hire purchase interests in vehicles. No other security interests in personal property were registered, so a prospective lender could not determine its priority against other lenders secured by the same property.

Self-enforcement. Where the collateral was securities, a summary procedure allowed the lender to hold the instruments with a blank instrument of transfer from the debtor. If the borrower defaulted, the lender had the power to complete the transfer instrument and register its new ownership without proceeding through court. For movable property, a lender could repossess the collateral using a close substitute to security called a "bill of sale of goods". This gave the lender title to the property but left the property with the debtor while giving the lender the explicit right to take back possession. A lender could also retain title through hire purchase and thus repossess. For land as collateral, when the owner was a corporation, the practice was for the lenders to use a "debenture" that could give them a security interest in any kind of company property, including land. They understood that, if the debtor defaulted, they could give a receiver the authority to sell without long court proceedings that used the mechanisms of the National Land Code.[3] In a foreclosure that act did not permit self-help, so the secured lender had to go through the courts rather than simply take possession of the collateral.

Enforcement. Collateral in the form of securities held in the creditor's possession could be dealt with through summary proceedings, which took 6-12 months. Enforcement of interests in other forms of personal property had to go through the courts and took 12-18 months. One function of the court was to value property. Foreclosure on land as security generally took 12-18 months. Appeals were more problematic, since case backlogs had grown, and one estimate in the mid-1990s was that a final appellate decision could take up to five years (La Porta 1997a). Courts gave debtors little or no protection. They would not, for example, strike a contract for unfair bargaining power or unfair contract. Nor did legislation specifically protect borrowers. A defaulting party who lost a case had to pay legal costs. Nevertheless, banks preferred renegotiating with debtors over litigation.

Execution. This was straightforward.

Clarity of Law. The priority of claims was clear. The types of security interests were few and straightforward, since the 1965 legislation substituted a few simple concepts for the multiplicity of security interests found in English common law. For example, the "charge" substituted for various types of mortgages and pledges. People continued to use the old labels, but the law itself was streamlined. Title to real property was clear from the registration system.

Costs. Modest stamp duties and notarization costs were imposed on each security interest. Registration fees were modest. None of these costs rose substantially after 1960. Enforcement costs were lowest for interests in land. Costs were low when securities were held by the lender as collateral, and much higher for floating interests in corporate assets because a receiver had to be appointed. A substitute, personal guarantees, was also expensive to enforce because the guarantor might escape through bankruptcy.

---

[3] Court cases in the late 1980s were interpreted as giving lenders this power. In June 1997, however, the Federal Court held that lenders had to pursue their claim through the formal court system. Since this decision could not be appealed, it was possible that challenges would be made retroactively to foreclosures that took place over the prior six years (La Porta 1997a).

Priority. A perfected security interest, called a charge in Malaysia, in land or personal property gave the holder priority over all other claimants, including the government claiming for tax. The major problem for a lender was assuring itself that it held the first security interest in personal property in the debtor's possession.

Use of Secured Loans. A 1989 law granted the central bank the authority to limit the ability of licensed financial intermediaries to lend without security. However, the central bank only exercised that authority to require finance companies to take security for loans above the equivalent of about US$4,000.[4] Malaysia did not publish statistics giving the secured portion of its banks' loans. Interviews suggest that banks generally relied on security and that an unsecured loan was rare. Banks preferred, in order of importance, land (which by one estimate secured 30 percent of bank loans in the mid-1990s), securities, which they held, and floating interests in the assets of large companies. Banks avoided security interests in other personal property, but finance companies generally used substitutes such as hire-purchase. The bill of sale of goods was rarely used. Banks commonly protected themselves further by obtaining guarantees.

Conclusion. Malaysia had a conservative regime favoring security interests in land and corporate property. It had a very wide range of well defined security interests in land and in all property owned by companies. The law was creditor friendly in the sense that a perfected security interest had the highest possible priority, neither the laws nor the courts gave debtors special treatment, self-enforcement powers were broad, and enforcement was timely (if not express) and not expensive. The weak point in the system was the use as security of personal property in the possession of a noncorporate debtor, for which no effective system of notice existed. Substitutes, notably hire purchase, addressed part of the problem. Tensions in the regime emerged after our period ended, with the challenge to self-help when foreclosing on corporate land.

Security Interests in Japan

The laws in Japan have been relatively easy to enforce and give creditors relatively high priority.

---

[4] For well capitalized finance companies, this ceiling was raised in 1996 to about US$200,000 if the borrower was a business. A general prudential rule placed ceilings on financial intermediaries' unsecured loans to related entities.

The Legal Regime. Japanese law was largely in place by 1910. In 1896, the country enacted a law for security interests as part of its civil code. Japan based its law on the French and German law. Special provisions for specific industries were created after that. A 1905 law provided for a security interest in all the assets at a factory site of a joint stock company. A few years later, Japan added laws permitting special interests for factories, railways, and mining; then in the 1950s, cars, aircraft, and construction machinery.

The Lenders. Among the major lenders in Japan were privately owned banks, of which there were a large number, including by the 1980s the largest in the world. Other major lenders included specialized institutions like long term credit banks, agricultural and other credit cooperatives, and trust banks. The markets were segmented by function and each was highly competitive. In the early years of our period, the Central Bank was able to influence the direction and cost of lending through its refinancing of the banks' loans, known as overloans. By the 1970s overloans died out and the government's power began to recede as it became a major borrower from the banks. But until 1995, the Central Bank continued to affect private banks' costs with extensive lending through the discount window. The government retained its power as regulator, exercised through administrative guidance from the finance ministry. Most of the major banks were part of at least one industrial/financial group linked by shareholding, common directors, and coordinated business strategies. These *keiretsus* varied greatly in cohesion and cooperation. A leading bank in the group would be the main bank for its members, privy to information about them that outsider banks could not have. From about 1980, the Japanese financial system slowly liberalized. Demand for credit shifted from the traditional borrowers, the large firms in major industries, because of disintermediation, a growing supply of funds, and opening to foreign markets. After the "asset bubble" in the real estate and stock markets during the middle to late 1980s swept across the financial system like a tidal wave, banks were left to untangle a large bad debt problem and the country called for a radical change in the structure and regulation of Japan's financial system.

Range of Collateral. Japanese law provided for security interests in a broad range of collateral, but the effectiveness of these interests depended on the need for possession and notice, which in turn varied according to type of collateral and debtor, as described below. Security interests in real property could include buildings but did not extend to income from land. Security interests in personal property could include accounts receivable and inventory. For a company's assets generally (as specified in the law), a debenture could give its holder a weak security interest.

Close substitutes for security interests relied on ownership. Some were created by statute; a conditional sale is an example. Case law recognized the *joto tampo*, in which the debtor transferred title to the creditor.

Possession. A pledge of personal property required continuous possession. Both pledges and close substitutes transferring ownership were weak when the debtor sold the collateral to a bona fide third party, who took priority over the secured creditor. Creditors often placed a sign on collateral in the debtor's possession identifying their interest in order to defeat a subsequent purchaser's assertion of good faith. So although a creditor could take a security interest in inventory, accounts receivable, and other unspecified property, the interest was weak if the collateral was not in the creditor's possession. Possession could, however, include possession by an agent of the secured creditor, and the debtor itself could be appointed as agent.

Registration/Publicity. Security interests in real property were perfected by registration. Special statutes enacted after 1905 strengthened security interests for certain kinds of firms or assets by providing registries for collateral. This was the case for real property and for personal property subject to the statutory exceptions, including inventory (but not accounts receivable) at the factory of a joint stock company, railways, mines, cars, aircraft, and construction machinery.

Where registration was not available, possession of the collateral by the creditor was required to perfect its interest against third parties and other secured creditors. Without registration or possession, the security interest still bound the debtor. In 1986, a law was passed to allow a creditor to register its ownership of the property provisionally, with ownership to vest upon default by the borrowers.

Self-enforcement. The parties to a contractual security interest might agree that if the debtor defaulted the creditor could auction property in the debtor's possession or receive ownership of the property through a provisional registration at the time the interest was created. If the creditor possessed the property, the code allowed the creditor to continue holding it after default, but not to auction it. The courts have allowed parties to contract around this statutory limitation since the 1920s and banks regularly did so in their standard loan contract.

The *joto tampo*, a close substitute, relied on self-enforcement. The creditor did not require court procedures but could simply sell the collateral.

Enforcement and Execution. Unlike an unsecured creditor, most secured creditors were not bound to use the courts to enforce their interest in collateral if the debtor defaulted. The unsecured creditor had to obtain a court judgment confirming its title in the property and then seize or auction the property in a formal execution procedure. Most holders of security interests needed neither to obtain a court judgment that they held title to the property nor to participate in the execution of the property. They could sell the property at a public auction or simply acquire ownership if that was provided for by contract. To foreclose on pledged property in the creditor's possession, however, the creditor had to use court procedures to establish its interest and auction the property. This requirement made the *joto tampo*, which did not require courts for enforcement, relatively more popular.

"Judicial compromise" settled most civil cases, rather than full litigation. The parties would settle, often under the guidance of the judge, and withdraw before the judge made an award in favor of one or the other. Banks preferred this as a way to avoid the public auction. Indeed, Mark Ramseyer (1991) argued that enforcement procedures might not be very relevant since banks might not want to take over management or force a sale. They would rather have a going concern they did not have to manage. So they used their enforcement powers to renegotiate terms and get more collateral, rather than foreclose.

Bankruptcy did not stay collection by a secured creditor. When the debtor was insolvent, the secured creditor was limited only by reorganization, which, in the case of a joint stock company, stayed collection. However, it gave just over 25 percent of the secured creditors the power to veto a proposal that would postpone repayment and just over 20 percent the veto power if reorganization would impair their rights.

Clarity of Law. The law was clear. Courts had interpreted the basic laws for almost a century.

Costs. Costs were modest but enforcement could be time-consuming. This explains the 1986 rule permitting provisional registration (see above).

Priority. A secured creditor had priority over unsecured creditors, later secured creditors, and almost all other claimants. Of the very few with higher priority, perhaps only one or two types of claim had some limited importance for secured creditors. Any subsequent purchaser of, or holder of, a security interest in specific property would have priority over a debenture holder. When the secured interest was in the debtor's property generally, higher priority was given to employees' owed salaries. Their claim had some value, but could be asserted only against the debtor's personal property. A senior priority given to the government for property taxes was not significant. When the secured interest was for specific property, secured lenders had priority over statutorily created preferences except for lessors of land or a house, also of very limited significance. When personal property in the possession of the debtor was auctioned, a creditor with a security interest had priority over other creditors for principal and interest due over the last two years; for debts due earlier, the lender was treated as unsecured. Creditors solved this problem by specifying in the loan contract that on the first default they could accelerate the loan so that the entire amount became due immediately.

Use of Secured Lending. From 1960 to 1995, real estate secured 24 percent to 31 percent of all banks' loans. Looking only at loans secured by real property, the share peaked in the mid 1970s, when the economy was in a post oil shock recession. During Japan's "property bubble" in the middle to late 1980s real property secured a lower share of bank loans, 24 percent, rising to 30 percent in 1990. After the property bubble burst, the share of loans secured by real property fell back to 26 percent by 1996. The collapse made banks much more conservative in their use of real property as collateral. Some observers argued that the system of security interests was to blame for much of the banks' problems in the early 1990s because it allowed the misplaced reliance on an overvalued asset.

Among types of personal property, accounts receivable were popular collateral.

Substitutes for security interests were largely in the form of third party guarantees and, perhaps, compensating balances. Guarantees were popular, but banks were reluctant to enforce completely for fear of getting a bad reputation as being too tough, so they often compromised at 50 percent of the guarantee. From 1960 to 1995, banks relied on guarantees (and collateral in the form of personal property) for 22-32 percent of all bank loans. The major increase in their use occurred in the mid-1970s. Compensating balances were another important security substitute. Banks would assert a right of set-off if the borrower defaulted.

Unsecured loans ranged from 28 to 35 percent of all bank loans between 1960 and 1995. Their greatest share was in the 1960s and again in the mid-1980s. Their lowest share was in the late 1970s. Banks said in interviews that they would do without collateral when lending to the biggest borrowers. As a general rule, however, banks wanted to secure all loans.

In short, throughout the period Japan had a system that allowed lenders a reasonably broad range of security interests. It did not, however, fully include intangibles like accounts receivable and did not provide opportunities to register interests in all personal property, relying instead on constructive possession to perfect some interests. This forced creditors to put a sign on equipment serving as collateral in the hope the sign would constitute adequate notice. The laws were relatively easy to enforce and creditors had relatively high priority.

Security Interests in Taipei,China

Taipei,China has offered security interests in a fair range of collateral but secured lenders have not had top priority in their claims on it.

The Legal Regime. The regime for mortgaging land and personal property in the creditor's possession was defined in the civil code of 1930, drawn from Japan and Germany. Periodically, the government restricted real estate lending to reduce speculation. Special laws were enacted for the use of ships and aircraft as collateral. In 1965, Taipei,China enacted the Chattel Secured Transactions Law to provide for collateral of personal property in the debtor's possession. The law provided a way to register and enforce a security interest in the collateral and created two close substitutes called conditional sale and trust receipts. This law was based on US laws in force before the Uniform Commercial Code standardized and rationalized the use of security interests in the US in the mid 1960s.

The Lenders. For most of the 35 years surveyed by this study, the major formal financial intermediaries were state owned banks: 9 of the 10 commercial banks were state owned in 1962 and, by 1989, 12 were state owned and 4 private. After 1989, the number of banks in the public sector fell as new private banks were registered. Foreign banks were restricted. Active locally were many private credit cooperatives, almost 300 credit unions, and regional savings corporations that were reorganized as 8 small and medium business banks, all but one private. As a share of total lending, that done by state owned financial intermediaries was almost 80 percent in 1968 and 67 percent in 1989; it was still over 50 percent in 1995.

Informal lenders in Taipei,China included businesses, households, employee deposits, and mutual credit clubs called *hui*. Informal lending accounted for 51 percent of business loans in 1964, fell to 28 percent in 1973, and rose again to 39 percent in 1981 as post-oil -shock inflation forced disintermediation from formal intermediaries subject to interest controls; it then fell to 32 percent in 1993 after the recession and financial crises of the mid 1980s.

Range of Collateral. Throughout the 35 years, and long before, security interests in Taipei,China could be taken in real estate, personal property in the possession of the lender, and monetary claims such as checks, government bonds, and publicly offered equity shares. From 1963, security interests were possible in machinery, equipment, tools, raw materials, semi-finished products, retail goods, vehicles, agricultural assets, and vessels up to a certain size. Interests in assets that were inputs to finished goods could extend to the finished goods. From 1960 to 1987, postdated checks used as a substitute for security interests carried criminal sanctions if funds in the account were not adequate to clear the check. Formal and informal lenders used the postdated checks as security and as a security substitute. After criminal sanctions ended in 1987, banks applied their own sanctions, jointly precluding new checking accounts for any depositor who defaulted on three promissory notes. Missing from Taipei,China's menu of security interests of assets in the debtor's possession was the use of collateral in the form of inventory and accounts receivable, since the assets to be registered had to be identified.

Registration/Publicity. Registration was required to perfect security interests in real property and for personal property not in the creditor's possession, which could serve as security.

Self-enforcement. Secured creditors did not have the power to take possession of collateral themselves and sell it. They did have the power to auction collateral already in their possession without going to court for a judgment authorizing the auction, but after notifying a defaulting debtor. In some cases, six months had to pass before the sale.

Enforcement and Execution. Secured creditors could recover their collateral within as little as four months if the debtor defaulted. The first step in enforcing a claim normally required a creditor to institute a civil suit, which would take 8-24 weeks and was subject to a court fee of 1 percent of the claim. A secured creditor could try a summary proceeding that took 3-4 weeks and carried very modest court costs, but if the debtor objected within 20 days of the summary action, the parties would shift to a civil suit. A creditor holding as security a promissory note from a third party could enforce it in a simplified procedure that took about 2-4 weeks and cost at most US$300. So opportunities to expedite the civil judgment were limited, but the delay caused by the standard procedure was not long.

To execute the judgment, the lender would again work through the courts, which charged a fee of 0.5 percent of the claim. With formal appraisal and auction, execution could take up to 10 weeks for real property and perhaps 7 weeks for personal property. Thus a secured creditor could reasonably anticipate taking between 10 and 34 weeks to execute its interest, depending on the security, and losing 1.5 percent of the value of the collateral to court fees, not a significant amount.

Secured creditors were not well situated when a corporate debtor was in reorganization. Reorganization gave an automatic stay to claims, including those of secured creditors, and managers could delay payments for a long time.

Clarity of law. Clarity of the law is not an issue.

Costs. See discussion under "Enforcement and Execution".

Priority. The first claimant on the proceeds was the government for land tax, followed by the court for its fees and the cost of execution. Then came secured creditors. If the debtor was a public company in reorganization, the cost of operations, reorganization, and wages up to six months took priority over secured creditors. In practice, secured creditors did not like reorganization.

Use of Secured Lending. The relative importance of secured and unsecured lending varied with the importance of postdated checks. Domestic banks' secured loans fell as a share of all their loans from a high of 65.6 percent at the end of 1966 to 52.2 percent in 1973. Between 1973 and 1983, banks' secured loans averaged 54.6 percent of all their loans, then started to rise. Private banks tended to lend to private borrowers, state banks to public borrowers. The private banks picked up an increasing market share of loans after 1987. If private banks relied more on security interests to reduce risk than did the state banks, the increasing market share of the private banks might have helped to account for the relative growth of secured lending compared to unsecured loans.

Real property was the most commonly used form of collateral for both businesses and consumers. Most commercial and consumer loans were mortgaged by real estate. In the 1990s, lending to individuals increased as per capita incomes rose and people acquired real property that could serve as collateral. Loans to individuals were 12 percent of total bank loans in 1961, fell to 9 percent in 1974, rose to 22 percent in 1982, then jumped to around 42 percent from 1987 to 1995. Offsetting this was a steep decline in lending to public sector borrowers.

Data about the use of close substitutes for security interests are limited. Postdated checks were the closest substitute and the impact of the change in the law is reflected in the rapid relative decline in informal lending after the change. Informal lenders had used postdated checks to reduce risk. When the criminal sanctions for bouncing postdated checks ended, informal lending fell in just two years from the high of 47.1 percent of all loans in 1986 to 34.6 percent in 1988, then slid to 32 percent by 1993.

Among substitutes for security interests, personal guarantees from the borrowing firm's directors were commonly taken by lenders in Taipei,China. They did so whether or not a loan was secured, but saw the guarantee as particularly important for unsecured loans to companies. Each director had unlimited liability and could not relinquish liability upon resigning from the board. Banks normally rejected any loan when even one of the directors refused to provide this guarantee. The banks saw as an additional benefit the impediment this created to directors who might want to siphon off some of the borrower's assets by transferring them to another company under their control.

Banks in Taipei,China were beginning to take group guarantees for loans to individuals by the end of the period. Employees of reputable firms would band together to guarantee mutually the debt of each borrower in the group. Each was liable if any defaulted. By October 1995, employee group loans were 1. 5 percent of all consumer loans by banks.

Conditional sales were another common substitute. The borrower had possession and acquired title upon payment of the debt. If the buyer defaulted or transferred the asset, the lender/seller could repossess and sell the goods unilaterally after 30 days.

Conclusion. Taipei,China balanced the interests of debtors and creditors more than Malaysia. It offered security interests in a fair range of collateral. A creditor could take a security interest in intangibles like accounts receivable by taking possession, but could not take an interest if the intangibles remained with the debtor. Taipei,China did not offer a general security interest in future assets of the debtor (often called a floating charge). Both the formal and informal sectors made extensive use of a substitute for security—the postdated check with criminal sanctions. Creditors were circumscribed in their ability to self-enforce, but could use the courts in procedures that took at most six months. Secured creditors caught in reorganization or bankruptcy could be delayed longer. Secured lenders did not have top priority in their claims on the collateral. The share of banks' loans that were secured grew to about 65 percent by 1995 and lenders extensively used other security substitutes, such as guarantees from directors.

Security Interests in the Republic of Korea

Security interests have not been an important tool in managing risk in the Republic of Korea during the period under review.

The Legal Regime. The Republic of Korea started our period in 1960 with a new civil code, including rules for security interests. The country's prior civil code dated from 1912, was borrowed from Japan, and so was based on the French civil code of 1805 and the German civil code of 1896. It had defined security interests and the mechanisms to enforce them. Then, effective 1960, the Republic of Korea adopted a new civil code modeled mainly on German law and partly on Swiss. This law, too, specified types of security interests and their enforcement. Also in 1960, the country adopted a law for real property registration and a year later enacted special laws governing security interests in factories, mining, cars, airplanes, and heavy machinery. With the 1962 passage of a law for auctions of secured property and a 1965 law to protect debtors from unscrupulous lenders, the legislative base was in place. Except for changes in the priority of secured creditors, discussed below, Korean law remained unchanged throughout the rest of the 35 years.

The Lenders. The legal basis for financial intermediaries in the Republic of Korea derived from Japan and the US for banking law, Germany for credit unions specializing in small business and agricultural lending, and the US for laws governing the central bank. In 1960, the formal financial system was simple: five commercial banks, five securities companies, and several insurance companies. The military government in 1961 created many specialized banks, including for housing and small and medium business.

Commercial banks were controlled de jure or de facto by the government into the early 1990s. The government used them as tools of credit allocation until accumulated bad debts impaired their operations. "Policy loans," as directed lending by the government was called, accounted for as much as 63 percent of bank loans in the 1970s, then fell slightly to about 60 percent through the period ending 1991.[5] The government also set ceilings on the banks' lending to industrial groups, the *chaebols*, and limited the groups' shareholding in the banks, effectively reducing relational loans. The government, having nationalized the largest banks in the 1960s, retained one of the five nationwide commercial banks as a state-controlled entity in 1972 and privatized the remaining four in the early 1980s, though it kept in place important methods of control that made it the de facto owner through the decade. But the banks remained plagued with bad loans that had resulted from the government's role for so long in their lending. The 1980s was a decade of serious problems with nonperforming loans, which peaked at 10.5 percent of all loans by these banks in mid decade. The government found ways to support them, such as through low cost funds from the Central Bank. Banks' efforts to enforce security interests in bad loans were slowed because many big debtors were in rehabilitation. Hamstrung, the banks saw other financial intermediaries, known as nonbank financial institutions, outstrip them. In the early 1990s, the government reduced its influence over the banks, which became much more subject to market forces than in the past.

Alongside the banks, the nonbank financial institutions developed largely free of government intervention and became the dynamic part of the financial system. New intermediaries opened during the 1980s as part of financial liberalization. The nonbank financial institutions' share of all domestic credit to the private sector rose steadily from a low of 22 percent in 1970, passing the commercial banks' share in 1990, to reach 62 percent in 1995.

Unregulated or informal lenders played an important but declining role throughout the 35 years. Data are hard to come by, but over ten years from 1963 the ratio of informal loans to bank loans rose from 38 percent to peak at 63 percent in 1966–1967, then fell to 29 percent in 1972. Estimates in 1994 placed their share between 6 percent and 21 percent. A seven year policy of financial liberalization instituted by the government in 1991 speeded up the long-term decline in the role of the informal lenders by gradually removing some of the officially created inefficiencies in the formal sector.

Range of collateral. Security interests could be created when the creditor took possession of personal property, securities, or other documentary rights belonging to the debtor. Security interests could be created in certain types of property that remained in the debtor's possession: land and buildings, and intangible rights such as intellectual property and, by special acts, in aircraft, ships, heavy equipment, and vehicles. A security interest could be created in inventories or accounts receivables.

Korean courts recognized an informal security interest called the *yangdo dambo.* This was a form of security used in the curb market, an informal money market that played a major role in the financial system for part of the 35 years. Borrowers gave lenders property worth much more than the loan they received. If they defaulted, case law required the lender to return any excess value to the borrower, but irregularities in the informal market often let the lender keep the full value of the property. Korean courts enforced the *yangdo dambo* even though the civil code did not provide for it. They treated it as a transfer of title to the property until the debt was discharged. In 1983, the government codified case law requiring the creditor, after liquidating the property, to return to the borrower any amount exceeding the debt (Kim K.S. 1996).

Registration/Publicity. Security in land or buildings must have been registered in the land registry to be effective. Special registries existed for interests in aircraft, ships, heavy equipment, and vehicles. No registries existed for other interests, such as inventories or accounts receivable. Registration costs were moderate.

Self-enforcement. Korean law did not allow a secured creditor to take possession of collateral, upon default by the debtor, without authority of the court. It did permit summary action for provisional attachment of the property by the court using procedures that varied by type of collateral.

---

[5] Narrower definitions of policy loans estimated shares somewhat lower but still high: e.g., 50 percent in 1975–1980, 35 percent in 1983–1988.

Enforcement and Execution. To enforce a security interest using the courts could be lengthy. The initial action could take three to four months, but appeals and the need for multiple auctions could extend the time so that it could take up to one year to recover on the collateral. If the security interest was registered and payment was not as agreed, the creditor asked the court to auction the property. If the interest was not registered, the creditor had to ask the court to determine its rights in the property and then auction the property. Generally a court officer took possession. A losing debtor had to pay interest at a statutory rate of only 5 percent or 6 percent from when the debt was due, unless the court permitted a higher rate agreed by the parties that was not usurious (25 percent was the statutory maximum in 1993). The number of cases enforcing security interests rose from 6,700 in 1961 to 74,700 in 1995, an increase of 10.1 times. During the same period, loans measured in constant 1990 won rose from W1.9 trillion to W285.9 trillion, an increase of 149 times. The growth in litigation fell far short of the growth of lending. This may suggest that secured lending was relatively less important over time. And indeed, we see it falling as a share of total loans after 1985 (see below). It may also suggest, however, that the need to litigate diminished as with experience people understood their rights better.

Clarity of law. Clarity of the law was not an issue.

Costs. The cost of securing a loan was about 1 percent of the amount secured.

Priority. Claimants with priority above secured creditors, even those registered, were the government for taxes and employees for wages. A creditor in possession of collateral had priority to that property above any other creditor of the debtor. For registered interests, priority among creditors was chronological. In extraordinary situations, government action weakened the position of secured creditors, along with all creditors. In the 1980s, the government initiated rationalization procedures to restructure the shipbuilding, overseas construction, textile, and lumber industries. These procedures prevented creditors from enforcing security interests against defaulting borrowers.

Use of Secured Lending. In the formal financial markets, secured loans have declined over at least the last ten years of our period, and possibly longer. The Republic of Korea reports three types of loans by commercial banks: secured, unsecured, and guaranteed. For all commercial banks, secured lending fell from 54 percent of total loans in 1985 to 49 percent in 1990 and 46 percent in 1995. Unsecured lending rose from 42 percent in 1985 to 46 percent in 1995, while guarantees, a substitute for security interests, rose from 4 percent to almost 8 percent, a small share compared to other economies. In addition, consumer loans, most secured by land, rose from 9 percent of total bank loans in 1985 to 18 percent in 1995. Banks would not require security from a state owned borrower or a large firm affiliated with a *chaebol* if the borrower had an acceptable credit rating. Nonbank financial institutions' secured loans seemed to have been a much smaller share, though comprehensive data were not available.

In the informal market, secured lending accounted for as much as two-thirds of all informal loans to licensed businesses in 1972, early in our period. This is interesting because one does not necessarily associate the informal market with formal techniques for securing loans. Studies at the time revealed that notarized property deeds were the principal collateral for loans in the curb market for short-term loans. Borrowers agreed in writing not to contest their cases in court if they defaulted.

Conclusion. Security interests in the Republic of Korea were perhaps not used as an important tool to manage risk throughout most of the period. A major group of lenders, the nonbank financial institutions, used security interests much less than banks, but even as a share of bank lending, secured lending fell, at least from 1985. Korean banks may have taken security interests when they made loans, but they relied very little on these interests to manage risk. This was because so much of their lending was in policy loans that carried an implicit government guarantee. Rather than taking an interest in collateral, they could satisfy formal prudential requirements for security with a guarantee from a borrower's affiliated company, which would lower transaction costs. However, at least from 1985 to 1995 guarantees were not a major substitute for security. For borrowers not in the privileged group of priority lending, the banks required land as collateral, as it was considered nearly "risk-free". This explained, in Kim's view, the relatively unsophisticated state of the Republic of Korea's security interests and the laws governing them. Certainly the Republic of Korea's use of policy loans did not differ radically from direct credit in Malaysia, Japan, or Taipei,China at the beginning of the period, the 1960s. But these other economies had liberalized their financial systems much more by the early 1990s than had the Republic of Korea. Policy lending may not have completely disappeared in Malaysia or Taipei,China, but it had declined significantly in importance.

Security Interests in India

India's system of secured lending has been much friendlier to debtors than to creditors, crippling efficiency and hurting both.

The Legal Regime. The law governing security interests in India was drawn from common law, latterly from court cases in India rather than England, and from a set of statutes. Unlike the other economies, India's statutory rules were scattered across many laws enacted between 1872 and 1908, mostly English, and other laws enacted from 1948 to 1992. Many of the laws were not written primarily to govern security interests (e.g., the Contract Act of 1872 or the Sick Industrial Companies Act of 1985). This patchwork created a set of rules, sometimes overlapping and at other times with gaps, that were difficult to interpret. In federal India, national and state legislation applied, contributing further to the patchwork effect.

The Lenders. One government owned bank dominated commercial banking in India: the State Bank of India provided at least 50 percent of all commercial bank loans throughout the 35 years. In 1960, all other banks were private. No prudential guidelines existed for commercial bank lending though the Central Bank provided some *ad hoc* guidelines from time to time. Interest rates were flexible. Informal "banks" and moneylenders dominated rural areas, which had no banks, and semiurban areas. In 1967, the government began issuing guidelines for lending by banks. In 1969, after it nationalized 14 major banks, the guidelines became much more detailed. The banks were pressed to expand throughout the economy and to lend more to the "priority sector," consisting of agriculture, smal scale business, and a few other activities. The government administered interest rates and expanded lending to the priority sector to 40 percent of all loans in the 1980s.

By 1995, a total of 27 commercial banks and 194 regional rural banks were government owned. Another 52 banks were private and regulated by the Central Bank. Commercial banks traditionally supplied working capital and other short-term loans, but expanded to medium-term loans in the 1960s, long-term loans in 1970, and equity investments in the 1990s. The private banks loaned relatively more than state-owned banks to private borrowers, particularly for longer maturities. Private nonbank financial institutions loaned medium- and long-term mainly to businesses, but also to individuals for car loans, for example—funding much of this by borrowing from the commercial banks. Government nonbank financial institutions were statutory entities providing long-term loans and equity for industrial use; some played a significant role. Government development banks financed different sectors of the economy, like agriculture. Rural cooperative banks made short- and medium-term loans for farmers and small scale businesses. But commercial banks had branches across even rural India.

Government's direct involvement in lending eased in the 1990s. It stopped administering interest rates in 1994 except for loans of less than about US$1,000. Loans to the priority sector fell to one third of all bank loans. The legacy of the managed financial system persisted. Over 40 percent of all priority loans were overdue in the early 1990s. Loans to "sick industries" were about 2-3 percent of all bank credit to industrial borrowers.

Range of Collateral. Security interests were taken in real property and identifiable personal property that might remain in the debtor's or creditor's possession; these included securities and life insurance policies. Security interests could be taken in inventory and accounts receivable. India had close substitutes for security interests, called trust receipts, that gave a trustee title to the collateral.

Indian law allowed creditors in all major cities to take a security interest in land by depositing the title to the land with a registry. Since 1971, state governments have increased the number of cities to which it applied. Banks came to insist almost always on this form of security for their loans.

Possession. Possession of collateral by creditors was possible.

Registration/Publicity. Registration procedures varied by state. In 1965, the law changed to require all security interests in a company's assets to be registered with the Registrar of Companies. The amendment was important because it set priorities among claimants. Approvals were necessary from government agencies in certain situations, such as creating an interest in urban land.

Self-enforcement. If the creditor possessed the collateral, it could sell, after default and after notifying the borrower. That happened only when the collateral was with the bank— as, for example, a pledge (such as gold, common for agricultural loans)—and a working capital loan against security on stock (a floating charge, common in trade loans). Legal battles occurred over mortgages, leases, and other paper collateral which the borrower possessed. India had a procedure for a secured creditor to take possession of collateral from a defaulting borrower. The procedure was prolonged, with legal battles at every stage. The main suit was followed by a first appeal, a second appeal, and then a special leave petition to the highest court. At each stage several subissues would cause further delays. The troubles were so great that where loans were secured by vehicles, at least, lenders would use extralegal means to take possession.

At least one specialized government owned financial intermediary had a qualified right to summary action. The State Financial Corporation, which loaned to industrial companies, could obtain a summary court hearing to sell collateral securing a loan in default.

Enforcement and Execution. Formal court proceedings took years, first to prove the validity of the security interest in the face of procedures that allowed the defendant to pursue many contradictory defenses and then another two to three years to acquire and sell the collateral. Secured creditors took 9-12 years to recover if the debtor was in bankruptcy and 8-10 years in a simple loan litigation. With appeals to the Supreme Court, the entire process could take 25 years. The typical process for enforcing a security interest in a loan, where bankruptcy was not underway, involved a wait as long as four years to a first hearing in the lowest court, two years for a decision there, further delays for two appeals, and then a long procedure to foreclose on the property. Interviewees said that the main reasons for the delays were inexperienced judges and receivers of the property, complex claims (for example, land records, including filings of security interests with the land registry, were incomplete and inconclusive), and lawyers' interests in delaying settlement. The delays stem in part from the low number of courts and resources for them, and the high rates of litigation in proportion to population. Output per judge is relatively high, compared with Western rates.

The costs of enforcement could be high. Court fees alone could reach 8 percent of the claim. Additional expenses, such as the cost of a receiver for the collateral, could raise the cost to 15 percent. Despite the long delays, the court had discretion to accept or reject liquidated damages agreed by the parties and to award reasonable costs, including interest on interest.

Indian courts would often help the debtor by remitting part of the loan or providing easy payment installments. Fairness might motivate some of this leniency: at the time of the loan, various legal and illegal cuts often reduced the amount actually transferred to the borrower, who might sometimes have received as little as 60 percent of the full face value of the loan.

Clarity of the Law. Lack of clarity was a serious problem. Title in real property was often not clear in the registries. As noted above, law had gaps and contradictions, multiple statutes existed, and at times case law alone was the basis for security interests in India. Thus one law governed property in the creditor's possession, another governed real property, a third and fourth the use of securities like shares as collateral, and a fifth the use of short-term debt instruments. The laws governing banks and securities were national, the others state, further complicating clarity. Legal battles often concerned the application of different statutes to the situation. No statutes governed security interests in personal property possessed by the debtor or close substitutes like hire-purchase, so lenders relied on common law. At the state level, laws governing ownership and leaseholds varied, as did fees and procedures. The variations raised administrative expense as well as the out-of-pocket costs of the transaction. The parties' rights and duties were often unclear or not even defined, nor were important concepts defined. All had to be set by contract. Extra-legal self-help, such as repossessing cars, grew in response.

Costs. Published rates for obtaining a variety of security interests ranged from 1 percent to 5 percent in 1995, but may have understated the cost to some of the borrowers. For real property, the cost of registering a security interest included a duty of up to 2 percent of the value of the loan, although banks were exempted for some years in the 1980s. In addition, since ownership of real property was often unclear, perfecting a security interest required a costly title search. For personal property, the lender could register interests in the assets of a company, but not an entity other than a company. Since many rates were still set by the government in 1995, market rates could be obtained by disbursing loan proceeds to the borrower less than the recorded amount of the loan. Thus the government's published rates would not necessarily have been the actual rates paid. Though costs may have been high, they did not affect the decision to take a security interest, since all loans were secured.

Priority. Priority rules varied according to the proceeding, the lender, and the debtor. A commercial bank, for example, could only hold a second charge on fixed assets. India had no bankruptcy law for any type of organization, but the company law prescribed winding up of insolvent companies by the court. Before 1985, secured creditors were entitled to the full proceeds of the sale of the collateral. After 1985, employees had a claim on the proceeds, so India does not protect secured property from all other claimants; employees and the secured creditors would divide the proceeds from collateral pro rata by the relative size of their claims on the company. A further complication is that registration alone would not prove priority in bankruptcy. Yet another twist is a procedure for "sick industrial companies," those that within five years of registering have losses equal to net worth. For these companies, even secured creditors were subject to reorganization directed by a special government agency, which would decide creditors' priority. Finally, the state government approval was needed to close any industry, introducing further uncertainty to a secured creditor's ability to collect from a bankrupt debtor.

India had an insolvency law for individuals that was rarely used. One state with a 40 million population had only 100 insolvencies a year in the 1990s. However, when insolvency was pressed, development finance institutions that loaned long-term had priority over secured creditors that were commercial banks.

Use of Secured Lending. Collateral was not considered important for lending to public sector borrowers in the late 1960s, after the banks were nationalized, but was seen as very important for loans to the private sector even then. Throughout most of the 35 years, 95-98 percent of all banks' loans were secured, often with multiple types of collateral and guarantees. One explanation is that given the uncertainty and delays creditors found it useful to diversify their risk across multiple types of security interests. The exception was loans less than about US$1,000 to borrowers in priority sectors. This nearly universal approach to taking security was not formally mandated by regulators. The central bank advised commercial banks to take adequate cover, but it issued no guidelines for the use of security interests. In 1986, however, the central bank advised the banks to take guarantees from directors of all borrowing companies. Banks used guarantees to supplement security interests in property that would turn over, such as inventory or accounts receivable.

As certain types of security interests became more costly, lenders switched to others over the period. For example, as registered mortgages on land became subject to higher stamp duties and other uncertainties, lenders relied less on them and more on a security interest in the property that could be perfected by taking possession of the title to the property (called equitable mortgage). Registration was not required. Then in 1995, states began to apply stamp duties to equitable mortgages. Also for reasons of cost, commercial banks relied more on interests in personal property. This is a very interesting shift in the use of security interests, since a mortgage of land is usually described as the best form of security (see, for example, the long quote from the World Bank's *World Development Report, 1989* at the beginning of this chapter).

During the 35 years, new types of lending became important as borrowers came into possession of acceptable collateral. Lending to individuals secured by their assets was negligible in 1970 but was 19 percent of all loans by banks in 1993/94.

Conclusion. India provided the classic case of deficiencies in the system for secured lending. Much friendlier to debtors than creditors in security interests, the system crippled efficiency and hurt both. The multiplicity of laws hindered assurance about rights and procedures, and slowed the process considerably. High taxes raised transaction costs. Certain security, like urban land, required government approvals that delayed perfection of the interest. Uncertainty about title undermined the use of land as security. Lack of publicity about security interests in personal property may have hampered their use, since a prospective lender could not assure itself about prior interests, but we cannot demonstrate this. The practice of overstating the loan to the borrower continued a vicious cycle: the lender effectively raised the cost of the loan by a large amount to offset high risk due at least in part to ineffective enforcement of security interests. The borrowers then used the courts to delay repayment of the full amount of the loan and reduce its real value to a level that their cash flows could absorb.

Security Interests in the PRC

The PRC's incremental approach to developing a regime for secured interest makes it difficult to compare with the other five economies but perhaps more relevant to economies in transition.

The Legal Regime. The PRC's legal regime for security interests was very new. There was no such law before 1978. Rules at the national level evolved slowly, so that until 1995 no general law governed security interests. The first step was to give creditors the right to receive guarantees through the Economic Contract Law (1981). The PRC sketched in more detail about the rules in the mid-1980s. Security for loans was recognized in the 1985 Regulations on a Loan Contract. Where one party was foreign, the contract could provide for the use of personal property as security, according to the Foreign Economic Contracts Law (1985). Courts began to accept cases after the General Principles of Civil Law (1986) set forth some principles for security interests and personal guarantees. The courts modified their rules for cases involving security interests in 1990, after the regime encountered many problems. A new civil procedures law took effect in 1991. All interests in land had to be notarized from 1992, to set higher standards for transfer. To fill some of the gaps in the laws, in the 1990s some large cities and provinces adopted local regulations for security interests and banks developed sample contracts.

Bankruptcy procedures also appeared late in our 35-year period and evolved slowly. For bankruptcy of state owned enterprises, a law effective in 1988 set priorities for claims. This was elaborated by a state council circular in 1995. For bankrupt nonstate borrowers, the Civil Procedures Law of 1991 established rules for claims. The laws of Japan and Germany mainly served as models.

The PRC's Security Law was passed on 1 October 1995, too late for it to affect behavior during our 35-year period. Along with the elements of laws in effect since the 1980s, we also sketch the elements of the 1995 law in this section to indicate the type of rules for security interests that the government believed necessary. Overall, the effect was seen as creditor friendly, at least as compared with prior law (this section draws on Xiangmin, Caldwell, and Epstein 1996, and Jones 1994).

The Lenders. State banks were the primary source of credit, lending mainly to state enterprises throughout the period. From 1978 on, state banks made up to 10 percent of their loans available to nonstate enterprises, notably TVEs and collective enterprises, with a small portion to households. Some of the state banks specialized by sector, such as agriculture or construction. Rural credit and urban cooperatives also loaned much smaller but growing amounts to the same groups of borrowers. As a share of total domestic lending by these three groups, loans to nonstate borrowers rose from 4 percent in 1978 to 15 percent in 1988, then fluctuated between 11 percent and 16 percent. The PRC had no private banks.

In much of their lending, the banks were essentially agents for the state. A large proportion of the banks' loans consisted of credit they extended because it was mandated (and funded) or "guided" by the state, or was part of a program agreed between the government and the bank. One estimate placed loans to support loss-making government enterprises at about 80 percent of all bank loans (Jones 1994). As a result, much of the contents of these banks' portfolios was in loans that were not being serviced.

Range of Collateral. From 1986, the General Principles of Civil Law provided for certain kinds of security interests. The creditor could have a security interest in personal property by written contract and possession of the property including, if the creditor were a bank, a deposit by the borrower. The creditor could have a security interest in the use of land, according to regulations promulgated by some provinces and cities. No law permitted security interests in such assets as inventory or accounts receivable, even after passage of the Security Law in 1995.

The 1995 Security Law permitted security interests in land use (but not ownership), fixtures on the land, machinery and equipment, and transport vehicles. Ownership could be by state or private entities. Certain property, such as health facilities, could not be used as collateral. The value of the collateral could not be less than the value of the loan. The new law also permitted interests in personal property and securities or intangible rights in the possession of, but not owned by, the creditor.

Registration/Publicity. Registration of a security interest in land required acceptance by the registry. Each step took from 3 to 30 days and required a nominal payment. Stamp duty was also nominal (0.5/10,000th of the contract value). Contracts for security interests in personal property were not registered.

The 1995 Security Law required registration of interests in the use of land and certain movable property to perfect the security interest. The registry varied according to the collateral. Different government agencies, at the local level, would register interests in land use, timber, plant and equipment, or vehicles, ships, and planes.

Self-enforcement. A creditor holding movable property as collateral could sell it by auction or otherwise. The 1995 Security Law authorized the creditor to sell the collateral, but in the case of land if the debtor objected then the creditor would have to turn to the courts to enforce its interest.

Enforcement and Execution. Enforcement through a civil suit would take less than one year, since courts were not crowded. Execution could be indefinite, since the PRC lacked adequate institutions to execute court judgments. Enforcement became less effective from the mid-1980s, according to two thirds of people we interviewed. Enforcement was somewhat problematic for creditors because of the government's active role in the economy even at the grassroots level. It was not simply that the executive interfered with the courts. The executive directed much of the lending by the formal financial sector. When borrowers of these loans defaulted, the bank was hardly in a position to take the debtor to court. The effect was seen in the limited use of bankruptcy.

Bankruptcy procedures existed for state owned enterprise from 1986 and were subject to government control. Payment of debts by bankrupt collectives, cooperatives, private enterprise, and joint ventures with foreign investors was governed by the Civil Procedures Law. The number of bankruptcy cases before the courts was small but rising: 940 from 1988 to 1993, 1,625 filed in 1994, and 2,583 in 1995. But most of the cases filed to obtain a bankruptcy decree were refused, which means they did not comply with the requirements for bringing suit. In 1994, for example, of the 1,625 cases filed, 995 were refused, 54 were mediated, and only 98 were tried. There were several explanations for this including the fact that local staff in the executive and judiciary collaborated to protect local interests (for example, the damage to local workers following a bankruptcy). Even without collaboration, the executive branch often interfered with the judiciary. The borrower may not have been able to service loans for reasons of government policy (for example, its products were prohibited).

The banks would gain little and probably lose more by pushing for bankruptcy. Given the weak security interests, the banks would be little better than unsecured creditors. Contemplating a very limited recovery in bankruptcy, the banks might see the procedure as a device to transfer losses from the state enterprises, most of which were attached to the local government.

A bank could keep all of a defaulting debtor's bank account, even if it exceeded the debt. This is broad compared with other economies.

Clarity of Law. This was a serious problem, at least from 1978 to 1995 when the new security law took effect. During this period, substantive rules and procedures changed frequently, as described above. The new laws themselves contradicted one another. For example, the 1986 General Principles of the Civil Law provided for security interests in real property and in movable property possessed by the creditor, as well as guarantees. The earlier Economic Contract Law of 1981 only provided for guarantees and was silent about security interests. Part of the problem was administrative: as new laws were enacted, the old ones remained unchanged on the books. Part was the sheer speed of the effort to put a thorough set of market oriented laws in place. Part was due to the PRC's use of a variety of countries as models for its legislation. Another cause of the problem was weakness in other laws. For example, the vague definition of property rights of urban enterprises made it difficult for them to offer effective collateral even after the law allowed urban land to be used as security.

Costs. Out-of-pocket costs were less substantial and less important to 10 professionals we interviewed than were the delays in perfecting and enforcing interests.

Priority. The 1995 Security Law gives priority among secured creditors in chronological order of registration. Even before 1995, the priority among claimants was, first, workers for unpaid wages and benefits; second, the government for taxes; and finally, secured creditors.

Use of Secured Lending. Though prudential rules required all bank loans to carry some form of security or guarantee, our interviews suggested that no more than 30-55 percent of loans to nonstate borrowers were secured. No comprehensive data described the volume of loans with security. Mandatory lending was only "secured" by personal guarantees of the borrower, and rarely were these enforced.

In the early years after 1978, creditors took possession of personal property as collateral, by contract, because no law defined substantive rights. Courts viewed security interests in real property negatively and they were rarely used. Security interests in land grew in importance, but were limited because the PRC recognized no private ownership of land.

Conclusion. The PRC adopted an incremental approach to developing a regime for security interests. In this respect it was very different from the other five economies, which started the period with existing regimes. This makes the PRC's experience difficult to compare, and perhaps more relevant for economies in transition. Only in 1995 did the economy get a rudimentary law for security interests. Prior to that time, serious questions existed about the content of the rules and procedures for applying them. Beyond problems with the law, the novelty of secured lending limited its use, since people took years to learn how it worked and accept its value. Supplementing this was a cultural preference for maintaining the property of one's ancestors, which made people reluctant to use such property as collateral.

COMPARATIVE EVOLUTION OF THE REGIMES GOVERNING SECURITY INTERESTS

The laws governing secured credit were in place by the mid-1960s for all economies except the PRC. No major changes occurred in the laws. Minor changes took place mainly in the 1980s. India briefly exempted banks from stamp duty on security interests in the mid-1980s. It extended to major cities a new type of collateral, in which the lender would receive a security interest in land simply by taking possession of the title and rationalized registration for security interests in a company's assets by requiring all interests to be recorded at the company registry. Japan allowed a lender to register its potential ownership in real estate collateral provisionally in 1985, providing a bit more protection. Workers' claims for salary and benefits received higher priority than secured creditors in the Republic of Korea in 1987 and a pro rata priority in India in 1985. The Republic of Korea had already given its government priority over secured creditors for tax due, in 1971. Only the PRC enacted major laws providing first for interests in a limited range of collateral and then a broader law, but the latter appeared only in 1995.

No economy had a single source for its security interest regime. The German civil law economies relied on various sources: Japan relied primarily on Germany but had tapped France earlier; Taipei,China relied on Japan (and Germany) and on the US for the Chattel Mortgage Law; and the Republic of Korea relied on Germany, France, Japan and, to some extent, Switzerland. The common law economies did not just rely on England: Malaysia drew its law for security interests from Australia and India diverged from English country law and practice during this period (though it used case law) as it developed its own approach. Each economy modified these laws itself, often through case law. Japan's courts, for example, made important changes as early as the 1920s. That said, Japan, Republic of Korea, and Taipei,China on the one hand, and India and Malaysia on the other have features of concept and technique in common.

We are interested in uses of the security interest regime as well as the law as written. These are described in the next sections.

OVERVIEW OF THE EFFECT OF SECURITY INTERESTS ON LENDING

Our research revealed several factors that influenced the way in which the regime for security interests affected the use of security and may also have affected lending. Since we want to know how security interests affected lending, we are interested in the factors that may have prevented the security interests from having the effect one would expect.

The factors influencing security interests were the availability of substitutes, the economic strategy, and economic development. Lines of causality were complex, bidirectional in some cases, and indirect in others. Figure 6.2 illustrates the relationships and shows how substitutes can displace the use of security interests and have a direct effect on lending under certain conditions.

Figure 6.2   Factors Affecting the Use of Security Interests

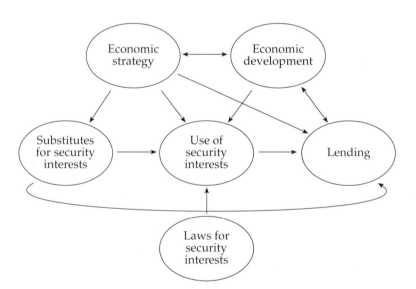

Source: Authors' compilation from country team reports.

The existence of a criminal sanction for default may reduce a creditor's need to take security, for example. The government's economic strategy can directly affect the use of security interests by, for example, making collateral unnecessary; it can affect the availability of substitutes and therefore the use of security interests, and can directly affect lending. Government strategy and economic development affect each other, as described in chapter 4, but this relationship is not of central importance to our story in this chapter. Events in economic development can affect the use of security and lending levels; for example, a serious recession can prompt lenders to require more security and also reduce demand for loans. We did not observe cases in which substitutes, the economic strategy, or economic development significantly influenced the legal regime, since no significant change in the regime occurred during the period.

The following sections explain these relationships, drawing on evidence from the six economies.

SUBSTITUTES AND THE REGIMES FOR SECURITY INTERESTS

Substitutes provide alternatives to formal security interests although some are used in conjunction with them. Substitutes include criminal sanctions on postdated checks that bounce, relational lending, guarantees, and transfer of ownership of collateral to a credit.

Substitutes may have played important roles in lending, but we find mixed evidence that they displaced formal security interest regimes. Criminal sanctions did displace the use of security interests until their repeal brought a resurgence of secured lending. Transfer of ownership was used in the absence of security interests under the law. Relational lending, less extensive than one might expect, and guarantees existed with the use of security interests. All substitutes rely on the legal system even where they displace the regime for security interests.

Criminal Sanctions for Bounced Checks

The use of criminal sanctions for bounced checks in Taipei,China suggests both the relevance of regimes for security interests and boundaries to their usefulness. This substitute supplanted security interests as lenders increasingly saw the advantages of sanctions imposed and paid for by the state, in contrast to security interests whose costs would be borne by the parties to the transaction. It is no surprise that lenders would increasingly choose to let the state protect their interests against defaulters. The relevance of security interests to lending in Taipei,China appears in their resurgent use after criminal sanctions are repealed in 1987.

Postdated checks were used in Taipei,China as a form of lending, and criminal sanctions acted as a substitute for collateral. The system worked as follows: first, a borrower wrote a postdated check to the lender, who then paid the borrower funds discounted to reflect the interest rate for the loan. The check could be traded. It was a promise to pay, not a security interest. Second, the checks came with a sanction serving as a substitute for collateral. In 1960, by amending the negotiable instruments law to impose a jail term on issuers of dishonored checks, the government made the postdated check a substitute for security interests provided by law. Debtors would be imprisoned for up to one year at first, then two years in 1973, and three years in 1977.

Lending on postdated checks became a major source of finance in Taipei,China. Both banks and informal lenders accepted postdated checks increasingly into the early 1980s. The banks classified these loans as unsecured and their unsecured loans rose as a share of all their loans from a low of 34.4 percent at the end of 1966 to 47.8 percent in 1973. They hovered around 45.4 percent between 1973 and 1983, then started to decline (as a recession developed and problem loans grew). Informal lenders started later to rely on sanctions for postdated checks, enabling them to capture market share from formal lenders. One sees their share of all loans in the financial sector rise from a low of 27 percent in 1973 to 47.1 percent of all loans in 1986.

Criminal sanctions ended in January 1987. Thousands of offenders had been indicted each year. The numbers convicted had risen dramatically, from 1,307 in 1960 to 8,830 in 1970 and reaching 26,704 in 1986. This was about half of all high court convictions in 1986. The pressure on the judicial system was so great that the law had to change. Postdated checks continued to be used by nonbank financial companies, but not by commercial banks or government lending agencies, as a substitute for security.

The end of criminal sanctions for dishonored checks in Taipei,China hastened the decline in the use of postdated checks as a substitute for security, led to banks' greater reliance on secured loans, and precipitated a steep decline in the share of informal lending after 14 years of growth. Informal lenders actively used the sanctions. Increasing concern about their riskiness was brought to a head by the 1985 bankruptcy of the largest credit cooperative in Taipei,China. This prompted savers to shift to the formal sector, which consisted of state-owned banks, and prompted the banks to rely increasingly on security. From year-end 1983 to 1995, two-year declines in the share of banks' unsecured loans averaged 1.75 percent except during 1986–1988. This was the two-year period around the repeal of the sanctions on dishonored checks, which took effect on 1 January 1987. We use a two-year period because lenders would anticipate the repeal before it took effect and adjust. From 1986 to 1988, the decline was 6.1 percent. This much larger drop in unsecured loans as a share of total loans seems directly related to the lenders' loss of criminal sanctions as a substitute for security. The proportion of secured loans by banks rose from 55 percent in 1982 to 57 percent in 1986 and 66 percent by 1994. The impact on the informal sector was even more dramatic. Informal lending fell in just two years from the high of 47.1 percent of all loans in 1986 to 34.6 percent in 1988, then slid to 32 percent by 1993.

The practice of postdating promissory notes like the postdated checks did not stop with the end of criminal sanctions. After the law changed, banks created their own sanctions. They accepted promissory notes as "secondary collateral against loans" even though the notes did not qualify as secured instruments according to the civil code. Lenders would require three notes, one for the principal and interest due. A second note for a multiple of the principal and a third blank note the lender could complete were both for use if the borrower defaulted. The three notes, when presented, would immediately place the borrower in violation of the banks' common rule that no one with three defaulted notes would be allowed access to basic banking services. Less effective than criminal sanctions, these were supplemented by the increasing use of security interests.

Several points emerge. Substitutes for security can play a significant role in reducing creditors' risks when they lend by employing sanctions that threaten a sufficiently unpleasant penalty that the borrower will try hard to avoid default. The prospect of jail is one sanction, though realizing the threat would seem self-defeating, since putting the debtor in jail would hamper its ability to earn enough to meet the payments. Taipei,China is hardly alone in using criminal sanctions (Fleisig, Aquilar, and de la Peña 1997). Second, the threat of losing one's ability to write checks may also be a useful threat, though perhaps not quite so draconian, since the practice continues, policed now by the banks and not the courts.

Substitutes appear to have serious problems that Taipei,China recognized—highlighting the importance of real security interests. Criminal sanctions for defaulted checks became too costly for the society as a whole when they occupied half the high court's time. With the end of criminal sanctions, the long-term shift from informal to formal markets speeded up in Taipei,China, along with the shift from unsecured to secured lending. This shift is perhaps the most dramatic evidence that secured lending is important.

The experience in Taipei,China may be relevant for other Asian economies, although it is not clear that they have learned from it. India imposed criminal sanctions for writing a check with insufficient funds about the same time Taipei,China ended its criminal sanctions. In Japan, banks also take promissory notes from small- and medium-sized borrowers. If the borrower defaults on the note, no bank will extend even basic services to the defaulter.

Relational Lending

Creditors lending to borrowers to whom they are related, either personally or through business ties, are often assumed to use the relation to reduce risk, making relational lending a substitute for secured lending. Relational lending is not "relationship lending," common in many parts of the world including the US. Relational lending occurs when the creditor and borrower share a formal ownership relationship.[6] The group may be organized around a family that owns controlling interests in all members. A bank owned by the family makes a relational loan when it lends to a firm also owned by the family. These groups, whether or not based on family relationships, are found in most Asian economies, as described in the chapter on business governance (chapter 7). The group also may exist by virtue of cross-shareholdings by each member in the others. The *keiretsus* in Japan are an example. Some are bank-centered conglomerates in which the bank lends to other members.

The relationship is assumed to reduce risk by giving the lender inside information about the borrower and an equity stake in the borrower's performance that increases its interest in the borrower as a going concern beyond that of a simple creditor. These stakes are the most well defined form of relationships that rely on the social and economic interests of the borrower to assure performance. The social and economic sanctions arise because the borrower is part of a community that will exclude him if he fails to meet his obligations. The sanctions have force because the borrower has no alternative to that community. It is extremely difficult to test these sanctions because the data are so confidential.

Relational lending may play a role in some credit decisions but it does not dominate credit in five of the six economies. It is not significant in economies dominated by banks owned or controlled by their governments: PRC, India, Republic of Korea (until the early 1990s), and Taipei,China. The Republic of Korea went furthest to restrict relational lending by imposing low ceilings on equity interests in banks and strictly limiting the lending of a bank to any one customer, particularly any customer from a *chaebol*. In India, although families make up important groups, relational lending is minimal because private banks play such a small role. Malaysia prohibits this sort of relational lending, though some may take place despite the rules. In Taipei,China, relational lending was important to credit cooperatives.

Japan is the only economy of the six where relational lending played a major role in finance over the 35 years, but even in Japan relational lending began to decline in the late 1970s as the financial system became increasingly liquid. Lending by the main bank to group members often required little or no collateral, since the main bank knew the borrowers. As such, the main bank had an information advantage over other potential lenders. Our Japanese team's efforts to test this lending to *keiretsu* members was stymied, however, by the fact that most Japanese banks belong to a group.

---

[6] Relational lending does not include, for our purposes, a long-standing commercial relationship based on the repeated extension of credit and possibly other services by the lender to the user. This is the lending Ramseyer examines in Japan (1991). Called relationship lending in the trade, this has been common in many parts of the world, including the US.

Even when relational lending occurred, the lenders took more security than one might expect. In Japan, banks took security (including guarantees, see below) in about 60 percent of their lending from 1960 to 1995. One might argue that banks exacting security from related borrowers may not expect to enforce their interest in court but we found no study of this issue. We did find evidence that as the relationships weakened, Japanese lenders turned to collateral. In India, banks with more relational lending took higher levels of security interests (and often had less serious bad loans) than banks without these relationships.

The declining trends in the prevalence of relational lending do not correlate with the changing use of security interests in any of the economies. In Japan, although demand from *keiretsu* members for bank credit had been on the decline for many years, there was no long-term change in the relative importance of secured and guaranteed lending (see next section). In the Republic of Korea, the power of the main bank has declined and as noted the government has limited some bank lending to the *chaebols*. In India, the role of the family business may be declining, but secured lending has not changed.

Guarantees

A third substitute for security interests is guarantees that others related in some way to the borrower give to lenders. Explicit guarantees would commonly include the formal guarantee of the patriarch of a family group to nonmember creditors. Implicit guarantees exist for *keiretsu* members, for example, when nonmember banks rely on the borrower's main bank either to assure the borrower's good financial health or, if health fails, to step in and bail out the borrower. The other banks look to the main bank because of its inside knowledge of the borrower. The credibility of the main bank affects the way other banks determine a company's strength.

Guarantees varied in importance across the six economies, according to interviews and published statistics. Despite a common belief that Asia was different, the numbers did not support the idea that guarantees were used at a consistently high level nor were the levels related to the creditor-friendliness of the economies. Guarantees were low in the Republic of Korea—barely 8 percent of all banks' loans by 1995. Guarantees were moderate in Japan, where banks making relational loans, such as to *keiretsu* members, relied on them rather than collateral. From 1975 to 1992, guarantees and secured lending fell relative to unsecured lending, then recovered, so one cannot say that guarantees displaced security interests in Japan. Guarantees were high in Taipei,China and India, according to interviews. In Taipei,China, banks routinely insisted that all a borrowing company's directors guarantee the loan. As noted earlier, if any director refused to sign or tried to withdraw a guarantee upon leaving the company, the bank would take that as a signal that the company was in trouble. This discussion assumes, of course, that the data about guarantees are reasonably accurate.

Delayed Transfers of Ownership

Delayed transfers of ownership, such as conditional sale or hire-purchase, are a close substitute for security interests. They are found in India, Malaysi, and Taipei,China, where they are frequently used for certain purposes (for example, consumer loans). These are not security interests, but very close. We lack statistics to compare their use. But if they were significant, their use would demonstrate the importance of the formal legal system, of which they are a part.

ECONOMIC STRATEGIES AND THE USE OF SECURITY INTERESTS

The use of security interests is less significant when economic strategies limit, rather than encourage, market operations. Three types of lending illustrate the direct role of the government in the economy: policy loans, loans to small- and medium-sized enterprises, and loans by state owned banks. The first two reveal the important effect of economic strategy on security interests when the government intervenes directly in the market. The third does not. Policy loans occur when the government directs banks (and others) to lend to favored sectors of the economy. A key element in many strategies of direct government control, policy loans prompt banks to rely less on security interests to manage risk when they make their decisions to lend. Lending to SMEs, which ought to be responsive to the strength of the security regime, seems to be partly a function of the role of the business in this type of economic strategy. Lending by state owned banks, often a key tool of the economic strategy, turns out to have no obvious effect on the use of security interests. This may be because ownership of the banks is a less direct form of intervention than are directives about lending.

Economic Strategies: Policy Loans and Secured Lending

Substantial government sponsored or mandated lending (called "policy loans") is integral to many economic strategies of direct government intervention and appears to reduce the use of security interests. Policy lending takes place with much less reliance on collateral to reduce risk even though collateral may be taken in a formal sense. This is important because during the 35-year period governments in many of the economies used policy loans. Japan moved away from policy lending in the early 1970s, having earlier used a system in which the Central Bank supplied funds to banks that allowed them to lend to targeted sectors substantially more than they raised through deposits and borrowing from other sources. Taipei,China reduced its policy lending in the mid-1980s, as did Malaysia as part of a liberalization process that began in the mid-1970s. Policy lending accounted for about 60 percent of lending in the Republic of Korea from 1973 to 1991 and only began to be reduced after reforms in 1993. India started to reduce priority loans in 1990s. Policy loans still account for much bank lending in the PRC.

Banks directed by their governments to lend to certain groups or for certain purposes usually must meet targets (perhaps by making such loans a designated portion of total loans) and provide concessional terms, such as low interest rates or long maturities. Failure to do so results in discipline, often in the form of fines. The government may help fund these loans through preferential access to the central bank's discount window.

Governments that direct lending could, in the abstract, have an interest in repayment and therefore want the bank to be able to collect if the borrower defaults. The interest would stem from concern about the viability of the financial system or possible claims on the state's treasury. Often the political strength of the borrowers offsets this potential concern, however, and in practice the government limits the banks' ability to enforce claims on defaulting borrowers of policy loans. As banks learn when political clout rules, they tailor their behavior to protect their own interests by looking to the government.

When banks lend as directed, interviews repeatedly confirmed, they anticipate that the government will bail them out if these loans become nonperforming in large volumes. The banks may take security, but do not expect to be able to levy on it at their discretion. In this situation, one would expect to see the number of cases enforcing security interests to decline as a share of all defaulting loans. We do not have these data, but in the Republic of Korea the number of cases where security was enforced declined dramatically relative to the real volume of loans over the 35 years.[7]

Under these circumstances, security interests neither increase efficiency nor do they affect loan volumes or allocation. Indeed, one study found that Korean banks passively followed government directions rather than do much to seek and evaluate credit opportunities (Dalla and Khatkhate 1995). It

---

[7] One must interpret these data with care. The decline in suits about security interests could also be due to the increasing effectiveness of the security interest regime, making suits less necessary because the parties' rights become clear or because self-enforcement works better over time.

appears that policy loans affect the use of security interests by obviating lenders' careful evaluation of risk. A bank that is directed to lend and has the prospect of government bailout will not develop the sophisticated system of risk analysis that is needed for a strong system of security interests.

Since policy loans are associated with periods of greater direct governmental role in the economy, one might expect to see relatively less unsecured lending during these periods and more as the economic strategy becomes more market-oriented. Only one economy, Taipei,China, offers a time series for secured and unsecured lending beginning in 1960. These data show precisely this trend. During the first economic strategy period, one of growing government control (1960–1972), unsecured loans averaged 41 percent of all bank loans. In the second period, with the greatest direct government involvement in the economy (1973–1985), unsecured loans rose to an average of 45 percent. As the economic strategy became more market oriented (1986–1995), unsecured loans fell to 38 percent of all loans. Unsecured lending was highest in the era of greatest government economic control, then fell. The Republic of Korea, however, with data only from 1985, shows the opposite: a relative increase in unsecured lending over the decade as the economy becomes more market oriented. This may be too short a time period to measure the shift, since it encompasses only one strategy period. It may indicate that factors other than government economic strategy (such as the loss of a powerful substitute in Taipei,China) drive secured lending more. Or it may simply indicate that our analysis is at too aggregate a level to mark the effect of strategy on secured lending.

Banks directed to lend may take security interests even though they do not expect to be allowed to use them much. This could explain why banks in the Republic of Korea, which had huge policy loans, consistently reported a much higher secured loan ratio than banks in Taipei,China, which had much lower policy loans. One should distinguish between the formal use of security interests to comply with prudential regulations (which one might call nominal security interests) and actual reliance on them to reduce risk (real security interests). Formal use occurs when law makes bank loan officers protect themselves on paper without needing to collect on defaulted debt. State bankers in India institute suits to protect themselves from criticism even though they only pursue the suits very slowly if at all. In the Republic of Korea, the bank is allowed to deduct from loans that are not expected to be recovered the value of the collateral for those loans. This means that the higher the bank values the collateral, the lower its nonperforming loans. Korean banks have an incentive to take security and overvalue it even if they do not expect to be able to foreclose on the collateral (Dalla and Khatkhate 1995). Here is an example of nominal security. Note that the practice occurs regardless of whether the government owns the banks.

Economic Strategies: SMEs, the Use of Security Interests, and Lending

To evaluate the effect of a security regime on secured lending to an economic sector, one must locate the sector in the government's economic strategy. This conclusion emerges from an analysis of secured lending to small- and medium-sized enterprises (SMEs). Even more than large firms, SMEs should benefit from effective security interest regimes. SMEs worldwide complain that their access to bank finance is limited, but it is worse in some economies than others and collateral is identified as a central concern. SMEs often lack the standard types of acceptable collateral (land, fixed equipment) but would have relatively more in the form of inventory or accounts receivable. SMEs often lack the relationships with the formal financial intermediaries, the commercial banks, that would give them access to credit.

The Republic of Korea and Malaysia revealed different ways in which the economic strategy affected the use of security interests by SMEs. The regimes differed in the two economies. Malaysia allowed a much broader range of security interests than the Republic of Korea, including registrable interests in inventory, accounts receivable, and future assets generally. But the two economies' development strategies differed, so the use of security interests varied. In Malaysia, SMEs were not central. They were not able to use the wide range of security interests just listed because few were corporations. SMEs had a problem raising funds from banks. In contrast, in the Republic of Korea, some SMEs were important and took substantial loans from banks. The government directed lending to them, making their use of security interests largely a formality even though lending to SMEs was high.

Malaysia. Malaysia's regime for security interests was most friendly toward larger firms, in that corporations, and no other form of business, could offer the full array of security interests. Malaysia's security interest regime was one tool of the economy's strategy to pursue export oriented growth through large firms. The economy relied on large foreign owned firms to add value in capital-intensive industries using imported technology and other inputs.

Thus, the SMEs organized as partnerships or sole proprietorships did not have the capacity to offer as collateral movable property that they possessed, or future assets. Malaysia's security regime did not help SMEs because it was not designed for them. They were not central to the government's growth strategy. Domestic owned firms were SMEs, mainly Chinese Malaysian but increasingly Malay since the 1971 "new economic policy," and produced for the low-income groups in the economy. SMEs grew with the economy and accounted for about the same share of output in 1995 as in 1985 (47 percent). But these SMEs did not play a major role in production for export and, in contrast to those in Taipei,China, did not lead Malaysia's growth, so they were not central to the economy's dynamism.

SMEs in Malaysia voiced the common complaint that financing was scarce partly because the law did not allow them to offer the banks the kind of collateral that they had. The SMEs were forced to use finance companies, which could provide hire-purchase finance, and informal markets such as the revolving credit schemes. To remedy this, the government tried various techniques. Banks were directed to lend no less than a specified portion of their total loans each year, at low fixed spreads above the cost of funds. At least some banks failed to meet these targets despite penalties, because the returns were low, administrative costs high, and losses significant. In 1989, the government switched to a policy designed to promote bank lending to SMEs even if they lacked security. The imperative for these policies was political, to increase the role of Malays in the domestic economy, rather than economic; the policies were not designed to support the SMEs in a battle for international market share.

Republic of Korea. Economic strategy in the Republic of Korea relied on those SMEs that would support its export drive in the 1980s and they were the ones that grew. Behind the 1980s' growth in the economy were SMEs producing machinery and equipment, which had accounted for 21 percent of value added by SMEs in 1980 and 31 percent in 1992. SMEs in other industries, such as chemicals, food processing, and textiles, lost share. The resurgent SMEs were subcontractors to the Republic of Korea's large exporting firms that were outsourcing more than before. As a group, SMEs (defined as enterprises with 5-200 employees) played an important but declining role in the economy's growth over much of the period (Kim and Nugent 1994).

SMEs received substantial funds from banks and others by government mandate. The government directed national commercial banks to allocate increasing shares of their new loans to SMEs: 30 percent in the 1970s, then 35 percent, and 45 percent in 1992. Local banks had much higher targets. In response, the commercial banks increased the share of their lending to SMEs from 33 percent in 1981 to 38 percent in 1989. The banks were important to SMEs, accounting in 1990 for 53 percent of private loans to SMEs, of which 22 percent was from commercial banks and the rest from specialized banks. For start-ups, only 15 percent was from banks, indicating that banks were cautious about lending to new ventures, which is typical of banks in many economies. Nonbank financial institutions, such as finance companies, leasing companies, and mutual credit funds, accounted for the remaining 47 percent (Kim and Nugent 1994).

These SMEs were in the anomalous position of providing security to banks that needed collateral for prudential purposes rather than the market.

This was because the banks were forced to lend by government mandate and therefore much less concerned about the quality of the security than would otherwise be true. Explicit government support for this lending was large. The Central Bank rediscounted commercial bills for SMEs. A government credit guarantee fund, created in 1976, guaranteed about 20 percent of loans to SMEs by 1990. Private guarantees supported about 25 percent of the debt of SMEs. The majority of loans to SMEs in the mid-1980s was backed by collateral: 66 percent in 1986, declining to 61 percent in 1988 (Kim and Nugent 1994). The collateral met prudential requirements rather than reducing risk. Behind all this was an implicit government obligation to help banks that encountered problems if the borrowers could not repay. Throughout the middle and late 1980s, Korean banks carried the weight of large bad loans, yet they continued to lend according to government mandate. The banks expected the government to bail them out. In these circumstances, collateral was of secondary importance to the lenders.

Economic Strategies: State Owned Banks and the Use of Security Interests

An integral part of many economic strategies is the use of state owned banks to collect savings and allocate credit. Government owned banks might be expected to differ from private banks in their approach to the use of collateral. One line of analysis is that because public sector banks lend more often for political reasons, they would require less security. The logic of this would be that to the extent government owned banks dominate lending, security interest regimes would be less important. According to this line of thought, since state banks dominated in five of the economies in the survey for most of the 35 years, security regimes should have played a less significant role than if private banks dominated, and unsecured lending by state banks would be higher. An opposite line of thinking is that private bankers want collateral to change the risk/reward profile of the transaction, but accept that losses will occur on some loans. State bankers, following such strategy, are more concerned that they not be held accountable in the event of any loss and therefore would require more security for their loans. The logic of this suggests that security regimes would be used more when state banks dominated and unsecured lending would be lower. To test these hypotheses, we would want to see within each economy if unsecured loans as a share of all loans are higher or lower in government owned banks than private banks. But banks rarely reveal this kind of information publicly, so we lack comparative data.

The limited data suggest that government or private ownership does not explain relative use of secured loans (see table 6.2). The one economy in which private banks dominated throughout the 35 years, Japan, reported a ratio of unsecured to total loans (38 percent in 1985) close to that in two of the economies (43 percent in Taipei,China and 46 percent in the Republic of Korea), and much higher than in another—India, with 2–5 percent— which is dominated by state owned or controlled banks. Public sector banks dominated in the three other economies, for which we have data about unsecured loans—PRC, India, and Taipei,China. They were dominant in Malaysia also, but we have no data about its unsecured loans. The Republic of Korea's government continued to control the privatized banks through the 1980s, so treating Korean banks as akin to public sector banks during this period is reasonable. From about 1990, some Korean banks became more subject to market forces than to the government, while others did not, but the gap with Japan grew. In fact, Japan did not disaggregate guarantees and movable property collateral. It reported in 1995 that loans supported by these together accounted for 32 percent of all loans. Japan looks much more like the other economies if we add half (16 percent) or three-quarters (24 percent) of those loans to the 33 percent share unsecured, which would become 49 percent or 57 percent.

Table 6.2   Unsecured Bank Loans as a Percentage of All Loans by State and Nonstate Banks

Economy	1985	1990	1995
PRC	—	—	45–70
Korea, Republic of	46	51	54
Taipei,China	43	39	34
Japan	38	34	33
India	2–5	2–5	2–5

— = not available
Note: Italics indicate very limited size of state owned banks.
Source: Team reports.

We did not find evidence that state owned banks required substantially more or less security than private banks. The degree of state ownership, then, should not affect the importance of the regime for security interests.

This observation is bolstered if one extends the analysis beyond government ownership to government control. In the Republic of Korea in 1995, the five government dominated banks our team studied had secured loans averaging 46 percent of all loans and ranging from 35 percent to 54 percent, while the three more independent banks reported an average of 48 percent in a 45-52 percent range. It is hard to argue that either group relied more on secured lending than the other. We do not know if the ratios would have been different earlier in the 35-year period, since the data were only published in 1994.

ECONOMIC DEVELOPMENT AND THE USE OF SECURITY INTERESTS

Economic development affects the role played by the regime for security interests in the use of security and in lending (see figure 6.2 above), primarily by affecting supply and demand conditions for loans. We did not set out to examine this linkage, but rather happened on it as at least a partial explanation for behavior resulting, or not, from the regime for security interests.

The use of security interests changed as the structure of the economy changed in many of the economies. For example, consumer loans, secured by land, rose recently in India, Republic of Korea, Malaysia, and Taipei,China as consumers' wealth increased to the point where they had assets that would allow them to take advantage of this kind of debt. Often financial intermediaries other than banks made the loans.

The declining use of security interests by banks in the Republic of Korea (described above) may have been due at least in part to changes in the supply and demand for credit, particularly from 1990 on. Slower economic growth and increasing access by the borrowers to offshore funds would have reduced demand for credit from banks at home. The continued growth of lending by nonbank financial institutions would increase the supply of credit at home. Compared with the 10 or 15 years leading up to 1990, banks were no longer in a lenders' market. The net effect was to reduce the market power of the banks so that they were no longer strong enough to require security as frequently as before.

In Taipei,China, though the repeal of criminal sanctions for bouncing postdated checks was important, economic development could also have influenced the relative decline in unsecured loans and loans by the informal sector. Export markets were very important to many of the small- and medium-sized firms that used these loans and markets. In 1986, Taipei,China revalued its currency, which would affect demand for its products by raising the cost on foreign markets. This would presumably increase the risk of lending to these smaller firms. The economic effect of revaluation could account for some of the decline in lending to them.

SECURITY INTEREST REGIMES AND THE USE OF SECURITY INTERESTS UNDER DIFFERENT MARKET CONDITIONS

To understand the effect of a regime for security interests, the prior sections demonstrate that one must look at the mitigating impact of cheaper substitutes, the economy's economic strategy, and its macroeconomy. The focus of our discussion in this chapter has been whether regimes for security interests have a greater effect on the use of secured lending and work for economic efficiency when market oriented policies prevail, or, conversely, whether their effect diminishes under controlled markets. In fact we find that, when markets are managed, regimes for security interests can have a negative effect and increase economic inefficiency. Two examples of the harm they can do under managed markets are found in India and Taipei,China. We start with these cases.

Security Interest Regimes that Contribute to Inefficiency

Though India demonstrates many of the problems a regime for security interests can cause, we start with Taipei,China, which demonstrates that security interest regimes with much less extreme problems can also undermine economic performance.

Taipei,China's Export Strategy and the Weakness of the Security Interest Regime

In Taipei,China, SMEs lacked conventional collateral, such as land, under a regime that did not allow the use as collateral of the assets they did have, such as inventory, accounts receivable, or other future assets. This undercut their access to credit and may have impeded their performance by hindering the growth of SMEs that could compete effectively in world markets. At the risk of describing a flaw in an export push some might say was so incredibly successful that any damage was minor, we use this case to illustrate how weaknesses in a regime for security interests can create inefficiencies that hurt an export strategy built on a certain type of firm (SMEs). This differs from the earlier section about SMEs, which examines the effect of the strategy on secured lending.

Taipei,China relied on SMEs to produce for export and used large monopolistic firms to supply domestic markets. Exports led GDP growth and SMEs accounted for 60-70 percent of total exports in the 1980s, declining after the currency revalued in 1986 to a still high share of 51 percent in 1995. And exports were 70 percent of output by SMEs in the mid-1980s, in contrast to the Malaysian SMEs, which produced for the domestic markets (Chou 1996).

Despite this impressive performance, the SMEs could have done better. Taipei,China's SMEs did not achieve the threshold scale economies needed to market their products abroad. They relied instead on foreign distributors, such as Japanese trading companies. Had they been able to grow, they could have expanded forward into marketing. Instead, their limited financing capped their ability to expand into international markets. SMEs funded their operations much less from formal financial institutions than large firms: 42 percent in 1985 (compared with 63 percent for large firms), rising to 56 percent in mid-1989 (76 percent for large firms). Unlike large firms, SMEs could not tap money and capital markets or foreign sources. Instead, the SMEs relied for financing on informal markets: 58 percent in 1985 (16 percent for large firms) and 44 percent in mid-1989 (14 percent for large firms).

A key problem for the SMEs was their lack of collateral acceptable to formal lenders. SMEs could use security substitutes, notably the postdated checks with criminal sanctions described above. These were a poor, very short-term substitute, made worse by interest rate ceilings that, although above the inflation rate and therefore real, were well below rates on the informal market. Since interest rates were not free formally until 1989 and may have continued to be managed by the Central Bank and leading banks, a spread continued to exist at least to 1990 between the rates on loans from banks and the market rates from informal lenders. The ceilings would prevent banks from pricing loans to SMEs according to risk. The limitations on possible collateral would prevent lenders from reducing the risk by offering security.

This combination of a weak security interest regime and interest ceilings forced the SMEs onto the informal market, where rates were much higher. SMEs paid more for their loans because of their greater dependence on the informal market. Had they been able to use a wider range of collateral, they could have reduced the cost of credit in the informal market at least and perhaps have had greater access to the formal market. This affected Taipei,China's economic strategy: few companies would mount an assault on international markets relying on short-term funds raised by discounting postdated checks. Here the regime for security interests could not deliver what the government managed economic strategy needed.

India's Inefficient Security Interest Regime

India offers a case study of a more extreme way in which a regime for security interests can increase operational and allocational inefficiency in the lending market under a controlled economy.

As described earlier in this chapter, the system was much friendlier to debtors than creditors with security interests. Multiple overlapping laws made it very hard for parties to a loan to be certain of the rights and procedures, slowing the process considerably. High taxes raised transaction costs. The government approvals for security like urban land delayed perfection of the interest. Uncertainty about title undermined the use of land as security. Lack of publicity about security interests in personal property hampered their use, since a prospective lender could not assure itself about prior interests. Lenders and borrowers overstated the value of the loan not only to get around interest rate ceilings but also to raise the cost of the loan by a large amount to offset high risk due at least in part to ineffective enforcement of security interests. The borrowers then used the courts to delay repayment of the full amount of the loan and reduce its real value to a level that their cash flows could absorb.

The effect on economic efficiency was severe. Operational efficiency was reduced. The practice of requiring security interests in at least 95 percent of the loans meant even prime borrowers that would normally not have to give security because of their high creditworthiness, had to do so. The costs they incurred as a result would have been unnecessary in a market oriented economy. Transaction costs also rose because of many of the individual problems, including title uncertainty, taxes, procedural delays, and uncertainty about other claims on the collateral. In such circumstances allocational efficiency is also reduced, since the regime locks out the promising new small borrowers who lack assets that qualify as collateral.

This sort of story is well known today. The point of our earlier analysis is to show that just rewriting the security interest laws will not solve the problem, nor will efforts to improve the legal procedures for administering the regime for security interests and dealing with its disputes. India must also attend to the economic policies that dovetail with the deficiencies of the regime. One example among many is the urban land policy. Without changes in this policy, it is hard to imagine that work on the laws governing security interests will yield much fruit.

When Markets Work: Security Interest Regimes and Bad Debt Problems

As the economies gradually adopted and implemented more market-oriented policies, their banks ran into bad debt problems that led to banking crises. The move to more liberal economic policies was far from the only cause; often an outside event like a decline in export prices or a shock precipitated the crisis. But the governments, withdrawing from a direct role in the economy, were less able or willing to resolve the crises on their own. So as the lenders moved into more of a market environment, they needed more market oriented tools to deal with the crises. One of these tools is secured lending.

Serious bad loan problems ought to be inversely related to the effectiveness of the regime for security interests. When security interests work as intended, they should reduce the impact of bad loans on lenders. If a borrower defaults, the secured lender can recoup much if not all of the debt by selling the collateral (assuming it has value). When the regime works poorly, or loans are unsecured, one should be more likely to see serious bad loan problems. It is not clear in the abstract that a regime extremely biased toward the secured creditor would be more likely to mitigate serious systemic loan problems than one that balanced the interests of borrowers and various types of claimants. Major financial institutions like banks are usually both secured and unsecured creditors. Moreover, any regime is subject to fluctuations in the market value of the collateral; if values fall precipitously, the bad debts remain on the bank's balance sheet regardless of whether the regime is extremely friendly to secured lenders.

All six economies reported that their banks encountered serious problems with nonperforming loans over at least one period of several years during the 35-year period. To put these in perspective, a recent review of bank problems around the world from 1980 to 1996 defined banking crises as "runs or other substantial portfolio shifts, massive government intervention, or collapses of financial firms." It defined significant banking problems as "extensive banking unsoundness short of a crisis." It reported 36 economies with banking crises, one of which was Malaysia. It reported 102 economies with significant banking problems. These included PRC (1980s on), India (1991 on), Japan (1992 on), Republic of Korea (mid-1980s), and Taipei,China (1995).[8] The study estimated total losses or costs in Japan at about 10 percent of GDP (Goldstein 1996). Thus, even the second tier "significant banking problem" was quite expensive.

Secured lending played a role in the bad loan problems of three economies: Japan to help create the problems, India to deepen and prolong the problems, and the Republic of Korea to protect banks that relied more on them. The first two economies exemplify circumstances in which market activity was restricted even in the resolution of the problems. The third shows the benefit to banks of lending on market principles. In the Republic of Korea, secured lending appears to have helped individual banks that took relatively more security than others and then were caught in a debt crisis.

In the other economies, security interests were not a major issue. Taipei,China professes to have encountered bad debts in the mid-1980s, but official statistics only identify foreign banks as being seriously hurt. Malaysia,

---

[8] We would add the problem loans in Taipei,China in the mid-1980s and the early 1990s. It is not at all clear that the reported nonperforming loans during the latter period accurately reflect the true volume, particularly for the state-owned intermediaries.

with a regime that favors secured creditors, had the most serious problem with bad loans. In the mid-1980s, a collapse in commodity prices cut exports, bringing the most severe recession since the mid-1950s, declining incomes, and a sharp fall in property prices, particularly in urban areas. The collapse of a Hong Kong bank prompted the first run on banks in Malaysia in 20 years. Sporadic runs on banks and other deposit-taking institutions in 1986 raised the possibility of contagion (Cole, Scott, and Wellons 1995). The Central Bank stepped in and gradually reduced the threat. In the PRC's bad debt problem, state owned banks reported a much higher level of nonperforming loans than nonstate banks. In a sample, five state banks reported 55 percent troubled loans and five private banks reported only 11 percent. The level of security interests was not identified by people interviewed in the PRC as being a major cause of serious loan losses. Indeed, only 15 percent of people interviewed in the troubled banks and 5 percent in the untroubled banks referred to it. Government lending priorities were overwhelmingly identified as the cause of the problems, and poor management was ranked second. Whether or not the security interest regime was doing its job, it did not cause or exacerbate these crisis.

Japan's Debt Problem: when the collateral is a cause

In Japan, the collateral helped cause the problems. Real property was the security for 25 percent of loans in Japan in 1960, rising to about 30 percent in the late 1970s. The banks carried the collateral at book value, but since land prices rose dramatically, the market value of the collateral would have been much higher. In 1970, for example, land prices rose 41 percent. But from 1974 on, land inflation was in the single digits, as low as 3 percent a year from 1983 to 1986. Then prices rose 10.6 percent in 1987, 6.2 percent in 1988, 9.7 percent in 1989, and 16.3 percent in 1990. This was part of the asset bubble that was even more dramatic in the stock market. It collapsed the following year. Land prices fell on average more than 4 percent a year from 1992 to 1995. As the bubble grew, banks loaned more, still using land as collateral. For all banks, loans secured by real property rose from 23.6 percent in 1985 to 29 percent in 1992; the percentages varied by bank. Thus exposed, the banks were at risk when land prices collapsed. The banks that had extended large amounts of loans with land as collateral encountered serious loan problems, according to an econometric analysis of 148 banks (Ueda 1996). The immediate reaction of the government was to try to manage the problems. Rather than let the banks work toward individual solutions, pursue defaulting debtors, and enforce security interests even in bankruptcy, the government initially encouraged the banks to help ailing borrowers. It applied the traditional convoy system, in which all lenders moved at a speed that the weakest member could handle. By the end of our period, however, the deficiencies of this system were apparent and the stronger banks began major writeoffs that would entail substantial claims on defaulting debtors. This crisis, and its management, are examples of what can happen when market mechanisms are not allowed to work well in both the lead up to a crisis and attempts to resolve it.

India's Serious Loan Losses: when the regime for security interests exacerbates the problem

The weakness of the security interest regime in India contributed to the serious loan losses of the banks in several ways, but the level of secured lending is not reflected in loan losses since almost all loans are secured. Banks suffered from huge loan losses during the 1980s but the seriousness of these losses was only revealed in 1991–1992.

Government owned banks had much higher levels of nonperforming loans than private banks. The government banks dominated lending and they admitted in interviews to experiencing to a much greater degree the problems described below. Politicians or government officials prodded them to lend with inadequate or sham collateral, to lend to borrowers already delinquent, and to lend to nonviable projects in priority sectors. The few unsecured loans were very small and made by government mandate to borrowers in priority sectors, notably agriculture. These had a very high failure rate. Banks could not foreclose on security interests or political loans when the borrowers became delinquent because the same policy or political reasons dictated that the borrower continue to operate. Banks seeking to enforce their security interests discovered many problems. Assets were depleted. Assets were sold, without notice, despite the bank's security interest. Guarantors disappeared. Enforcement took years, as described earlier in this chapter. A bureaucratic imperative drove much of the behavior of government owned banks. For example, as related above in the section on India, to protect himself from criticism, a low-paid bank employee might feel compelled to launch a suit against a delinquent debtor, yet the same employee might accept bribes from the debtor to push the suit no further. As a result, the suit would languish unresolved for years. In contrast, the 52 private banks were much freer to select customers and enforce security interests. They had nonperforming loan ratios in an acceptable range of 3–6 percent, much lower than those of government banks.

Republic of Korea's Bad Debt Crisis: when secured creditors are safer

One might anticipate that the security interest regime was largely irrelevant to restoring the Republic of Korea's serious bad loan problems, given the economy's history of commercial banking. However, some correlation can in fact be found between the level of security and bad loans. As described above, the government directed about 60 percent of the lending of commercial banks from 1973 to 1991. A recession in the early 1980s hit the industries targeted earlier by the government: overseas construction, shipping, textiles, and lumber. So the government restructured these industries, writing off debts and directing even more loans from the banks to these troubled sectors. The banks relied on low-cost funds from the Central Bank to support the directed credit and managed interest rates. Under these circumstances, the banks were hardly in a position to call in their collateral for bad loans. Nonperforming loans rose from 2.4 percent of all loans during 1976–1980 to 10.5 percent during1984–1986 and declined after that to 5.9 percent in 1989, by official count. The numbers probably understate the volume of bad loans, since Korean banks report bad loans after deducting the collateral value, even though they have not levied on the collateral. If this value were included, the bad loan values could be much higher than reported (Dalla and Khatkhate 1995). In any event, the banks' return on assets fell as low as 0.20 during 1987–1995, very low indeed.

Despite this sad history, our economy team found a loose inverse correlation in 1995 between the share of secured loans and nonperforming loans for the 13 banks shown in figure 6.3. The data only begin in 1994, so analysis of trends is not possible.

Figure 6.3   Relation of Nonperfoming Loans to Secured Loans for Each of 13 Commercial Banks in the Republic of Korea, 1995

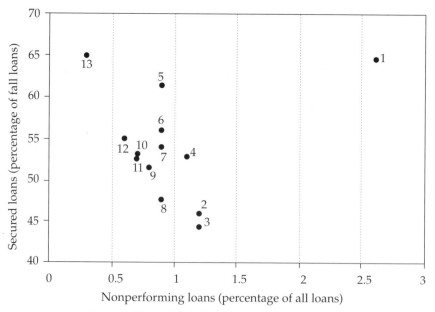

Source: Office of Bank Supervision, Bank of Korea.

At the same time, eight Korean banks with both unsecured assets and a range of nonperforming loans revealed a close correlation between the two, with one striking exception and another minor one (table 6.3). In general, the higher the share of nonperforming loans, the higher the proportion of unsecured assets. That is, the more a bank had secured its loans, the lower its nonperforming loan ratio. The banks with higher government intervention, in the form of appointment of top executives and asset management (interviews informed us of this), had the greatest number of nonperforming loans and the most unsecured lending, so that government ownership may drive the levels of both nonperforming loans and security. The striking exception is bank 1, with high nonperforming loans and low unsecured lending. It was hurt by the failure of a few large construction companies even though it held a relatively high proportion of secured loans and was relatively well diversified among borrowers by size of firm. The minor exception, bank 4, does not depart far from the rankings by unsecured assets.

Table 6.3   Eight Commercial Banks in the Republic of Korea:
Their Shares of Nonperforming Loans and
Proportions of Unsecured Lending
(percentage)

Type of bank	Bank's share of nonperforming loans	Bank's proportion of unsecured lending
Higher government intervention		
Bank 1	2.6	35.7
Bank 2	1.2	55.7
Bank 3	1.2	54.1
Bank 4	1.1	47.2
Bank 5	0.9	52.4
Lower government intervention		
Bank 6	0.7	47.4
Bank 7	0.6	45.0
Bank 8	0.3	35.1

Source: Korea team report.

Korean banks, then, reveal a relationship between bad loans and unsecured lending, and this correlation seems to be driven by the degree of the government's intervention in each bank's operations.

The Republic of Korea's nonbank financial institutions were said in interviews to have relied even less than the banks on the security regime and their share of lending to the private sector grew. The government policies that locked in the banks largely ignored the nonbank financial institutions. Policy loans fell from 49 percent of their lending in 1973–1981 to 15 percent in 1991. They could compete in financial markets. They saw their share of private sector lending rise from 22 percent in 1970 to 62 percent in 1995. Unfortunately, we do not have data describing the proportion of their loans that were secured.

In short, regimes for security interests can affect the seriousness of bad loan problems. Many factors cause bad loans, many precipitate a crisis, and there are limits to the ability even of a regime that is very friendly to secured lenders to protect banks in a crisis. With this caveat, we do find evidence that secured lending helps individual banks in a crisis. The example from the Republic of Korea is of no small significance because the economy's regime is not the friendliest to secured lenders. Even in those circumstances, banks able to take and enforce security interests according to market principles reported lower bad debts than banks that could not do so.

When Markets Work: Security Interest Regimes and Informal Markets

Informal lenders operate in markets even when the formal economy is gnarled by government edict. They might be expected to rely less than formal lenders on the regime for security interest because they operate outside of the formal financial system and its regulatory framework. If so, the security interest regimes would not play a significant role in economies with relatively large informal sectors. This assumption is borne out in a study of informal credit in Malaysia in the late 1970s. Informal lenders in Malaysia accounted for 75 percent of credit in rural areas in 1979. Of this proportion, almost 75 percent were moneylenders. Most of the credit, both formal and informal, was used for operating costs (65 percent) and consumption (20 percent). The formal moneylenders, who accounted for less than 5 percent, took gold and jewelry as collateral. The informal moneylenders, who accounted for about 70 percent, took no collateral and charged interest rates 60 percent higher than those for the secured loans. In urban areas, the rotating savings and credit associations were an important source of informal credit. Called *hui* in Chinese, they relied on relations among the participants rather than on collateral.

As informal lending declined as a share of total loans in most of the six economies, one might expect, perhaps incorrectly, that one sector of the financial system that used the law relatively less is on the wane. Certainly relative to formal lending, informal lending fell in the Republic of Korea, so that by 1995 the curb market was practically extinct. In Taipei,China it declined from 46 percent of all financial institutions' loans in 1964 to 27 percent in 1973, rose to 47 percent in 1987, then fell again to 30 percent in the early 1990s. Informal lending dropped in India and is not significant in Japan. Data for

Malaysia are not available. The assumption that informal markets do not use security interests, however, seems to be misleading

A contrary hypothesis is that in a highly managed economy the informal markets operate more closely to market principles than the formal markets. Since the regime for security interests is designed to function in a market economy, one would expect players in the informal markets to use security interests.

In practice, informal lenders did use the formal legal system more than one would expect from the original assumption, though they were not reported to use security interests much. In the Republic of Korea, informal lenders secured as much as two thirds of their loans to licensed businesses in 1972. The notarized property deeds called *yangdo dambo*, described above in the section on the Republic of Korea, were the principal collateral for loans in the curb market for short-term loans. Borrowers agreed in writing not to contest their cases in court if they defaulted. Korean courts enforced the *yangdo dambo* even though the civil code did not provide for it. In Taipei,China, informal lenders relied on courts to impose criminal sanctions on borrowers whose checks bounced.When the criminal sanctions were withdrawn in 1987, informal lending declined as a share of all loans. Informal lenders in India use the security interest regime to foreclose on collateral they hold.

CONCLUSION: THE ROLE OF LAW IN MARKETS FOR SECURED LOANS

The insight that the informal markets used the formal legal system more than they use the regime for security interest may be generalized. Regimes for security interests played an ambiguous role throughout most of the 35 years. Since markets were only allowed to work near the end of that period, it is not surprising that we do not see a clear effect of the regimes on the use of security interests and on lending and cannot easily distinguish among major elements of the various regimes.

During this period, the effects of the specific elements of a security regime are not apparent. As markets operate more freely, however, differences among the regimes may become more relevant to the use of security interests and to lending. In the period covered by this chapter, a constant refrain about the limitations of a security regime has been that it failed to provide for interests in inventory, accounts receivable, or future assets in general. The lack of a facility to register interests and the priority of the secured lender consistently appeared as problems. We did not establish many strong direct causal links between deficiencies in range of collateral, registries, or priority, though we did identify cases such as that involving Taipei,China's SMEs. Perhaps this is because the factors were not significant enough in their own right or perhaps we lacked the data to show their importance.

The formal legal system played an active role throughout, however. Weak security interest laws could hinder economic activity, which is not a surprise. The informal markets used law, as described above. Substitutes relied on law: relational lending on equity ownership, guarantees on contract law, sanctions for bouncing checks or promissory notes on the criminal code, and delayed transfers of ownership on special laws creating, for example, conditional sales. Prudential regulations encouraged banks to make nominal use of security interests, at least. Most broadly, the economic strategies were largely embodied in law. The regime for security interests was part of this array.

Chapter 7

THE SETTLING OF COMMERCIAL AND ADMINISTRATIVE DISPUTES

Historical experience suggests that the availability of effective and low cost dispute settlement is an important condition for expanding markets, for meeting the increasing complexity of economic development, and thus for economic development itself (Milgrom et al. 1990). In this chapter we analyze the role of legal processes and legal institutions, in particular the role of courts in Asian economic development. The chapter is divided into two subsections. The first deals with the role of dispute settlement institutions (DSIs) in resolving commercial disputes between nonstate parties. The second addresses the question of whether nonstate (private) parties have been vested with legal rights to take recourse against state actions; it analyzes available data that reflect the extent to which nonstate parties have made use of these rights.

Our findings for this section can be summarized as follows:

• Over the long term, rates for litigation concerning civil and commercial disputes increased in all economies. We find a positive and statistically significant correlation between per capita litigation rates and several indicators for the division of labor. This lends support to our Convergence Hypothesis, which suggests that with economic development, legal institutions will perform increasingly similar functions throughout the world.

• Still, litigation rates vary considerably across economies. The variations cannot be explained by economic development, or the extent to which division of labor has been achieved in these economies. For example, litigation rates in Japan in particular have remained much lower than in the other high performing economies.

• Nor do institutional constraints explain differences in litigation rates. We see this in comparing litigation rates in Japan with those of the Republic of Korea and Taipei,China. The comparison demonstrates that even when we control for a shared civil law tradition and a legacy of state imposed ceilings for the legal profession, litigation rates can vary considerably. We do not solve this puzzle of persistent divergence.

• With respect to administrative litigation, we find a stronger tradition of court adjudication over these matters in the two common law countries than in the countries that have a civil law tradition. However, even in India and Malaysia, administrative agency adjudication and tribunals often substituted for courts as a result of economic policies that allocated extensive control rights to the state.

The increase in administrative litigation required a change on the supply side. Only after political changes gave way to greater accountability of the state and its agents to law, were administrative procedures made available or put into effect. This supply met an increasing demand by nonstate agents to reduce the costs of state interference and assert their legal rights. The increase in the demand side is the result of socioeconomic change.

Data on the number of judges and the allocation of budgetary resources to the judiciary show that the supply side for court institutions over the 35 years has changed only marginally. Even in countries where the case load of courts increased substantially, the volume of human and financial resources extended to the court system did not reflect this. This provides further evidence for our proposition that legal institutions evolve at a slower pace than substantive law, which supports our Differentiation Hypothesis.

COMMERCIAL DISPUTE SETTLEMENT AND CONTRACT ENFORCEMENT

Existing theories on the evolution of DSIs suggest that these institutions evolve in response to changes in the socioeconomic environment. In small markets where market participants can easily monitor other market participants, who often belong to the same ethnic group or trade or settle in the same locality, disputes can be settled for the most part by informal mechanisms (Landa 1981; Bernstein 1992). They include implicit guarantees by persons whose reputation is their most important asset (reputation bonds), and ad hoc arbitration by members of the same community or trade. As markets expand in terms of geography and the number of market participants, these mechanisms become less reliable. Formal institutions that have the power to enforce their rulings against parties unwilling to comply voluntarily become more important. These institutions also fulfill an important function in providing access to information about unreliable business contacts (Milgrom 1990). In the West, courts have come to play an important role in solving commercial disputes. Although established by the state, their credibility as neutral arbiters between nonstate parties has been enhanced by vesting them with independence.

The formal court system as it exists in Asia today is the result of the comprehensive transplantation of legal systems from the West. Where they were transplanted by colonial powers—as in the case of India and Malaysia—they initially served primarily members of the colonial power. Subsequently, courts were staffed with local legal professionals most of whom were trained in England. Local legal training began only much later. In Malaysia, for example, domestic bar exams were introduced only in the 1980s. In the other countries, old and new traditions were merged. Legal training was based on the new codes, but traditional systems of civil service exams were used to regulate the number of candidates to be admitted to the legal profession.

In most economies a formal court system endowed with the means to enforce disputes between previously unrelated parties already existed before any socioeconomic developments created a demand for state institutions to enforce commercial contracts. The key question for dispute settlement in Asia therefore is not if and how formal DSIs evolved; it is whether the institutions that were transplanted from the West have come to play an important role for settling commercial disputes as the economies grew more complex. Ideally, we would compare commercial dispute settlement inside and outside the courts for each economy. However, we lack empirical data on informal dispute settlement. We therefore rely primarily on the rate of litigation concerning civil and commercial disputes in the formal court system.

When Western style court systems were transplanted to Asia, a host of dispute settlement systems was already in place. Systems included both informal institutions relying primarily on voluntary compliance and formal institutions vested with the power to use coercion to enforce primarily criminal and administrative law.

In many countries, DSIs outside the court system remain in operation. Some of them have their origins in traditional DSIs, including village elders and religious courts. In other cases, traditional dispute settlement mechanisms were institutionalized by political interest groups. Mediation committees in the PRC were first established in parts of the mainland that were under Communist Party of China (CPC) control (Clarke 1991). To this date, mediation committees play an important role in settling minor civil disputes in the PRC as well as in Taipei, China. In India, informal DSIs are commonly used in rural areas. Traditional institutions predating Western transplants have been revived in an attempt to provide alternatives to an increasingly inefficient court system. Finally, in Malaysia, traditional *penghulu* (or headman) courts have become part of the formal court system, and native courts in Borneo have jurisdiction in cases arising from the breach of native law or custom. The *penghulu* courts were established to provide the rural population with accessible courts when poor transportation made it difficult to reach magistrates' courts in the major towns. Economic development over the past decades has reduced the need for these courts, which have largely gone out of use. The two economies where traditional DSIs appear to be least prevalent are the Republic of Korea and Japan, although this may reflect only the absence of reliable data.

An important feature of DSIs whose roots can be traced back to pre-Western DSIs is that parties have been given access to the court system to enforce awards rendered by these institutions. In fact, as will be discussed below, there is evidence that over the years, parties have made increasing use of this option. This shows that although mediation and conciliation may—possibly for cultural reasons—be a preferred mechanism for settling disputes, these institutions have benefited from the possibility of piggy-backing on the enforcement mechanisms made available by the formal court system.

Mediation procedures are also frequently used by the courts. Cases can be transferred within the court to special mediation procedures, or the presiding judge may offer to arbitrate a settlement. Cultural factors may play an important role in the common use of nonadversarial procedures. The relentless pursuit of one's rights is often perceived negatively and parties that do so may lose face. In addition, the high costs of adversarial settlement make it attractive to pursue other ways to settle not only for the parties to the dispute, but also for the judges involved. Resolving disputes through settlement relieves the judge of the necessity to write a formal ruling. It also relieves the court system of appeal cases, as voluntary settlements are typically final and binding. Where a low number of judges has to cope with an increasing case load, the incentives to pressure parties to settle voluntarily are high.

EVOLUTION OF CIVIL AND COMMERCIAL LITIGATION IN ASIA, 1960–1995

To analyze the importance of formal DSIs, we have collected data on litigation. Where possible, the total number of civil cases has been broken down into cases involving commercial matters and property rights, and other cases such as family and inheritance matters. Although changes in the volume of litigation concerning the latter may be indicative of socioeconomic change, we are more interested in the role played by courts in entrepreneurial activities. Litigation rates indicate the demand for DSIs. However, the demand for dispute settlements in courts may be determined not only by the willingness of nonstate parties to use formal legal procedures to enforce contracts, but also by the availability of DSIs. We therefore also present data on the number of courts at different levels, the number of judges, and—where available—budgetary expenditures on the courts.

A comparison of legal institutions, such as courts, poses a number of problems, because the structure and jurisdiction of courts differs from country to country. Courts are for the most part organized into three or more different levels, headed by a supreme court. The jurisdiction of different court levels may be defined by the value and nature of a claim, by their function as first instance or trial courts as opposed to courts that review decisions taken by other courts (appeal courts), or a combination of both. We refer to lower or higher level courts when the jurisdiction of courts at different levels as trial or first instance courts is at stake and to first or second instance courts when discussing the appeal function of courts.

As court structures and legal procedures are similar in economies that share the same legal tradition (common law or civil law), we present the data first for the two common law countries in our sample followed by the economies that share a civil law tradition.

Dispute Settlement Institutions in India

India inherited its formal court system from the British colonial powers. It consists of three levels, the supreme court, the high courts, and lower level courts, including district courts, subdivisional courts, and local courts that are served by subordinate judges. The increase in civil litigation in the Indian court system has been modest for most of the period under investigation, although it accelerated over the last five years. There is little systematic data to show the trend in commercial litigation in detail. Available evidence suggests that between 1960 and 1995, the number of civil cases filed with subordinate judges increased from 270,000 to 472,000. In nominal terms this represents an increase of 74.8 percent. In real terms the number of suits filed per capita actually declined during this period. The 1960 figure represents 610.4 court cases in civil matters per million people (PMP), but in 1995 there were only 507.9 civil cases. Still, this does not necessarily imply a lower propensity to file commercial disputes as the number of active entrepreneurs and firms may not have increased in proportion to the increase in population.

A breakdown of civil cases into civil cases of commercial nature and other civil cases has not been available for courts at all levels. At the supreme court level, commercial disputes accounted for 5,319 cases in 1995 (table 7.1), or 8 percent of all cases that were registered. As table 7.1 shows, the number of commercial cases pending at the Supreme Court increased substantially in 1993. A possible explanation is the change in economic policies introduced in the mid-1980s, which freed up private sector activities, and may have fueled litigation.

Indian courts face severe capacity problem. The number of cases decided by the courts, especially at the lower levels, falls far behind the number of new cases filed each year. This problem existed already in 1960. Of every one hundred cases pending at the high courts in that year, 59 were newly filed cases, and only 41 were decided. At the lower level courts the gap was less severe at 25 to 75. The gap did not increase over the years. However, this is mostly due to the fact that for many types of disputes additional DSIs in the form of tribunals were established. In addition, the long duration of court procedures—it can take up to 12 years to take a case through the court system—gives ample evidence of the inefficiency of India's court system.

Table 7.1   Commercial Disputes in the Supreme Court of India, 1993–1995

Year	Registered cases			Share of cases decided (percentage)
	Number	PMP	Percentage change	
1993	3,268	3.6	—	66.8
1994	4,165	4.6	27.8	80.9
1995	5,319	5.7	23.9	73.5

— = not available
PMP = per million people
Source: India team report.

Despite these problems, the capacity of the court system was not improved substantially. In 1960, there were 5.59 judges per million people. By 1995, the ratio had increased only to 10.9 judges per million people (table 7.2), still low by comparative standards. Budgetary expenditure on the judiciary increased slightly over the years, from 1.25 percent of total government expenditure in 1960 to 1.7 percent in 1995. More than 50 percent of budget resources allocation to the judiciary are covered by court fees.

Table 7.2   Number of Judges in Indian Courts, 1960–1995

Year	Supreme court		High courts		Subordinate courts		Total	
	Number	PMP	Number	PMP	Number	PMP	Number	PMP
1960	8	0.02	284	64	2,182	4.93	2,474	5.59
1970	14	0.03	—	—	—	—	—	—
1980	18	0.03	362	0.53	7,625	11.06	8,005	11.62
1990	26	0.03	486	0.58	8,380	9.91	8,892	10.52
1995	26	0.03	538	0.58	9,000	9.68	9,564	10.29

— = not available
PMP = per million people
Source: India team report.

A majority of lawsuits in India are between state and nonstate parties. A specific feature of the Indian political economy over the last 35 years has been the extensive state intervention in the economy. Although this fell short of a centrally planned economy, until recently most private activities required state licenses and approvals and were subject to extensive regulations. Most regulations were passed by the executive whose rule-making authority expanded significantly over the years through delegation from the legislature.[1] In contrast to the centrally planned economies of Eastern Europe and the former Soviet Union, citizens and entities retained the right to have recourse to the courts against the state. In addition, citizens were increasingly vested with substantive legal rights, including the right to a work place and the right to housing, which enabled them to defend these rights in the court system. This combination of extensive regulation of nonstate, especially commercial activities, the elevation of social rights to legally defensible private property rights, and the right to extensive judicial review led to a substantial increase in litigation in Indian courts. In the 1970s, over 60 percent of cases pending in the court system concerned litigation between the state and nonstate parties, including individuals and commercial entities.

In order to cope with the heavy case load involving state-private transactions, tribunals were created with special jurisdiction—a phenomenon which has been referred to as "tribunalized justice." These tribunals have jurisdiction over, among other things, levying, assessment, collection, and enforcement of taxes; import and export of foreign exchange; industrial and labor disputes; land reform and enforcement of ceilings imposed on the maximum size of land plots nonstate parties could acquire; and production, procurement, supply, and distribution of food and other goods. Tribunals are part of the formal court system. Consequently, parties have recourse to legal review.

India has a rich history of indigenous DSIs that long precede British colonization. The creation of a formal court system based on the British model did not completely supplant indigenous institutions. In many areas of India, informal DSIs survive to this day. However, the relative importance of formal versus informal DSIs differs across India. Informal DSIs are most prevalent in rural areas. In more developed areas of India, by contrast, there are fewer traces of informal dispute settlement. However, well functioning DSIs outside the court system exist in significant numbers, including some of those whose origins may be traced to traditional institutions.

Several agricultural trading associations have DSIs whose jurisdiction is defined by membership. Many of these associations are organized under the umbrella of the Federation of the Indian Chamber of Commerce and Industries. The DSIs have been remarkably successful in settling disputes among their members. A sample study revealed that the Wholesale Rice Dealers Association in Bangalore, for example, has been able to settle disputes among its members so effectively that over the past ten years, not a single case was referred to the courts for further review or enforcement (Mitra 1989). Other DSIs that were originally established as informal institutions received statutory backing

---

[1] As early as 1959, a High Court judge in India described this practice as an "abdication of power by legislature and an escape from the duty imposed on them by the values of democracy" (quoted in country team report).

after they had proliferated and proved to be effective. An example is the *Lok Adalat*, which started as a people's movement in Gujarat in the late seventies with the purpose of providing the poor with cheap and expeditious legal services. Other regions quickly followed suit. The number of cases resolved in *Lok Adalats* between 1982 and 1993 amounted to almost 3 million (see table 7.3)—an annual average of 270,000 cases. This is more than half the number of cases in civil matters that were filed at the lower level courts in 1995. Moreover, the number of *Lok Adalats* equals more than half the number of subordinate judges working in the official court system in 1995. The active use of these institutions and their spread indicates that for many predominantly local cases, the *Lok Adalat* is a viable alternative to formal dispute settlement in the court system.

Table 7.3   **Informal Dispute Settlement for the Poor:**
Lok Adalats in India, 1982–1993

State	Lok Adalats		Cases settled	
	Number	PMP	Number	PMP
Gujarat	355	9.2	52,497	1,359.4
Maharashtra	553	7.8	19,245	269.8
Utter Pradesh	1,349	10.7	1,366,869	10,807.1
Andhra Pradesh	65	1.1	53,153	881.6
Orissa	174	5.9	97,017	3,283.5
Rajasthan	293	7.2	464,366	11,441.8
Assam	16	—	1,456	—
Tamil Nadu	131	2.4	15,025	280.0
Kerala	12	0.4	784	27.5
Karnataka	965	22.7	139,034	3,277.2
Bihar	41	0.5	41,354	576.9
Madhya Pradesh	344	5.8	510,354	8,532.4
Haryana	310	20.3	103,666	6,780.9
Union Territory	148	15.0	22,957	2,324.3
Total	4,756	6.0	2,987,777	3,759.8

— = not available
PMP = per million people
Source: India team report.

To summarize, available information on dispute settlement in India offers mixed evidence of the importance of courts in settling civil and commercial disputes. The higher level courts, including the high courts and the supreme court, have made important contributions to the development of new legal precedents. However, the lower level courts have been remarkably inefficient. The per capita number of cases is low. Contrary to expectations, it has decreased rather than increased over the course of the past 35 years. The weakness of the court system appears to be an important explanation for the relatively low number of cases settled inside the courts. The proliferation of tribunals and DSIs outside the court system suggests that there is a great demand for effectively functioning DSIs. However, the state has by and large failed to provide such institutions. Although Indian courts particularly at the higher levels enjoy a high reputation, at lower levels, courts are understaffed and therefore overwhelmed by their case load and personnel frequently lack adequate legal training to deal with more complex commercial matters. Still, there are some signs that since the mid-1980s, the demand for commercial dispute settlement has increased (i.e., the increase in the number of cases pending at the supreme court). This appears to be largely the result of changes in economic policies, which allocated greater room to market activities. The supply side response has been to establish new DSIs that provide alternative dispute resolution. In 1995, the Indian Council for Alternative Dispute Resolution (ICADR) was established. A new arbitration code, enacted in 1996, revised the procedure for arbitration. So far, these institutions have not been very active. In fact, one may speculate that the inefficiency of the court system has affected alternative dispute resolution as well. Unless parties comply voluntarily with a verdict reached by the ICADR, its judgment will need to be executed by the courts. And where parties know that courts are inefficient they may have incentives not to comply voluntarily.

Dispute Settlement Institutions in Malaysia

Malaysia's court system and legal procedures reflect its pre-colonial legal tradition as well as the influence of English law. A formal court system based on Islamic law existed in parts of the territories that comprise today's Malaysia prior to the arrival of the colonial power. New courts were established which were staffed with judges trained in English common law. The two court systems existed next to each other. The first supreme court of the Federated Malay States was established in 1906. With independence in 1957 and the merging of Sarawak, Malaya, and Singapore to form Malaysia in 1963, the court system was restructured.

Native courts are part of the official court system, but their jurisdiction is limited to the application of Malay customary law. There are three important bodies of native law; a patriarchal system of customary law (*adat temenggong*); a matrilineal system of customary law (*adata perpateh*); and native laws and customs among the natives of Sabah and Sarawak.

Malaysia's court system can be divided into superior and subordinate courts. The federal court is Malaysia's highest court. High courts are the highest courts in the member states of the federation. In 1963, three high courts were created, the High Court of Malaya, the High Court of Singapore, and the High Court of Borneo. With the breaking away of Singapore in 1965, the number of high courts was reduced to two. The system of subordinate courts in the peninsula of Malaya is different from the one in Borneo. In Malaya, the lower level courts consist of penghulu courts, magistrates' courts and sessions courts. *Penghulu* courts are headed by a *penghulu*, or head-man, appointed by the state government. The *penghulu's* jurisdiction is re-stricted to civil cases of lower value and minor criminal offenses. Most cases at *penghulu* courts are settled through informal settlement rather than for-mal legal ruling. Magistrates' and sessions courts also have jurisdiction over civil and criminal matters (with the exception of cases that are punishable by death sentence), with sessions courts handling higher value civil cases and criminal offenses. In Sabah and Sarawak, the two territories comprising Borneo, lower level courts include native courts as well as *kathis* and *syariah* courts that apply Muslim law.

The jurisdiction of subordinate courts has increased over time, with the exception of *penghulu* courts whose jurisdiction in real terms has actually declined. In 1953, the maximum value of claims that could be referred to a *penghulu* court was Malaysian ringgit (RM) 50, for magistrates' courts up to RM1,000 and for sessions courts up to RM5,000. In 1994, the jurisdiction of the *penghulu* court was still unchanged, reflecting an actual decline in jurisdic-tion in real terms (from a 1994 claims value of RM123 to RM43, based on 1990 real RM). By contrast, the jurisdiction of magistrate's courts had expanded to RM25,000 and that of sessions courts to RM250,000.

Civil litigation has increased considerably in Malaysia since the early 1970s (table 7.4; earlier data are not available). Between 1972 and 1995, the number of cases at the magistrates' courts increased from 1,258 (PMP) to 9,482 (PMP) and at the sessions courts from 317 (PMP) to 3,531 (PMP).

Similarly, the high courts experienced an increase from 1,488 cases (PMP) in 1972 to almost 5,000 (PMP) in 1995. For the high courts we also have some information about the share of commercial cases. They made up roughly 30 percent of all civil cases between 1972 and 1983. During the 1980s, commer-cial litigation fluctuated substantially. Although we lack data for all courts, this is reflected in available data for the high court in Kuala Lumpur, where the most significant cases are typically filed (table 7.5).

The biggest increase in commercial litigation in the capital occurred in the mid 1980s, when numbers soared to over 13,000 cases in a single year, up from less than 2,000 in 1980. By 1995, the number of court cases was back where it had been in 1982 (less than 3,000 cases). These changes in commer-cial litigation closely follow the economic cycle Malaysia experienced in the 1980s. In the mid-1980s the economy experienced a severe recession and as a result many firms and entrepreneurs were unable to meet their contractual obligations. Once the economic situation had stabilized and growth resumed, litigation rates came down to their precrisis level.

Table 7.4   Registered Civil Cases in Malaysia, 1972–1995

Years	Magistrates courts		Sessions courts	
	Number	PMP	Number	PMP
1972	14,388	1,258.3	3,612	317.0
1973	14,488	1,240.9	3,802	325.6
1974	15,256	1,275.2	4,371	365.4
1975	16,628	1,356.5	5,384	439.2
1976	20,010	1,595.0	7,142	569.3
1977	18,570	1,446.4	7,960	620.0
1978	31,961	2,432.4	5,512	419.5
1979	38,905	2,893.0	6,326	470.4
1980	36,442	2,647.8	6,906	501.8
1981	32,557	2,307.2	7,726	547.5
1982	43,861	3,031.5	9,739	673.1
1983	44,168	2,977.3	11,088	747.4
1993	76,607	4,022.0	—	—
1994	164,739	8,375.7	67,870	3,450.7
1995	190,967	9,482.0	71,124	3,531.5

— = not available
PMP = per million people
Source: Malaysia team report.

**Table 7.5   Cases Filed in
Commercial Division of Kuala Lumpur High Court, 1979–1996**

Year	Cases
1979	1,068
1980	1,757
1981	2,296
1982	2,928
1983	3,958
1984	5,473
1985	9,426
1986	13,367
1987	9,912
1988	4,761
1989	4,170
1990	3,324
1991	2,925
1992	2,847
1993	2,534
1994	2,114
1995	2,987

Source: Malaysia team report.

Overall, the number of judges has kept pace with increasing litigation over the years. In 1960, the number of judicial and legal officers serving at subordinate courts on the Malayan peninsula and in Borneo was 45. In 1990, it had multiplied by a factor of 5. The superior courts had only 12 judges in 1960 (excluding Sabah and Sarawak which joined the federation only in 1963). In 1970, when Malaysia in its current borders had been consolidated, there were 21 judges. In 1995, the number had increased to 74, including 15 judicial commissioners (see table 7.6 below). The function of judicial commissioners (JCs) at different court levels is similar. However, while the tenure of high court judges is permanent and guaranteed by the constitution, lower level JCs serve only a contractual term.

Changes in the supply side of legal institutions are also reflected in the increase in government expenditure. In nominal terms, expenditure on the judiciary has increased quite substantially beginning in the early 1970s. However, this reflects only the overall increase in government expenditure. In real terms, the share of the judiciary was 0.23 percent in 1972, and only 0.25 percent in 1995. Still, the Malaysian statistics reveal an interesting aspect of government expenditure; prior to 1972, the state budget included allotments only for the operation of the judiciary, but not for development, such as the costs of constructing court buildings, repairs, equipment, and training. This is not an uncommon feature in countries with a recent regime change. Operational costs of existing institutions are covered, but the need to invest in basic infrastructure to keep these institutions afloat is recognized often only much later. When development costs were first added to the budget, they amounted only to 17.3 percent of total expenditure on the judiciary. In 1980, they had reached 41.9 percent of total expenditure. By 1995, the fraction spent on development had fallen back to 28.5 percent (table 7.7).

In addition to the court system, Malaysia has a number of arbitration tribunals, including the Kuala Lumpur Regional Center for Arbitration and specialized arbitration tribunals for the association of architects, and the association of engineers. Evidence on the use of these institutions as well as evidence on informal or customary dispute settlement has not been available. In view of the large Chinese business community in Malaysia, one may suspect that disputes among members of these family businesses are resolved on the basis of Chinese customary law rather than being referred to the courts. There is evidence that this is common practice in other economies in Asia with large Chinese communities (Jones 1994).

The influence of Islamic law in business matters has increased since the early 1980s. Islamic business law has increasingly been incorporated into formal law. Examples include the 1983 Islamic Banking Act, and the 1986 Takaful Act on the Islamic insurance industry. Matters related to these laws may be tried in the official court system, but we lack evidence of the extent to which this

Table 7.6   Judicial and Legal Officers Personnel at Malaysian Courts, 1960–1995

Year	Subordinate courts			High courts			Total		
	Number	PMP	Percentage change	Number	PMP	Percentage change	Number	PMP	Percentage change
1960	45	5.5	n.a.	12	1.5	n.a.	57	8.1	n.a.
1970	69	6.4	16.4	21	1.9	26.7	90	10.4	18.6
1980	164	11.9	85.9	33	2.4	26.3	197	17.9	72.3
1990	233	13.2	10.9	50	2.3	-4.2	274	15.3	8.4
1995	—	—	—	74	3.4	47.8	—	—	—

— = not available
n.a. = not applicable
PMP = per million people
Source: Malaysia team report.

Table 7.7   Government Expenditure on the Judiciary, in Malaysia, 1960–1995

| | Total expenditure on judiciary | | | Operations | | Development | |
Year	Amount	Percentage change	Percentage of total expenditure[a]	Amount	Share (percentage of total expenditure)	Amount	Share (percentage of total expenditure)
1960	4,430,289	—	—	4,430,289	100.0	0	—
1970	6,016,442	35.8	—	6,016,442	100.0	0	—
1972	8,732,732	45.1	0.23	7,223,232	82.7	1,509,500	17.3
1980	30,051,600	244.1	0.20	17,450,800	58.1	12,600,800	41.9
1990	65,938,100	119.4	0.19	48,268,100	73.2	17,670,000	26.8
1995	124,089,400	88.2	0.25	88,668,400	71.5	35,421,000	28.5

— = not available

a. Percentage of total central government expenditure.

Source: Malaysia team report.

might be the case. Another indication of the growing importance of Islamic law is the constitutional amendment of 1988, which expanded the jurisdiction of the Muslim *syariah* courts by providing that high courts shall no longer have jurisdiction over matters that fall within the jurisdiction of the *syariah* courts.

The case of Malaysia is an interesting one for the evolution of DSIs. Formerly informal DSIs such as the *penghulu* court and the native and Islamic courts in Borneo have been integrated into the formal court system. In many of the lower level courts, mediation dominates over a formal legal procedure that ends with a court verdict. However, a formal outcome may be reached and, in addition, parties have access to appeal procedures in the magistrates' courts, if necessary. We lack the data to analyze the extent to which private parties are making use of mediation or litigation procedures at the lower level. Data on litigation rates in the high courts support the proposition that with the growing complexity of social and economic life, the need for formal institutions with coercive power to enforce contracts among previously unrelated parties increases. However, during economic downturn, courts provide an important fallback mechanism to resolve commercial disputes.

Dispute Settlement Institutions in Japan

As part of its comprehensive reception of continental European law at the end of the nineteenth century, Japan copied civil procedure laws and the structure of a formal court system mostly from German models. The general courts have jurisdiction over civil (including commercial) and criminal matters. The record of civil, including commercial, litigation in Japan between 1960 and 1995 casts some doubt on theories that suggest that commercial litigation increases with the expansion and increasing complexity of markets. Japan was already a well developed market economy in 1960. However, the number of cases filed per million people was relatively low then and increased only slightly over the course of the 35 years during which Japan clearly established itself as one of the most prosperous industrialized economies in the world. The comparatively low litigation rate in Japan has often been attributed to cultural preferences, a leaning toward mediation and conciliation rather than the litigation and enforcement of rights.

However, limiting the analysis of litigation rates to the past 35 years may be misleading. A review of civil litigation in first instance courts since 1892 shows considerably higher litigation rates for part of the prewar period (table 7.8).

Compared with prewar Japan, where litigation rates fluctuated considerably, litigation rates in postwar Japan have remained almost stable, with the exception of a relatively sharp increase in the second half of the 1980s. We may attribute this to the fact that in terms of socioeconomic development, the prewar period witnessed much more dramatic changes than the postwar period. As Japan emerged as a highly industrialized economy, litigation rates stabilized. Major downturns in the economy of the scale experienced during the worldwide depression of the late 1920s, which may have triggered higher litigation rates, were absent during this period. This would suggest that factors other than culture contribute to the propensity to litigate.

Even though we may explain the fluctuation in litigation rates in Japan over time, the fact remains that in comparison with other highly industrialized economies in the West, but also, as we will see below, in comparison with other Asian economies, the propensity to litigate in Japan has been low. Two factors are commonly held responsible for this result; culture and institutional barriers (Haley 1978; Ramseyer 1985). Both factors are intertwined.

Table 7.8   Civil Litigation Rates in Japan, 1892–1990

	Cases filed	
Year	Number	PMP
1892	118,474	29.3
1896	79,546	18.9
1900	104,739	23.9
1904	127,004	27.5
1908	90,570	18.9
1912	117,049	23.1
1916	159,351	29.8
1920	129,152	23.3
1924	208,774	35.8
1928	248,406	40.0
1932	255,157	38.7
1936	180,501	27.4
1940	88,160	12.3
1950	68,488	0.8
1954	133,595	15.7
1958	162,786	18.4
1962	132,191	14.0
1966	169,979	17.3
1970	175,164	17.0
1974	149,688	13.5
1978	156,505	13.6
1982	244,069	20.5
1986	335,679	27.6
1990	210,178	17.0
Average 1892–1940	146,683	26.8
Average 1950–1990	176,211	16.6

PMP = per million people
Source: Yanagida et al. (1994).

Institutional barriers are often shaped by culture, but they may also reflect the political interests of the governing elite, as opposed to the economic or cultural preferences of disputing nonstate parties.

The strongest evidence for the existence of institutional barriers is the control over the size of the legal profession, including judges and attorneys. In particular, the supply of judges has been very low. The total number of judges increased by 20.5 percent between 1960 and 1995, but the number of judges PMP decreased from 25.2 judges PMP in 1960 to 22.8 in 1995. In comparison with other developed market economies this number is extremely low. Table 7.9 below shows comparable data for five industrialized economies in the late 1970s. The number of judges PMP in France was more than twice the total number of judges in Japan. The UK had by far the largest number of judges per capita, which is mostly the result of a high number of summary court judges. In Germany and the US, the number of judges PMP was roughly 10 times higher than the number of judges in Japan.

Table 7.9 Judges in Industrialized Economies in the late 1970s

Country	Number of judges	PMP	Year
France	3,590	67.6	1977
Japan	2,731	23.7	1979
United Kingdom	24,802	504.9	1976
United States	45,000	206.3	1976
West Germany	14,765	240.5	1977

PMP = per million people
Source: Yuhikaku quoted in Yoon (1990).

The main reason for the real decline in the number of judges is the control over the size of the judicial profession exercised by the state. To become eligible for a position as a judge, prospective candidates must pass the national law examination. A fixed ceiling is established for the number of candidates that may pass in any given year. Until 1994, the number was fixed at 500 per annum, it is now 700 per annum. Efforts are being made to further relax the ceiling and allow more candidates to pass the exam. However, change has been gradual rather than decisive.

Other constraints include indirect control mechanisms the state exercises over the judiciary. The independence of the judiciary is formally guaranteed by the constitution, but the placement of judges who rotate between different positions during their career is an important indirect control mechanism to ensure judicial self-restraint (Ramseyer 1994). Although this is most likely to affect the outcome of cases that might be of political relevance, including administrative cases, it may also have an effect on the use of the courts by nonstate parties. Upham has called the way in which the state has governed legal processes and institutions "bureaucratic informalism" (Upham 1987). While not controlling the judiciary in a strict sense of the word, the state asserts an important role in managing social conflict and change.

Informal dispute settlement is likely to play an important role in many commercial cases that are not brought to the courts or not settled in arbitration tribunals. Japan is known for long term contractual relations among parties who often belong to the same business group (Foote 1994). For the members of these groups, this implies that the size of the market in terms of the number of market participants is relatively small. Moreover, reputation is an important asset for parties with long-term relations. Informal dispute settlement can reasonably be expected to provide an important alternative for solving disputes among members of the same business groups. Because of their informality, ad hoc renegotiation or mediation is difficult to document. Other forms of informal DSI in local affairs or for members of trading and other commercial associations appear to be of little importance in modern day Japan.

To summarize, the history of dispute settlement in Japan presents us with a puzzle, which we cannot solve by analyzing court data and socioeconomic development alone. Litigation rates are low and have hardly increased over time. The more dramatic increases and fluctuations were recorded during the first decades after the establishment of the courts. However, in the postwar period, litigation rates have stabilized at a low equilibrium. An important reason for this seems to be the state's control over the supply side of the judiciary. However, as similar constraints have not led to the same outcome in other economies (see the discussion on the Republic of Korea as well as on Taipei,China below), this alone is not a sufficient explanation.

Dispute Settlement Institutions in the Republic of Korea

In 1960 the Republic of Korea had a formal court system in place whose origins go back to continental European models. The general courts have jurisdiction over civil (including commercial) and criminal matters. There are three court levels: the district courts (lower level courts), high courts (intermediate courts), and the supreme court (highest court). Parties may appeal to the supreme court against decisions taken by high courts or the appellate division of district courts. Appeals to the supreme court are limited to a review of legal as opposed to factual matters. In 1994, special tribunals were established in the Seoul district court to handle disputes concerning international transactions, as well as economic disputes for which specialized knowledge is required, such as disputes involving maritime, insurance, patent, and securities law.

Table 7.10   Civil Litigation in Republic of Korea, 1960–1995

Years	First instance court			Appellate court			Supreme court		
	Number	PMP	Change (percentage)	Number	PMP	Change (percentage)	Number	PMP	Change (percentage)
1960	25,112	1,004.4	n.a.	3,817	152.7	n.a.	934	37.4	n.a.
1965	62,426	2,188.1	117.9	8,288	290.5	90.2	2,686	94.1	151.6
1970	58,134	1,821.1	-16.8	7,535	236.0	-18.8	3,178	99.6	5.8
1975	91,523	2,594.1	42.4	8,035	227.7	-3.5	2,380	67.5	-32.2
1980	120,330	3,156.3	21.7	10,546	276.6	21.5	3,328	87.3	29.3
1985	297,999	7,302.8	131.4	17,272	423.3	53.0	906	22.2	-74.6
1990	279,948	6,530.3	-10.6	19,338	451.1	6.6	2,870	66.9	201.4
1995	614,946	13,710.9	110.0	36,322	809.8	80.0	8,608	191.9	186.8

n.a. = not applicable
PMP = per million people
Source: Korea team report.

Available data on the number of civil disputes filed with the courts suggests that civil litigation has increased significantly since 1960.

Between 1960 and 1995 the total number of cases filed with the courts increased by a factor of 24 from 25,112 to over 600,000 cases over half of which concerned dispute over moveable property. The number PMP amounted to 1,194 in 1960 and increased to 14,712.6 in 1995. A breakdown of these numbers over time shows that litigation rates have fluctuated widely (see table 7.10 below). Periods of significant increase have alternated with only very modest growth in litigation rates, or even decline. In terms of rapid growth, three periods stand out: the period between 1960 and 1965, between 1980 and 1985 and between 1990 and 1995. Without a further breakdown into the nature of disputes, it is difficult to analyze the causes of this wide fluctuation. The steep increase in litigation rates in the early 1980s could be explained by the contraction of the economy leading to business failures and inability of contractual parties to fulfill their contractual obligations. However, this explanation fits less well with the early 1960s and the early 1990s.

Data on the number of disputes that were disposed of by the courts are not available to demonstrate the ability of courts to meet the growing demand for litigation. However, the number of judges has increased only comparatively slowly. This suggests that their case load must have increased considerably over the years. A simple calculation supports this proposition. While in 1960, there were on average 102.62 civil cases per judge, the ratio had increased to 544.5 in 1995 (table 7.11). Most probably, these numbers under-

Table 7.11   The Number of Judges in Relation to Case Load and Population Growth in Republic of Korea, 1960–1995

	Republic of Korea				Seoul		
Year	Judges	Change (percentage)	PMP	Cases per judge	Judges	Change (percentage)	PMP
1960	291	n.a.	11.6	102.6	72	n.a.	29.4
1965	372	27.8	13.0	197.3	118	63	31.0
1970	413	11.0	12.9	166.7	118	0	21.3
1975	517	5.2	14.7	197.2	161	36	23.4
1980	562	8.7	14.7	214.1	195	21	23.3
1985	794	41.3	19.5	398.2	205	5	21.3
1990	1,028	29.5	24.0	293.9	298	44	28.1
1995	1,212	17.9	27.0	544.5	382	28	35.6

n.a. = not applicable
PMP = per million people
Source: Korea team report.

state the actual case load of judges, because apparently a large number of judges sit on benches for family or criminal matters rather than on those settling economic disputes. Moreover, the case load at lower level courts has increased much more than at higher level courts. The major reason for the low increase in the number of judges in the Republic of Korea, as in Japan and Taipei,China, has been the ceiling on the number of candidates that are allowed to pass the national legal exam each year. An interesting finding is that despite comparable institutional constraints, the number of judges has increased more in the Republic of Korea than in Japan. In Seoul, which hosts roughly a quarter of the Korean population today, the number of judges in 1995 was over 35.6 PMP. Although there were only 11.6 judges PMP in the Republic of Korea in 1960 (similar to the number of judges in India in 1995), the number had increased to 27 by 1995 and today exceeds the number of judges PMP in Japan.

There is little documentary evidence on informal dispute settlement in the Republic of Korea. Commercial arbitration has come to play a more important role in recent years, but cases referred to arbitration are only a fraction in number of those filed with the court system. The Korean Commercial Arbitration Board (KCAB) is the only institution authorized to provide standing arbitration for domestic and foreign commercial disputes. The KCAB has relatively far-reaching powers and may, for example, request administrative sanctions from relevant government authorities. Disputes that are filed with the KCAB are first mediated, and many disputes are resolved at this early stage. The subsequent arbitration procedure leads to a ruling which is final and binding and can be appealed in the courts only in narrowly specified circumstances. Awards granted by the KCAB are enforceable through the courts. In addition to arbitration, the KCAB offers legal counseling as well as conciliation. Legal counseling involves a formal request for a legal opinion on a specific case, which can be provided over the phone. Conciliation offers parties an opinion on how to settle a case without rendering a final verdict. Conciliation can also be applied in court proceedings. In court, a judge typically suggests a settlement based on his view of the potential outcome of the case. Parties frequently settle on this basis in order to save time and money. By contrast, conciliation at the KCAB is frequently undertaken with conciliators who may not be trained lawyers, but have expertise in the business area at hand. Thus, they offer the parties a wider range of practical rather than purely legal solutions. In the practice of the KCAB, legal counseling occupies by far the most important place followed by mediation/conciliation. Relatively few cases proceed to arbitration.

To summarize, the Republic of Korea has witnessed a dramatic increase in civil litigation involving commercial cases over the past 35 years. Thus, the case of the Republic of Korea supports theories that suggest that with increasing division of labor, formal institutions that serve as neutral third party arbiters and have the power to enforce verdicts gain in importance. The capacity of legal institutions to settle disputes has only barely matched the significant rise in the case load for judges that has resulted from the demand for formal litigation.

Dispute Settlement Institutions in Taipei,China

As in Japan and the Republic of Korea, the formal court system of Taipei,China has its origin in continental European models. It consists of a unified court system with three levels: district courts (lower level courts), high courts (intermediate level courts) and the supreme court (highest level court). The general courts have jurisdiction over criminal and civil matters, including family, property, maritime, and commercial cases. Commercial cases are filed with the court branches in charge of civil law.

Civil litigation has increased substantially since 1960 (table 7.12). The total number of civil cases filed with the courts increased from 188,004 in 1960 to 802,168 in 1995, or from 17,420 cases per million people to 37,660. However, the share of commercial cases at courts of first instance has been relatively small. This is different at the high court and supreme court level, where appeals are handled. There commercial cases have accounted for over 80 percent of all cases filed. This shows that commercial cases are less likely to be referred to the courts than other civil cases, but that parties to commercial disputes are more likely to file an appeal. Despite the overall low share of commercial cases in total litigation, it is worth noting that the growth rate of commercial cases has been higher than that of other court cases. Between 1960 and 1995 the total number of civil cases decided by courts tripled, but the number of commercial cases increased tenfold.

Litigation rates increased, despite the fact that Taipei,China was—like Japan—placing limits on the size of the legal profession. The number of judges also increased from 28.1 PMP in 1960 to 59.3 PMP in 1995 (table 7.13 below). Although the number is lower than in many otherWestern market economies, it rivals that of France, and is more twice the number in Japan. The government has also allocated substantial resources to the judiciary over the years. The budget allocated to the judiciary accounted for 0.84 percent of total expenditure in 1960 and 1.24 percent (2.3 percent of total national budget) in 1995, which is significantly more than in Malaysia.

Many of the additional judges that were hired appear to have been assigned to settle the soaring number of criminal cases. As a result, in 1993, civil court judges at district courts still had to handle a monthly case load of 111.77 cases, while the case load for criminal judges was reduced to only 60.4 cases. The number of criminal cases punishing the dishonoring of negotiable

Table 7.12 Civil Cases Disposed of by Taipei,China Courts, 1960–1995 (share of commercial cases)

	District courts			High courts			Supreme court		
Year	Number	PMP	Commercial case share percentage	Number	PMP	Commercial case share percentage	Number	PMP	Commercial case share percentage
1960	35,174	3,259.3	2.8	6,888	638.3	95	—	—	—
1965	35,093	2,779.0	3.3	7,863	622.7	94	—	—	—
1970	41,671	2,839.4	3.6	7,590	517.2	95	—	—	—
1975	39,899	2,470.5	4.1	5,576	345.3	93	4,147	256.8	n.a.
1980	63,044	3,540.8	5.4	7,111	399.4	92	4,218	236.9	95
1985	90,042	4,675.6	6.5	8,041	417.5	87	2,883	149.7	88
1990	69,797	3,429.3	10.6	7,741	380.3	86	3,296	161.9	87
1995	91,901	4,350.1	10.0	7,203	341.0	89	2,653	125.6	81

n.a. = not applicable
— = not available
PMP = per million people
Source: Taipei,China team report.

Table 7.13   Number of Judges in Taipei,China's Courts, 1960–1995

Year	District courts		High courts		Supreme court		Total	
	Number	PMP	Number	PMP	Number	PMP	Number	PMP
1960	239	22.1	64	5.9	—	—	303	28.1
1965	289	22.9	87	6.9	—	—	376	29.8
1970	251	17.1	127	8.7	—	—	378	25.8
1975	345	21.4	154	9.5	51	3.2	550	34.1
1980	394	22.1	156	8.8	62	3.5	472	26.5
1985	532	27.6	229	11.9	74	3.8	835	43.4
1990	639	31.4	274	13.5	120	5.9	1,033	50.8
1995	813	38.5	340	16.1	99	4.7	1,252	59.3
Total increase (percent)	227.5	73.7	431	172.9	86.2	46.5	313.2	111.0

— = not available
PMP = per million people
Source: Taipei,China team report.

instruments also provides evidence for the resources the state has allocated to criminal prosecution. Until 1987 it was a criminal offense to dishonor a check. Before the law was repealed private parties made extensive use of post-dated checks as a quasi collateral, and benefited from the enforcement provided by the state at no cost. The total number of cases concerning the dishonoring of postdated checks that were prosecuted is quite staggering both in terms of total number and as a share of criminal cases (table 7.14 below). In 1984, these cases accounted for over 70 percent of all criminal cases. The data also suggest that the official legal system played a much larger role in enforcing commercial matters than suggested by the number of commercial cases filed in the civil courts. In fact, criminal cases dealing with dishonoring commercial instruments outnumber commercial cases filed at first instance courts between 1960 and 1986 on average by a factor of 32.

The history of criminal sanctions for dishonored negotiable instruments is impressive evidence of how a legal system can create an "endogenous legal boom" by criminalizing economic behavior which, though undesirable, is a

Table 7.14   Dishonoring Negotiable Instruments as Breach of Contract: Criminal Enforcement in Taipei,China, 1970–1990

Year	Number of criminal cases of dishonoring negotiable instruments	Percentage of all criminal cases	Commercial cases disposed at district courts	Ratio of criminal cases for dishonoring negotiable instruments to commercial cases at first instance courts
1970	59,563	56.88	1,488	40/1
1972	42,924	49.52	1,380	31/1
1974	36,560	43.44	1,523	24/1
1976	100,788	69.34	1,757	57/1
1978	71,382	60.52	2,267	31/1
1980	98,443	65.25	3,409	29/1
1982	132,069	69.52	4,519	29/1
1984	160,079	70.71	5,011	31/1
1986	110,985	58.48	6,035	18/1
1988	14	0.02	6,219	.002/1
1990	0	0	7,387	0

Source: Taipei,China team report.

very common side effect of economic transactions in complex markets.[2] It seems to reflect a Chinese legal tradition of using law almost exclusively as a means to punish undesirable behavior rather than to provide mechanisms for nonstate parties to initiate enforcement of their rights. One may even speculate that this has left its mark on the disposition of nonstate parties to use the state courts for settling commercial disputes. Because of the extensive criminalization of business activities, entrepreneurs may have preferred to resolve their disputes elsewhere and not to bring them to the courts. We lack sufficient information to understand how disputes are resolved outside the courts. However, the fact that commercial litigation did not increase after the criminal sanction for dishonoring postdated checks was repealed suggests that the repeal alone has not increased the propensity to use state courts for commercial disputes.

Available data on the way in which civil disputes are settled show that, over time, mediation has lost ground in favor of litigious procedures that result in a final and binding decision by a court. This can be taken as a sign that the compliance rate with rulings issued by mediation bodies has decreased. Further evidence is that the number of court cases parties have settled voluntarily after they were filed or that were referred to mediation procedures has decreased substantially between 1960 and 1995. Although there was another sudden upswing in the cases referred to mediation between 1990 and 1995 (from 7.2 to 30 percent), the share of cases accepting the outcome of mediation was substantially lower than in previous years. In nominal terms in 1990, mediation finally settled 36,783 cases; in 1995 only 13,049. Given the rapid economic development in Taipei,China this piece of evidence supports the proposition that in complex markets, DSIs relying predominantly on noncoercive means do not suffice. Most cases that are decided by mediation committees are referred to the courts for final approval. Still, as the relatively low number of commercial cases litigated in the courts demonstrates, state courts have not fully filled the gap left by increasingly ineffective means for enforcing contracts.

To summarize, the history of dispute settlement by the courts in Taipei,China shows that courts have played an important role in enforcing criminal sanctions against parties in breach of contract where the law provided for such sanctions. However, they have been only modestly important in settling commercial disputes among nonstate parties despite a recent increase in commercial litigation rates. These two aspects may be two sides of the same coin. Parties who must fear prosecution should certain aspects of a contractual relation be revealed in a court procedure are likely to avoid filing a suit to begin with.

---

[2] The term "endogenous legal boom" was coined by Wolf in his analysis of civil litigation in Germany during the hyperinflationary years of 1920–1923, when the failure of courts to index contracts for inflation contributed to the huge increase in litigation and almost led to the collapse of the court system (Wolf 1993).

Criminal sanctions for breach of contract provided a very effective deterrent for breach of contract for some time. However, in the long term, this has proved to be ineffective. Courts became overloaded with cases dealing with postdated checks and prisons overpopulated with delinquents whose deed was to breach a contract. As a result, the state finally repealed criminal sanctions. This is important evidence that in the long term, state controls are not effective in ensuring that private parties do not breach contracts.

Dispute Settlement Institutions in the People's Republic of China

The court system of the PRC was established in 1954. In line with the centralized system of political control, courts were not established as institutions independent of other branches of the government, but are controlled by the governments at the corresponding levels. They control the appointment of judges and finances of the courts. The highest court in the PRC is the supreme people's court. Higher level people's courts (HLPCs) exist at the provincial level. For each of the 30 provinces, autonomous regions, and centrally administered cities there is one HLPC. Below the HLPCs, at the level of prefectures, are the intermediate people's courts. Finally, at the county level there are over 3,000 lower people's courts. The function of the supreme people's court goes beyond judicial review. It includes the active supervision of the operation of courts at lower levels and the issuance of guidelines to other courts.

The history of dispute settlement in the PRC has been deeply influenced by politics. In the second half of the 1950s, legal institutions experienced a major upheaval (table 7.15). A political campaign led to a drastic reduction in the number of courts and judges and resulted in a serious drop in cases settled by the

Table 7.15   Courts and Litigation in the PRC before 1960

Year	Total court personnel			Civil cases filed		
	Number	PMP	Change (percentage)	Number	PMP	Change (percentage)
1956	41,483	66.0	n.a.	—	—	n.a.
1957	—	—	—	818,669	1,266.3	n.a.
1958	—	—	—	427,496	647.8	-48.8
1959	—	—	—	377,345	561.4	-13.3
1960	32,058	48.1	-27.1	308,024	461.8	-17.7

— = not available
n.a. = not applicable
PMP = per million people
Note: Civil cases include monetary claims, housing disputes, torts, and others.
Source: PRC team report.

courts. People's mediation committees rather than courts became the primary institution for handling civil disputes. The procedure and enforcement mechanisms used by these institutions differ from court proceedings. They consist of social control and indirect coercion rather than litigation and seizure of assets in accordance with legal procedures. Disputes between state owned enterprises were referred neither to courts nor to people's mediation committees, but were settled inside the regional or national administration depending on the affiliation of the company and the parties to the dispute. The effects of these events are clearly reflected in the development of litigation rates between 1956 and 1960.

Courts continued to exist after 1960, but their function was curtailed. This changed again with the introduction of economic reforms in 1978. With the opening of the economy to activities outside the economic plan and the policy explicitly to "separate government from enterprise" the need for institutions that could settle economic disputes became apparent. In 1983 the Organic Law of the People's Court was amended to include economic benches at people's courts at all levels. By 1986, 97 percent of the PRC's 3,400 courts had established a bench for economic disputes.

The number of economic cases filed with the courts in the years since 1983 clearly reflects a growing demand for dispute settlement in the courts both in nominal terms and on a per capita basis (table 7.16). Between 1983

Table 7.16   First Instance Economic Disputes in the PRC, 1983–1995

	Cases filed			Share of	Average
			Change	cases decided	claim per
Year	Number	PMP	(percentage)	(percentage)	case (US$)
1983	44,080	43.1	n.a.	—	—
1984	85,796	82.8	92.1	—	—
1985	226,695	215.7	160.5	—	—
1986	322,153	302.0	40.0	95.0	—
1987	367,156	338.7	12.2	99.6	—
1988	513,615	466.2	37.6	94.7	—
1989	690,765	617.5	32.5	96.9	4,499
1990	588,143	518.1	-16.1	101.7	6,686
1991	563,260	489.5	-5.5	103.6	8,905
1992	650,601	558.5	14.1	99.6	9,210
1993	894,410	759.0	35.9	98.8	13,688
1994	1,053,701	884.8	16.6	99.2	12,129
1995	1,278,806	1065.5	20.4	99.4	15,933

— = not available
n.a. = not applicable
PMP = per million people
Source: PRC team report.

and 1988, the number of cases per capita filed increased on average by 68.48 percent per year. The increasing importance of litigation is reflected not only in the number of cases filed with the courts, but also in the value of claims.

The actual year to year change in litigation rates has fluctuated quite dramatically—from a 92.1 percent increase in 1984 to a 16.1 percent drop in 1990. The increase in 1984 can be explained by the opening of the new economic benches for which an excess demand already existed. The decrease in 1990 may reflect a slowdown in economic growth during this year, but may also be attributed to a more cautious use of state courts in the wake of the Tiananmen incident. Overall the courts have coped quite well with the increasing case load. Partly this is the result of an improvement on the supply side. The total number of court personnel, including judges, was substantially increased and additional benches to settle economic cases established. In 1979 total court staff amounted to 58,000. By 1995, the number had quintupled to 292,000, 165,089 of whom are judges.

Despite the fact that most cases appear to be settled without considerable delays, courts in the PRC are facing several problems that may undermine their credibility in the eyes of business people seeking their help in contract enforcement. A major concern for Chinese courts remains the qualification and training of court personnel. To this day, many judges lack full legal training. Salaries of judges are comparably low and many of the brightest young lawyers prefer to become private attorneys rather than judges (Lubman 1995). Another major concern is the enforcement of court verdicts, in particular local protectionism. This refers to the practice of courts in any of the 30 provinces, autonomous regions, or cities refusing the execution of judgments rendered by courts in any of the other provinces (Clarke 1995). The economic interests behind local protectionism are quite apparent. Verdicts that are enforced against local enterprises can have a direct impact on the budget of the regional government, especially if they concern enterprises that are owned or whose financial resources are controlled by the local government. The court judges are appointed by the government and people's congresses at the corresponding level and depend on financial support from the regional government. This affects not only their salaries, but also housing, promotion, employment of their children, and other benefits. To alleviate the problem of enforcement, some courts—presumably with approval of the governments in their province—have entered into treaties with other courts, by which they grant enforcement of that court's rulings on a basis of reciprocity (Clarke 1995). This process parallels that of international treaties, that attempt to ensure enforcement of the court verdicts of one nation in another nation's courts. Within one country, a system of bilateral treaties between courts puts the plaintiff at a serious disadvantage. He will not only have to establish that a court has jurisdiction over the case, but that the court's verdict—should it be in his favor—will be enforceable in the court district where the defendant is located.

To summarize, our data suggest that DSIs have become increasingly important with economic development in the PRC. Indeed litigation rates reflect the expansion of the Chinese economy since 1978. By creating economic benches inside the court system and establishing new arbitration tribunals in 1995, the state has gone a long way in improving the supply side of DSIs. The renewed use of the courts is the result of political as well as socioeconomic change. When the state committed to provide credible and effective contract enforcement among nonstate parties, litigation rates increased.

COMPARISONS ACROSS ECONOMIES

In the previous sections we have discussed in detail the development of civil and commercial litigation in the six economies in our sample and explained it in the context of the sociopolitical development of each. In this section we attempt a comparison across all the six economies. In addition, we want to test the proposition that formal dispute settlement will become more important with increasing division of labor. We therefore rank the six economies on a common scale. To measure the division of labor, we have selected three indicators that are summarized in a cumulative index on a scale from zero to ten, called the *Division of Labor Index* (table 7.17). The three indicators are (1) the share of the population in urban areas; (2) the share of the population in agriculture (negative indicator); and (3) the proportion of the population above the age of 25 that has completed primary and secondary education. These indicators measure the diversification of economic activities, which is typically higher in urban than in rural areas as well as in sectors outside agriculture. Education levels reflect the level of human capital available for more diverse economic activities.

We use data for 1960 as a common base line to show relative change over time. The economies are ranked on a worldwide basis.

The ranking of the six economies according to the *Division of Labor Index* shows that in 1960, the PRC and India ranked low on a worldwide scale. Data on education levels for the PRC were not available until 1975, but high investment in education by the Communist regime is probably why the PRC ranked above India in 1960. Japan had by far the greatest division of labor in 1960, followed by Taipei,China, Republic of Korea, and Malaysia. The relatively low level of the division of labor in Malaysia in 1960 stands out among other economies which at that point were in the process of taking off on their high speed economic growth track. Using the cumulative index for 1960 as a base line we can observe a substantial increase in the division of labor in all economies. On a 1–10 scale, the lowest ranking economy (India) in 1995 scores 5

Table 7.17   Division of Labor Index, 1960 and 1995

Economy	Share of population in urban areas (percent)		Share of labor force in agricultural sectors (percent)		Mean years of secondary education		Cumulative index	
	1960	1995	1960	1995	1960	1995	1960	1995
PRC	18.2	30.3	80.8	73.5	0.96[a]	1.56	4.0	5.3
Index	2	4	2	3	8	9		
India	18.8	26.8	72.9	64.1	0.12	0.84	2.3	5.0
Index	2	3	3	4	2	8		
Japan	67.3	77.6	26.4	7.2	1.87	3.06	9.0	10.0
Index	9	10	8	10	10	10		
Korea, Republic of	32.4	81.3	55.1	18.1	0.97	3.47	5.7	9.7
Index	4	10	5	9	8	10		
Malaysia	29.9	53.7	58.6	64.0	0.49	1.63	4.7	8.3
Index	4	8	4	8	6	9		
Taipei,China	51.0[b]	63.0	46.5	12.8	0.92	2.49	7.3	9.3
Index	8	9	6	9	8	10		

a. Education estimate for PRC is based on 1975 data.
b. Population estimate for Taipei,China is based on 1974 data.
Source: Authors' calculations based on World Bank (1997).

points and has doubled its score since 1960. The Republic of Korea has moved ahead of Taipei,China and comes close to a 10 score.

To compare the division of labor with the propensity to litigate, we have used the raw data on urbanization, on share of the labor force in agriculture, and education levels, and run a simple regression with time series for data on civil and commercial litigation from five of the six countries (data were not available for India). To account for the different levels in litigation, all models were controlled for fixed effects within countries. We found a positive correlation that was statistically significant between litigation rates and the three measurements for the division of labor.[3]

If the division of labor is an important factor in determining the demand of DSIs, we would also expect economies with a similar rank on the *Division of Labor Index* to show a comparable propensity to litigate. As the comparative overview of litigation rates in the six economies presented in table 7.18 below indicates, however, this does not appear to be the case. The

Table 7.18   Demand and Supply of DSIs in Lower and Intermediate Level Courts in Asia, 1960 and 1995

Economy	Type of cases	Litigation rates (PMP)		Number of judges (PMP)	
		1960	*1995*	*1960*	*1995*
PRC [a]	Commercial at lower and intermediate levels	461.8	1,124.0	—	137.5[a]
India	Civil at lower levels	489.6	1,209.0	5.5	10.9
Japan	Civil at all levels	1,782.7	3,386.8	25.2	22.8
Korea, Republic of	All civil except family cases	1,194.0	14,713.0	11.6	27.0
Malaysia	Civil at lower and intermediate levels	—	17,850.0	7.1	15.3[b]
Taipei,China	All civil including family	17,420.0	37,660.0	32.4	57.1
	Commercial only	694.4	865.5		

PMP = per million people
a. Numbers for PRC are based on estimates. Note that many who serve as judges do not have full legal training.
b. Data for Malaysia are for 1990.
Source: Team report.

---

[3] We regressed the cumulative index and each of the indicators separately. For each regression we obtained a p-value > 0.0.

data presented in the table are not strictly comparable across the six economies. For some we have data on civil cases only. Others have all civil cases
except family cases, yet others have commercial cases only. Moreover, in
some economies we have data for all court levels (lower, intermediate, high),
while for others we are primarily relying on courts of first instance. Nevertheless, the data allow us to observe general trends with respect to the propensity to litigate.

The low civil and commercial litigation rates in the PRC and India in 1960
and in 1995 are consistent with their low score on the division of labor index.
In both countries we see an increase in litigation, but overall, the numbers are
much lower than in the other countries. As lower level courts had the highest
case load in both countries, including data on courts at all levels would not
substantially change this result.

In the Republic of Korea, Malaysia, and Taipei,China litigation rates increased substantially over the years—looking at civil litigation only.
Taipei,China's civil litigation rates in 1960 were considerably higher than in
any of the other economies and litigation increased further over the next 35
years. However, commercial litigation has remained low and relatively stable.
We lack data for 1960 in Malaysia. However, based on our earlier discussion of
litigation rates in Malaysia since the early 1970s, we may assume that they
have increased over the years, with some major fluctuations, but more gradually in the long term. The Republic of Korea is the country that witnessed the
steepest increase in litigation from only 1,194 (PMP) in 1960 to over 14,000
(PMP) in 1995. Japan has experienced the least change with respect to civil
litigation rates. In part this can be attributed to the fact that Japan was already
a well developed economy in 1960. Although growth rates have been high,
especially during the 1960s, the country did not undergo the dramatic socioeconomic change experienced by Republic of Korea, Malaysia, and
Taipei,China. However, in light of the fact that Japan is the most developed
economy in our sample and received the highest scores in the division of
labor index in 1960 and 1995, one would expect much higher litigation rates
than we can observe. The comparison of litigation rates in Japan, Republic of
Korea, and Taipei,China presents us with an interesting puzzle, because the
three economies share similarities with respect to the history and structure of
their court system and the general legal system, but show different outcome
variables in litigation rates. All three have copied extensively from continental European models. All three have continued to use the traditional civil
service exam method to ensure quality and to control the size of the judicial
profession. However, while in Japan litigation rates *in general* have remained
low, civil litigation has soared in the Republic of Korea and in Taipei,China,
although commercial litigation has also remained low in the latter.

The number of judges differs quite substantially across different economies. The comparison of the number of judges in Japan with other developed
market economies has shown that the supply side of courts has been significantly lower than in the West. This is also true for the other economies. Ironi-
cally, the number of judges in the two common law economies in our sample,
India and Malaysia, has remained lowest over the years. This is in contrast to
the high number of judges in the UK, which ranked first among the Western
market economies (see table 7.9 above). This evidence sheds further doubt
on suggestions discussed earlier that the supply side is primarily responsible
for low litigation rates in Japan.

Our comparative analysis of litigation rates shows that civil and commercial litigation is a more complex matter than a simple function of the division
of labor in society, and the supply of court institutions. Culture may be an
important explanatory variable, but to show its relevance, we would need to
explain significant differences not only between East and West, but between
the Republic of Korea and Taipei,China on the one hand and Japan on the
other hand. Future research would also need to analyze the interaction between the propensity to litigate—within the specific environment of a given
country—and outcome variables, such as the choice of contractual parties
and the use of other mechanisms to settle disputes. A proposition that could
be tested is that low litigation rates correlate positively with relational as opposed to arm's length contracting. Relational contracting has been identified
as an important element of contractual relationships in Japan. However, it is
also common in other economies, as has been documented in a study on
entrepreneurs in Wisconsin in the early 1960s (Macaulay 1963). So far little
understood are the tradeoffs between relational and arm's length contracting
for different sectors in the economy and for the economy as a whole. It is often
suggested that relational contracting, especially if based exclusively on kinship, has limitations. In particular, it may constrain the size of the market and
may bar new participants from entry. However, for stable markets it can provide a low cost alternative to formal legal relations, including formalized dispute settlement.

ADMINISTRATIVE LITIGATION

In modern economies interactions between state and market are common. This is true even in market based economies where the state control is
comparatively limited. The most obvious case for state-market interaction is
the collection of taxes and the supply of public goods. Other areas include the
regulation of market failures (antitrust measures), banking supervision and

capital market oversight, zoning rules, environmental and health protection measures, the supply of information systems such as land and security registers, and dispute settlement and contract enforcement. This list is not comprehensive. It comprises only the bare bones of state-market interaction. In many economies, including the economies in our sample, the state has been much more involved in the economy.

The state and nonstate parties that are subjected to state rules and regulations may pursue conflicting interests. Construction plans may run counter to zoning rules. The expansion of businesses may be limited by antitrust regulations. Environmental and health standards may increase the cost of production, and companies may resist internalizing these costs. Moreover, where the state seeks to support one economic agent, this may have negative effects on others. Subsidies extended to some companies may disadvantage others. Cheap credits may benefit targeted industries, but come at high costs to banks. Where banks are state owned this is less of a problem, because they can count on additional support from the state budget. However, where banks are privately owned, they risk their own economic resources.

This potential for conflict of interest raises the question of whether state actions affecting the business interests of nonstate parties may be challenged. This could take various forms. First, parties may protest informally or file a petition with the state agency that endorsed the state action against them. Second, they may petition the immediate superior agency of the state official who rendered the original ruling, or file a formal appeal for internal administrative review of the state action. Third, nonstate parties may take the state to court and seek a formal review of the legality of the state action.

Which of these measure nonstate parties may choose depends largely on the procedures and institutions made available to them by the state. In other words, in order to provide nonstate parties with the opportunity to challenge state actions, the state has to volunteer the institutional framework necessary to pursue these actions. Historically, states have been quite reluctant to offer checks and balances, including full judicial review of state actions, to nonstate parties, as this limits their discretionary powers. In the US, full judicial review of state actions has always been available. In continental Europe, legal review of administrative actions became available only in the nineteenth century and judicial review over constitutional matters much later. The purpose of these measures was to make the state more accountable. The principle that actions by the executive should not be undertaken unless a legal basis in the form of a law that was passed by the legislature had been provided for and that state acts should comply with the law was increasingly recognized. By the middle of the nineteenth century, leading jurists in Germany were debating whether the general courts should be vested with the power to review the legality of state acts taken by the executive. The outcome of this debate was that general courts retained jurisdiction over civil and criminal matters and special courts were created to deal with legal review of administrative acts (Nolte 1994). Although these courts were formally independent, it took until after World War II for them to play an important role in the review of the legality and propriety of state acts based on substantive constitutional principles and procedural rights.

When Japan imported continental European law at the end of the nineteenth century, it was this model of special administrative courts, in addition to the courts with general jurisdiction, that was copied. Taipei,China followed a similar model. Under American occupation, administrative courts were abolished in Japan and jurisdiction over executive acts was vested with the general courts. Although today in Japan and the Republic of Korea, general courts have jurisdiction over administrative matters, they have made use of this right only very cautiously. The Republic of Korea is currently establishing a new system of special administrative courts, which will take effect in 1998.

The history of the development of administrative courts in Europe suggests that—even in the absence of fully democratic regimes—a demand for greater accountability of state actions is created as the economy develops. MaxWeber has called the "rationality of the bureaucracy" as well as a "rational legal system" a precondition for capitalism to emerge (Weber 1980 [1921 first German edition]). Rational state action enhances the predictability of state actions and reduces uncertainty for entrepreneurs. The experience of theWest suggests that for ensuring rationality of the bureaucracy and rationality of the legal system, a set of institutional constraints and checks should exist. These constraints include not only legal principles, such as the principle that state actions must comply with the law, but also the availability of effective recourse against state actions.

In this section, we analyze whether similar institutional constraints have evolved in the six Asian economies in our sample and how these constraints have been used. Our findings show considerable differences between, on the one hand, the two economies with a common law tradition and on the other the remaining four economies whose legal framework for administrative law and procedure was influenced by nineteenth century continental European law. In the former, extensive judicial review was already practiced at the time the economies became politically independent. In the latter, effective legal institutions and procedures that provide nonstate parties with legal recourse against state actions were much weaker and were strengthened only over time. The supply of these institutions was primarily the result of legal change that itself fueled demand by market participants for further legal processes that would allow them to assert their rights and enforce the legal boundaries of state intervention.

ADMINISTRATIVE LITIGATION IN ASIA, 1960–1995

Disputes between state and nonstate parties provide a clear case of unequal access to information and sources that can be mobilized for investigation. If nonstate parties are to be given a fair chance in these proceedings, this should be reflected in the rules governing the burden of proof. As listed above, of the six countries, India and Malaysia—the two common law countries—were further advanced toward legal accountability than the other four at the time of independence. We start the discussion with them.

Administrative Litigation in India

A strong bureaucracy that was held accountable to the law was established in India under the British rule. Most high level bureaucrats in the Indian civil service during that period were trained in England. A strong and independent judiciary was also created under British rule. After independence, a major conflict developed between the legislature and the judiciary. The supreme court has comprehensive jurisdiction to review legislative acts. Similarly, lower level courts can review administrative acts and regulations. In its defense of legality and constitutionality, the supreme court has repeatedly invalidated legislative acts issued by the parliament. Parliament, in turn, has repeatedly sought to limit the court's ability to review legislative acts, in particular legislative acts to amend the constitution (VanderMay 1996). What is remarkable in this context is the degree of independence the supreme court has retained throughout this struggle as well as the high respect it commends.

At the lower level, the creation of special tribunals with jurisdiction over a variety of essentially administrative matters has helped in dealing with the flood of administrative cases. Still, since the middle of the 1970s, the share of total court cases in which the government was a party has been over 60 percent. This case flood can be attributed in part to the number of regulations, licenses, and state approvals citizens and economic agents are subjected to. The extensive delegation of lawmaking authority to the executive has resulted in a proliferation of rulemaking at all levels. The major check on the legality of these rules has been the judiciary, and citizens have made ample use of this institution. Sample studies on the outcome of cases in which the state is a party suggest that the nonstate parties have a high chance of winning such cases. In appeal cases against the tax administration, the courts reversed agency adjudication in 95 percent of all cases. In land matters, nonstate parties win in 60 to 65 percent of the cases, and in other matters the success rate may even be higher. These numbers are very high by comparative standards. They may be seen either as evidence of the independence of Indian courts or the low level of compliance with the law by state bureaucrats.

Recent economic reforms that have begun to do away with many state imposed restrictions may substantially reduce the amount of administrative litigation. However, we lack sufficient evidence at this point to prove this.

Administrative Litigation in Malaysia

The common law Malaysia received from Great Britain provided that nonstate parties, including individuals and entities, have the right to take legal actions against the state. This right has never been curtailed by law. Administrative cases are treated just like other cases among nonstate parties. This applies to the statute of limitations as much as for rules governing the locus standi. Decisions concerning the constitutionality of laws is a prerogative of the federal court; all other courts are excluded from taking such decisions.

In general, courts have jurisdiction over all administrative matters. However, in recent times, the number of state agencies has proliferated. Within their jurisdiction, they have the right to decide on questions of fact and law in claims and disputes between two citizens or a citizen and a state agency or department. The proliferation of administrative agencies and the increase of their decisionmaking power is closely related to the changes in economic policies introduced in the early 1970s ("new economic policy"). General clauses, broad discretion for the state bureaucracy, and flexibility were favored over the formal procedures and technicalities the traditional court system implied. Although parties still have the option to challenge agency adju-

Table 7.19   Administrative Litigation in Malaysia
(High Courts Only), 1961–1995

Years	Cases decided			Reversal of agency adjudication (percentage)
	Number	PMP	Change (percentage)	
1989	66	3.8	n.a.	—
1990	82	4.6	21.1	—
1991	53	2.9	-37.0	—
1992	38	2.0	-31.0	—
1993	75	3.9	95.0	—
1994	54	2.7	-30.8	—

— = not available
n.a. = not applicable
PMP = per million people
Source: Malaysia team report.

dication in the courts, the scope of discretion allocated to state bureaucrats has in effect reduced the ability of the courts to undertake legal review. This is also reflected in data on administrative litigation, which have been low. We lack full time-series data. Over the last five years the number of cases decided at high courts fluctuated between 38 and 82 cases, or between 2 and 4.6 cases per million people (see table 7.19).

Once parties initiated cases against the state, they were also ready to take a case through appeal procedures. The court of appeal, which was established only in 1994, received an increasing number of appeals in cases where one of the parties was the state. During the first year of operation, the number was only 38, in 1995 it increased to 196 cases, and by 1996 it had reached 308 cases. The numbers both in real terms and on a per capita basis are quite low, but we lack data from lower level courts to draw final conclusions.

Administrative Litigation in Japan

Japan copied the European model of the nineteenth century, which allocated judicial supervision over administrative state acts to special courts. These courts were abolished under the US occupation and jurisdiction over administrative matters was allocated to the general courts. Since the early 1950s several attempts have been made to enact a comprehensive law on administrative procedure that sets forth standards for administrative decisionmaking and review processes. It took until 1994 for such a law to take effect. However, elements of this law have been incorporated in some— though not all—special administrative laws and have been anticipated by judicial case law especially since the 1980s.

The major feature of state-private interaction in Japan during the postwar era has been the widespread use of "administrative guidance." Administrative guidance is not a clearly defined concept. It refers to the practice of using nonlegal means to persuade private parties to conduct their affairs in a certain manner or to refrain from certain action. Administrative guidance can be expressed in writing, but oral communication has been perhaps the more frequent use of administrative guidance (Upham 1987; Kodderitzsch 1994). The origins of this practice go back to the banking and exchange rate regulations that were enacted in the late 1920s and 1930s (Ueda 1994). It was intended to give the state discretion to control the financial sector, but at the same time to abstain to the greatest extent possible from using legal or explicitly coercive means. In the postwar era, this practice continued. In many ways it served as a substitute for a well developed regulatory framework in an economy that expanded too rapidly for the state to keep pace in creating specific legal instruments for dealing with market failures. Moreover, administrative guidance was much less rigid than the legal framework for industrial policy proposed by MITI in the early 1960s,[4] which would have equipped MITI with strong authority for market intervention. At the same time, the use of administrative guidance has limited the ability of nonstate parties to invoke judicial supervision over administrative acts. By definition, administrative guidance is not a legal act. The 1994 administrative procedure law for the first time established principles for the use of administrative guidance and thus has, to some extent, "legalized" this concept. Existing legal rules narrowly define when a party has standing in an administrative case and rest the burden of proof with the plaintiff—that is with the nonstate party. Finally, the Japanese judiciary has exercised extensive self-restraint in cases that could potentially be of political significance. This was less true in the 1960s, but has influenced judicial decisionmaking since then. Throughout the 1960s, the judiciary had asserted its independence and came to play an active role in some widely publicized cases including the Minamata pollution cases, but also the oil cartel cases of the early 1970s, which challenged the legality of administrative guidance. Companies that were found to have engaged in cartel building were held liable and a high court invoked criminal sanctions despite the fact that MITI had approved and accepted this practice. The court even stated that MITI had induced illegal private behavior (Upham 1987). These cases had an

Table 7.20   Administrative Litigation at Japanese District
Courts, 1961–1995

| Years | Cases decided | | | Reversal of agency adjudication (percentage) |
	Number	PMP	Change (percentage)	
1961	656	6.9	n.a.	5.5
1965	644	6.5	-5.8	4.2
1970	822	7.9	21.5	17.9
1975	1,736	15.6	97.5	1.8
1980	—	—	—	—
1985	919	7.6	-51.3	5.1
1990	963	7.8	2.6	4.4
1995	954	7.6	-2.6	7.8

— = not available
n.a. = not applicable
PMP = per million people
Note: Data for 1980 unavailable because of changes in the organization of judicial statistics. Data include the number of cases decided by district courts only.
Source: Government statistical yearbooks (various issues).

---

[4] Japan team report, Part I, section 4.

important impact on the use of administrative guidance in areas that had violated existing legislation, such as antitrust rules. However, the appointment of a new chief justice signaled a new trend for the courts. Since the mid-1970s they have played a less equivocal role and taken a rather formalistic view on cases of potentially political relevance. This is reflected in administrative litigation rates (at district courts), which increased steadily until the mid 1970s, but decreased afterwards. Even stronger evidence is provided by the reversal of agency adjudication in Japan (see table 7.20). The share of cases won by the nonstate party increased to 17.0 percent by 1970, but dropped to only 1.8 percent of all cases in 1975.

Administrative Litigation in the Republic of Korea

In the Republic of Korea, a law allowing nonstate parties to take judicial recourse after having exhausted all internal review processes was enacted in 1951. In 1975, a special court, the National Tax Tribunal, staffed with trained judges, legal scholars, civil servants, and tax officials was created to deal with tax matters.[5] Although not a full court, this tribunal served as a court of first instance in tax matters. In 1984, the right to sue the state in general administrative matters was expanded. The recent Administrative Procedure Act, which was passed in 1995, further improves procedural checks on government actions and establishes special administrative courts. This law will take effect in 1998.

Table 7.21   Administrative Litigation in the Republic of Korea, 1961–1995

Years	Cases decided			Reversal of agency adjudication (percentage)
	Number	PMP	Change (percentage)	
1961	340	13.2	n.a.	n.a.
1965	531	18.6	40.9	—
1970	664	20.8	11.8	—
1975	647	18.3	-12.0	—
1980	1,218	31.9	74.3	—
1985	1,913	46.9	47.0	—
1990	3,116	72.7	55.0	—
1995	9,640	214.9	195.6	33.9

— = not available
n.a. = not applicable
PMP = per million people
Source: Korea team report.

---

[5] The tribunal still exists, but its function may be transferred to the new administrative courts.

Available evidence on administrative litigation presented in table 7.21 below shows that until the second half of the 1970s nonstate parties have made only cautious use of the possibility of suing the state although, on a per capita basis, litigation rates have been higher than in Japan. (See table 7.20 above.) Over the next 15 years, administrative litigation increased by 50-100 percent over 5 year intervals. The most significant increase in litigation occurred during the past five years when the number of administrative cases almost tripled. In 1995 more than 214 cases per million people were decided by the courts. The per capita number is considerably higher than in either Malaysia or Japan, even accounting for differences in data. The largest category of cases to be referred to the courts concern taxes and other state fees, followed by cases dealing with the refusal or withdrawal of licenses.

The increase in administrative litigation coincides with important political changes in the Republic of Korea. The first direct presidential elections in 1987 and the creation of the Sixth Republic in 1988 marked a turning point in the country's political history towards greater adherence to legal checks on state power. Change has been gradual and has not affected all areas of the law. For example, lower judges continue to be appointed only for an initial term of 10 years. Although the process of reappointment has been used in the past to ensure that the judiciary exercised considerable self-restraint vis-a-vis the executive, the importance of the limited term of judges is said to be of little relevance today and does not appear to undermine the independence of the judiciary. The greater self-confidence of the judiciary and the law enforcement apparatus is also reflected in the high rate at which agency adjudication has been reversed by the courts in the latter part of the review period. In 1994, the state lost in 36.7 percent and in 1995 in 33.9 percent of all adjudicated cases. According to available data, the high reversal rates during these years primarily resulted from wrongful initial administrative measures (80 percent of all reversed cases). In the remaining 20 percent of the cases the courts reversed because of a different legal opinion.

Administrative Litigation in Taipei,China

The 1947 Constitution of Taipei,China established the Judicial Yuan as one of five branches of the state government. The Council of Great Justices (CGJ) was created to render interpretations on the constitutionality of laws. In addition, an administrative court modeled after the French Conseil d'État was established. A law on administrative appeal establishing the rules for internal administrative review of state acts, as well as an administrative litigation law, had been established in 1930. These laws were substantially revised in 1937 and again in the early 1970s. However, in actual legal practice the role of judicial supervision of administrative acts as well as the review of the constitutionality of laws was severely curtailed during the period of martial law. Until 1992, when the organic law of the CGJ was amended, it remained unclear whether the right of the CGJ to render interpretations amounted to the right of full judicial review. Administrative review was limited in part by the applications of legal doctrines that originate in German administrative law, which subject certain people—including civil servants, teachers in public schools and universities, students, and prisoners—to a "special power relation." This status limits their rights to appeal against state actions and gives the bureaucracy great discretion in handling matters that relate to them. Only since the 1980s has the judiciary been able to assert its independence and thus generate the credibility to settle disputes between state and nonstate parties impartially. In the late 1980s a minister of justice had to resign after attempting to influence the decision of judges. Data on administrative litigation are included in table 7.22. The data show that administrative litigation increased over the years. After 1980, growth rates clearly accelerated. Moreover, after agency reversal had reached a low point in 1970, the chance for nonstate parties of winning a suit against the state increased substantially. In some localities, reversal rates have increased even more substantially (from 95.1 cases per million people in 1980 to over 160 cases in 1988, and further to 291.5 cases in 1995) which seems to correlate with a change in government. By 1995, the per capita litigation rate in Taipei,China was almost equal to that in the Republic of Korea.

Table 7.22   Administrative Litigation in Taipei,China, 1960–1995

Years	Cases decided			Reversal of agency adjudication (percentage)
	Number	PMP	Change (percentage)	
1960	256	23.7	n.a.	10.34
1965	360	28.5	20.3	7.88
1970	987	67.3	136.1	3.85
1975	1,230	76.2	13.2	5.32
1980	1,693	95.1	24.8	7.83
1985	3,082	160.0	68.2	9.44
1990	—	—	—	11.98
1995	6,159	291.5	82.2	12.45

— = not available
n.a. = not applicable
PMP = per million people
Source: Taipei,China team report.

Administrative Litigation in the People's Republic of China

In the PRC, a general rule that allows citizens and organizations to bring the government or public officials to court on suspicion of having violated the law was included in the 1982 Civil Procedure Code. This resulted in an increasing number of administrative cases filed with the people's courts. To cope with the growing case load, administrative tribunals were first created in 1986. As of 1990, all high courts and intermediate courts as well as 91 percent of the lower level courts had established administrative tribunals. A law setting forth the procedure for judicial review of state actions was adopted in 1990. The law was an important achievement, but it falls short of comprehensive administrative procedure law as known in Western legal systems. It also limits the scope of judicial supervision (Potter 1994). Judges may only review the legality of administrative acts, not their propriety. Moreover, they may not review the legality of administrative regulations that provide the basis for that act, as this power rests solely with the National People's Congress legislature or with administrative departments of the state council that were authorized to review the legality of normative acts. Still, the acceptance of the mere concept of subjecting public officials to legal review and court proceedings is a significant development in China's history. Not surprisingly, public officials have not always welcomed this change. They have been reluctant to appear in court and state agencies have frequently refused to pay court expenses. In Hainan province, the local government went as far as threatening to cut the salaries of the judges on the tribunal.[6] Judges in other provinces have reported similar threats. In spite of this and other incidents that might discourage citizens and organizations from seeking justice, administrative cases have increased substantially in recent years.

On a per capita basis, the propensity to litigate in PRC remains lower than in the Republic of Korea and Taipei,China, since there were only 47 cases PMP in 1995 (see table 7.23 below). But is not much lower than in either Japan or Malaysia. A breakdown of administrative cases reveals that the majority of cases that were classified deal with general issues of public security and law and order, followed by land issues. Data on reversal of agency adjudication have been scarce. The only year for which data are available is 1990. As the comparison with Japan and Taipei,China shows, the number of cases where courts reversed agency adjudication during this year is relatively high.

---

[6] People's Daily, 25 December 1996, p. 4.

COMPARISON OF ADMINISTRATIVE LITIGATION ACROSS ECONOMIES

Our analysis of the development of judicial review over state acts in the previous sections suggests that over time states have tended to create more institutions and procedures that enabled nonstate parties to appeal against such acts. The development is more clear in PRC, Japan, Republic of Korea, and Taipei,China than in India or Malaysia. The latter two economies have inherited the relevant institutional and procedural infrastructure for extensive judicial review from the common law system, which has placed them at a comparative advantage vis-a-vis the other economies. The judiciary in India, above all the Supreme Court, has retained this independence even during the years of high state intervention in the economic and social life and in spite of major attacks by the legislature against its independence. Still, the effectiveness of judicial supervision over administrative acts and regulations at lower levels has been undermined by excessive administrative rulemaking. Meanwhile, Malaysia has effectively curtailed the rather comprehensive rights to judicial review the 1956 Constitution had vested with the judiciary. It is too early to judge whether this is a lasting reversal of judicial authority, among the economies in our sample, but so far Malaysia is the only case where judicial independence and judicial review have been curtailed rather than expanded after the mid-1980s. The development in the other four economies has not been linear, but has fluctuated over time. Some economies established substantial review rights relatively early, but took them back in times of political crisis. Politics has been an important factor in determining the commitment of the state to judicial review of state acts in PRC, Republic of Korea, and Taipei,China. The political decision to make administrative litigation available or to revive existing processes is likely to have been influenced by economic development. Economic development generates prosperity. As a result, the relative costs of state interference increase. Administrative litigation provides a procedural mechanism to reduce the costs to what is legally permissible and enhances the accountability of state agents to the law. The growing demand for these legal processes is reflected in the rise in litigation rates in recent years.

Overall, the results of civil and commercial litigation on the one hand, and administrative litigation on the other, suggest that we see signs of increasing litigation with socioeconomic development and political change. However, these signs are not strong enough to conclude that dispute settlement in Asia converges with similar practices in the West. The propensity to litigate remains considerably lower than in many countries in the West. In light of the political developments and the economic policies pursued during

Table 7.23   Administrative Litigation in PRC, 1983–1995

Year	Total		Public security			Land			Reversal of agency adjudication (percentage)
	Number	PMP	Number	PMP	Share (percentage)	Number	PMP	Share (percentage)	
1988	8,575	7.8	3,385	3.1	39.5	2,719	2.5	31.7	—
1989	9,934	8.9	3,336	3.0	33.6	3,347	3.0	33.7	—
1990	13,006	11.5	4,519	4.0	34.75	4,038	3.6	31.05	18.9
1991	25,667	22.3	7,720	6.7	30.08	8,162	7.1	31.80	—
1992	21,125	18.1	7,863	6.0	28.99	8,330	7.2	30.71	—
1993	27,911	23.7	7,018	6.0	25.14	8,063	6.8	28.89	—
1994	35,083	29.5	8,623	7.2	24.58	7,962	6.7	22.69	—
1995	53,596	44.7	11,633	9.7	21.70	10,012	8.3	18.68	—

— = not available
PMP = per million people
Source: PRC team report.

the period under investigation, it is difficult to draw conclusions about the causes for these differences. Culture may be an important factor. However, changes in litigation rates over time suggest that culture alone does not explain the functioning or use of formal dispute settlement institutions.

Chapter 8

CONVERGENCE AND DIVERGENCE IN LEGAL AND ECONOMIC DEVELOPMENT

At the outset of our analysis we proposed four hypotheses that test the role of law in economic development and address the question of whether the development of law and legal institutions in Asia differs from the West. The Convergence Hypothesis suggests that as a result of economic convergence, law and legal institutions also converge across economies. The Divergence Hypothesis suggests that legal development in each country is idiosyncratic. This may in turn influence economic development, because different legal arrangements may be more or less conducive to economic growth. A middle ground between these two extreme views about law and economic development is the Differentiation Hypothesis, according to which some areas of the law may converge with economic development, while others may persistently diverge. Based on the analysis in the previous chapters, we can dismiss the Irrelevance Hypothesis. In light of the changes in laws and legal institutions that have taken place over the course of the 35 years investigated in this study, there is little basis for arguing that law has not played an important part in Asian economic development.

To falsify or verify the three remaining hypothesis, we need to address two questions. First, whether economic development converges, and second, whether we also see signs of legal convergence. Both questions are addressed in this chapter. In addition, we seek to point out the areas of the law where we see stronger signs of convergence with the West and those that still show little resemblance to comparable rules and legal processes in the West. Our analysis tends to support our Differentiation Hypothesis, though this must be qualified by the potential we see for institutional evolution. While we see strong signs of economic convergence, laws, and in particular, legal processes have not fully converged. Industrialization and urbanization have transformed the economies surveyed in this book. Those that began the economic transformation earlier are more advanced than are the late developers.

Economic convergence does not necessarily imply convergence of legal systems. Indeed, our discussion of the patterns of legal change in chapter 4 has shown that for convergence of laws, economic policies rather than the stage of economic development were primarily responsible. Nevertheless, a closer examination of patterns of change in the legal systems along the procedural and the allocative dimensions of law suggests a general trend towards convergence of legal systems. Convergence has been stronger along the allocative dimension of law than the procedural dimension.

CONVERGENCE AND DIVERGENCE IN ECONOMIC DEVELOPMENT

Empirical evidence reveals a huge divergence in levels of national income around the world. However, the gap between rich and poor need not persist. The experience of the high performing economies in Asia over the past decades is the best evidence that those with relatively low income levels are able to catch up with the richer ones (World Bank 1993; ADB 1997). Economic convergence does not occur automatically, but is the product of a variety of factors, including initial conditions, policy variables, demography, resources, and geography. In the context of Asian economic growth and development over the past 30 years, policy choices have been shown to be crucial for achieving high growth rates (ADB 1997). Policy choices affect key economic growth factors, such as savings rates, the ability to engage in international trade, and the quality of institutions.

Indicators for Economic Convergence

For the purpose of our analysis we are particularly interested in economic variables that indicate the allocation of resources in the economy. If Asian economic development does in fact converge with economies of the Western model, we would expect to see comparable policy variables, and thus a shift from state controls over the allocation of resources to the market. To capture changes in the state's allocative role, we have collected data on the extent of state control over the means of production and government spending, the state's role in allocating financial resources, and state controls over cross-boarder trade. These indicators do not capture the entire scope of possible state involvement in the economy. Rather they reflect the most direct forms of state involvement in the allocation of resources. Other forms of state involvement, which have been common in many economies, including those in this study, take the form of negotiation between the state and private businesses, or state guidance over the use of economic resources. A good example is Japan, where common interests of state officials and the business community resulted in bargained national policies that essentially sheltered the domestic market against too much foreign intrusion. These measures, which may be referred to as "indirect" as opposed to "direct" state controls, are not captured by the indicators described below. They are hardly accessible to economic data analysis. For the purpose of this study, whose primary focus is on legal, not economic development, we limit the analysis to direct state controls. There are huge data problems even here, as we will show. The purpose of the presentation of these data is to indicate that at least with respect to direct state controls, the involvement of the state in the economy has changed considerably over the years, and that these changes suggest economic convergence across Asian economies and between Asia and the West.

Extent of State Control

The extent of state controls in the form of state ownership and government expenditure has important implications for the structure of the economy, as resources used by the state sector are not available for private sector growth. To measure the size of the state, we use government expenditure as a share of GDP. We present total government expenditure, including expenditure by the central as well as provincial governments and municipalities. A well-known feature of economic development is that government expenditure increases with economic development. However, we are also interested in the extent to which economic policy periods influence the level of government expenditures. A more direct measure of the involvement of the state in the economy is the extent of state ownership of enterprises. We measure the extent of state ownership using three variables: state-owned enterprises' (SOEs') share of value added, SOEs' share of investment, and SOEs' share in employment (World Bank 1995).[1] Data are based on the World Bank's Policy Research Report, *Bureaucrats in Business* (World Bank 1995) and are available for the period from 1978 to 1991 (for some economies for shorter periods only). Using all three indicators allows us to assess the effects of policy changes on the SOE sector. The SOEs' share in total investment reflects state policies that devote substantial resources to SOE investments. The SOEs' share in value added reflects the competitiveness of the SOE sector. Finally, the SOEs' share in total employment shows whether reversals in state policies that promoted the growth of the SOE sector have resulted in the closure of SOEs or whether the existing sector lingers on even after its share in total investment and value added has declined.

For a comparison of the extent of direct state controls across the six economies, we have created a worldwide index and ranked the six economies in our sample accordingly. The index is based on a scale from zero to ten. Table 8.1 gives the scores for each economy on government expenditure and the size of the state-owned sector and a cumulative score for the two indicators. A lower score indicates a larger and a higher score a smaller state sector.

As higher scores indicate smaller state sectors, the relatively high scores obtained by the economies in our sample on this worldwide scale indicate that the state sector in other economies has often been considerably larger.[2]

---

[1] SOEs' share of value added is defined as the contribution by SOEs to gross domestic product. SOE investment is the contribution of the SOE sector to fixed capital formation. SOE employment gives the share of full time SOE employees in total formal sector employment.

[2] See also table 5.3 above.

Table 8.1   Cumulative Index: Direct State Controls

Economy	1980			1985			1990		
	Government expenditure	SOE	Score	Government expenditure	SOE	Score	Government expenditure	SOE	Score
PRC	7.0	1.0	4.0	9.0	1.0	5.0	9.0	1.0	5.0
India	7.0	3.3	5.2	7.0	2.3	4.7	5.0	2.3	3.7
Japan	7.0	8.0	7.5	7.0	9.0	7.0	7.0	10.0	8.5
Korea, Republic of	7.0	5.0	6.0	8.0	6.0	7.0	7.0	7.3	7.2
Malaysia	5.0	10.0	7.5	5.0	—	—	6.0	7.0	6.5
Taipei,China	8.0	5.3	6.7	8.0	5.7	6.9	7.0	7.0	7.0

— = not available

SOE = state owned enterprise

Note: The cumulative score is an unweighted average of the expenditure and the SOE score.

Source: Authors' calculations based on World Bank (1995, 1997). Government statistical yearbooks (various issues).

Throughout the 1980s scores have improved in most economies. One exception is Malaysia where the expansion of the state in the first half of the 1980s resulted in a growing SOE sector. Although these policies were partially reversed in the late 1980s, the 1990 score still reflects earlier policies. Another exception is India where data suggest a smaller state sector in 1980 than in 1990. This reflects the slow pace of reform in India relative to other economies. Although government expenditure appears to have decreased slightly over the last few years, its share of GDP remains much higher than in other economies.

A comparison of the six economies shows that Japan stands out as the one with the smallest state sector. The PRC had the largest state sector in 1980, India in 1990. The PRC's low scores are the result of the large enterprise sector, which has not declined in absolute terms, even though its share in productivity is plummeting. India scores only slightly better than the PRC for the SOE sector, but worst for government expenditure in 1990 .

In all economies, the downsizing of the state sector has been gradual. Privatization measures have had a direct impact on indicators that measure the size of the state. By contrast, where enterprises have remained in the state sector, investment has often fallen, but the number of employees remained unchanged. This shows that changes in economic policies takes place unevenly. They signal future change, but the reversal of the result of past policies is often difficult, although not impossible. In an important shift in policies, the PRC announced in October 1997 the reform of the state-owned sector, including far reaching privatization measures.

Financial Resource Allocation

In economies where the state owns all or most of the financial institutions, the state directly controls the allocation of financial resources. It can direct banks to lend to specific enterprises or sectors and enforce economic policies through its ownership rights.

Other less intrusive forms of state controls over the flow of financial resources include interest rate controls and credits. The latter encompass credits dispersed on the basis of policy directives that may apply to state as well as privately owned banks. Interest rate controls deprive banks of the ability to set interest rates according to market rates. Policy credits often target loans for specific economic sectors. Both measures are likely to change the relative costs of financing for companies in industries with different demands for external and internal finance. A recent study about sources of finance and growth provides empirical evidence that different industry sectors have different demands for external finance. Some are highly dependent on external finance, while others rely primarily on retained earnings. Moreover, the ease with which companies may obtain financial resources influences their growth potential. In economies that limit access to external finance, and, in particular, equity finance, sectors with a high demand for external finance contribute less to capital formation than in economies that do not restrict access (Rajan and Zingales 1997). Similarly, interest rate controls and policy credits are likely to affect the relative growth of different sectors in the economy and will influence the preference for credit over equity as a source of external finance for enterprises. As a result, state controls over the allocation of financial resources are likely to skew economic development.

All six economies have made extensive use of financial controls in the past. In some economies most controls have been removed already. This is the case in Japan, where interest rate controls were common until the early 1970s, but have been gradually relaxed since. In other economies, controls have shifted from direct to more indirect controls. In the Republic of Korea, for example, the four largest banks were privatized in 1983 and the entry requirements for financial institutions have been relaxed. Interest rate controls and policy credits are still used by the state to control the allocation of financial resources, even though they may be less prevalent today than they were until the early 1990s. Taipei,China has been more cautious in privatizing banks, but has opened the market to new entries and as a result, the financial sector has become more diversified. Interest rate controls were largely abolished in the second half of the 1980s and the use of policy credits limited to enterprises controlled by the military sector.

In the PRC and India, change has been more gradual, but change has taken place even here. In the PRC the state controlled financial sector, has become more diversified. Although state banks are still required to lend to priority sectors, in particular to the state owned sector, they have also been required to become profitable and, as a result, many banks have expanded lending to the nonstate sector. The recently announced reforms of the state owned sector are likely to further this trend. India pursued policies that expanded state controls over the financial sector until the early 1980s, when eight additional banks were nationalized. Although in 1995 state owned banks still accounted for some 85 percent of deposits and 92 percent of bank branches, reforms are under way. State owned banks have been allowed to sell equity to the private sector and entry barriers have been relaxed. In addition, several measures were introduced in the early 1990s to reduce interest rate controls and to scale down policy credits.

The changes in state controls over the allocation of financial resources in five of the six economies are reflected in table 8.2 below. They are based on a qualitative comparison of financial liberalization in Japan; Republic of Korea; and Taipei,China from 1965 to 1990 (Patrick and Park 1994). Data for the other two economies are assessed relative to these three economies and changes between 1990 and 1995 have been added. Data for Malaysia have been too scant to include this economy in the overview.

Table 8.2   State Controls of the Allocation of Financial Resources Compared, 1965, 1990, and 1995

	PRC	India	Japan	Republic of Korea	Taipei,China
1965					
Ownership of banks	NA	H	L	H	H
Credit allocation	NA	HH	M	H	H
Interest rate controls	NA	HH	H	H	H
1990					
Ownership of banks	HH	HH	L	L	M
Credit allocation	HH	H	L	H	L
Interest rate controls	HH	HH	L	H	M
1995					
Ownership of banks	HH	HH	L	L	M
Credit allocation	HH	H	L	M	L
Interest rate controls	HH	H	L	NA	L

NA = not applicable
— = not available
Note: Data for Malaysia are not available. H = High; M = Medium ; L = Low. Double entries denote extreme values.
Source: Patrick and Park (1994); Authors' compilation based on team reports.

By 1990, only Japan had moved to few state controls according to all three indicators. Taipei,China had higher controls in place in 1965 and had lowered them only slightly in 1990. Further reforms in subsequent years suggest that Taipei,China is following Japan in liberalizing the financial sector. By contrast, the Republic of Korea substantially reduced state ownership over the banking sector, but retained interest rates controls and policy credits. As a result, controls remain substantially higher than in Taipei,China. India shows some change in the last couple of years, while the PRC is only now embarking on reforms that may in the long-term lead to structural reforms of the financial sector.

Trade Controls. Controls over the ability of economic agents to engage in trade are a third major indicator of the state's role in the economy. We measure the extent to which states control trade by the openness of economies to international trade. Although domestic trade may also be subject to state controls, we lack sufficient data to measure, for example, the extent of licensing and approval requirements for marketing different products across economies. First, we measure the number of years an economy has been rated an "open" as opposed to a "closed" economy since 1960 (Sachs and Warner 1995). This variable does not indicate the degree of openness across economies or relative change over time. We therefore use three additional indicators, the share of total imports that are subject to tariffs, the share of total imports that are subject to quotas, and the black market premium over the official exchange rate as an indicator of government controls over the exchange rate market. All three indicators influence the classification of an economy as open or closed according to the criteria listed above. We present data only for several points in time (table 8.3) since we lack time series data for the first two indicators. The black market premium is presented as the average for different periods as indicated.

On the basis of these indicators, Japan, Republic of Korea, Malaysia, and Taipei,China are rated open economies for most of the period between 1960 and 1996. The degree of openness varied across economies, but the variations decreased over time. In 1992, differences in tariff restrictions were still considerable in some economies, but the four economies almost converged with respect to quota restrictions and black market premium. Japan was the most open economy in 1980 and has retained this high level of openness according to all measures. The second most open economy in 1980 was Malaysia, although import restrictions were substantially higher than in Japan. Tariff restrictions increased between 1980 and 1992 in Malaysia, while the share of imports subject to quotas declined. The Republic of Korea bypassed Malaysia in 1992 as the second most open economy after Japan even though the black market premium in 1992 was still twice as high as in Malaysia. Finally, in Taipei,China import restrictions were lower in 1985 than in the Republic of Korea or Malaysia, but have declined more slowly. The black market premium in Taipei,China did not decline substantially.

India and the PRC were rated as open economies in 1994 and 1995, respectively. The data on import restrictions document that both economies are much less open than any of the other four. This is an important indicator of the slow reversal of economic policies and laws that previously allocated strong controls to the state in both economies. Although trade policies appear to have been easier to reverse than direct controls in the form of state ownership, controls over imports in particular have proved to be quite persistent. Quantitative restrictions imposed in 1992 were still considerably higher than were in place in Japan, Republic of Korea, Malaysia, or Taipei,China in 1978. However, reforms have been introduced in the meantime, which have further opened the economies of India and the PRC.

Comparison of Economic Indicators

The three indicators of state control discussed above point in a similar direction. Economic policies that promoted state controls over the allocation of resources were often comprehensive; that is, they affected not only the

Table 8.3   Trade Controls in Asia, 1981–1992

Economy	Years of openness to international trade before 1995	Share of imports subject to tariffs				Share of imports subject to quotas			Black market premium			
		1981	1985	1989	1992	1985	1989	1992	1976–80	1981–85	1986–89	1990–92
PRC	0	31.9	29.20	29.20	30.60	1.80	29.10	26.40	—	—	—	—
India	1.00	59.9	90.00	62.40	42.60	71.60	54.20	48.90	13.80	16.50	11.50	14.30
Japan	33.00	—	0.02	—	—	0.06	—	—	0.08	0.30	0.50	0.85
Korea, Republic of	27.00	—	20.20	11.30	10.00	14.20	13.20	2.90	13.20	0.62	9.50	2.70
Malaysia	35.00	9.7	14.70	11.50	11.20	8.20	6.00	5.00	0.60	0.20	1.64	1.40
Taipei,China	32.00	—	7.00	—	—	5.95a	—	5.14b	3.30	2.70	2.60	2.60

— = not available
a. Data are from 1982.
b. Data are from 1990.
Source: For tariff and quota data , Sachs and Warner (1995); Barro (1994); for black market premium, Cowitt (1986).

allocation of financial resources, but also the state ownership and the state's controls over trade. Changes in economic policies aimed at reducing the role of the state also tend to affect all sectors, but they do so at a different pace. The controls that are most readily reversed are trade controls. Downsizing the state owned enterprise or banking sectors poses more substantial problems. An interim policy measure in many economies has been the opening of markets to new entries, which has substantially reduced the relative share of the state controlled sectors. However, most economies have realized the need for further structural reforms in order to provide a sound basis for market led economic development strategies.

CONVERGENCE AND DIVERGENCE IN LEGAL DEVELOPMENT

Our Convergence Hypothesis suggests that domestic development, together with growing internationalization of markets, results in the creation and development of law and legal institutions that, if not identical on paper, perform largely similar functions around the world. Conversely, the Divergence Hypothesis holds that irrespective of economic convergence, legal systems may diverge as a result of culture or legal tradition. We are also suggesting a halfway-house in which different parts of the legal system might converge, while others persistently diverge (Differentiation Hypothesis).

In the following sections we explore in detail the evidence for convergence, divergence, and differentiation between legal systems in Asia and in the West. We also point out differences between the six Asian economies. These differences suggest that legal systems in Asia are themselves much more diversified than is suggested by arguments that stress the peculiar nature of Asian legal culture based on, for example, ubiquitous Confucian norms. This diversity makes generalizations about Asian legal development difficult. However, it also has the effect of diminishing the often stressed difference between Asia and the West, because we find that the variation among Asian economies, or among Western economies for that matter, is often as great as between individual economies in Asia and in the West.

If we analyze the broad patterns of legal change along the procedural and allocative dimensions of law, we find strong signs of convergence. However, a closer analysis of legal processes shows that behind this broad pattern of convergence, processes continue to work quite differently from those in the West.

The legal reforms at the end of the nineteenth and the beginning of the twentieth century resulted in the incorporation of Western law into Asian legal systems. Most of the laws governing basic economic transactions were market/rule-based laws. By contrast, the legal systems that existed in most of Asia at that time can be classified as primarily state/discretionary. Law was used as an instrument for upholding order and it left ample discretionary power for the state to do so. In this period, the legal framework for market based transactions was developing mostly outside the scope of the state enforced law.

The incorporation of Western law by Asia did not change the overall quality of the legal system. Based on the European experience, Weber noted (1980, 1921 first edition in German) that economic development does not simply give birth to new legal forms. The Asian experience demonstrates that conversely, legal forms do not automatically result in economic development. New law offers a potential whose realization depends on many other factors. An important factor in Asian legal development was the emergence of independent nation states. The colonial regimes established by Britain in India and Malaysia and by Japan in Korea and on the island of Taiwan were state/discretionary legal systems for the local population, even though members of the colonial power may have benefited from rule-based law. Another important factor was the economic policies pursued by the governments in Asia. As we have seen in chapter 4, these policies became the key determinants for changes in the nature of legal systems between 1960 and 1995.

During this period, the economic laws that were on the books remained largely unchanged, and with the exception of the PRC, formal legal convergence between East and West had already been achieved in 1960. Although amendments altered many a transplanted law, there were more similarities than differences. However, legal and business practices differed substantially from the laws on the books, and as economic policies constrained market activities, the market based law was marginalized. Laws, rules, and regulations that were adopted after 1960 in effect established a parallel legal system to the one that already existed. The purpose of these rules was to ensure that the state could play an important role in allocating resources and governing economic activities.

A second policy shift occurred in most economies around 1980. Economic policies expanded the scope of market activities, and the discretionary power of state officials in charge of enforcing the laws was reduced. As discussed in the previous sections, economic indicators for this policy shift include privatization measures, opening of trade and, in particular, of foreign direct and portfolio investments and liberalization of financial markets. One may add that at least in some economies this shift was accompanied by political changes, which—with the exception of Malaysia—tended to move towards opening and democratization. The following sections explore in more detail this policy shift, because it is this development that informs our conclusion about the role of law and legal institutions in Asian economic development.

From State- to Market-Allocative Law

As a result of the shift in policies around 1980 the use of the market-allocative law that was already on the books increased. As indicated earlier, market-allocative law already played an important role in some sectors of the economy prior to 1980. It was extensively used in the export sectors and practiced in areas where there were few state controls. Still, markets remained relatively closed to foreign investors as state controls provided extensive checks on the scope of permitted investment activities. The same applies to the financial sector, where state ownership or other more indirect forms of state controls were used widely. The initial shift to market based law was uneven across economies, but the expansion of markets generated new demands for legal change.

The deregulation of economic activities, which signaled the trend from state- to market -allocative law, exposed weaknesses in the existing legal frame-work, with respect to the contents of both legal rules and legal procedures, although in this section we will concentrate on the former. Weakness is evident, for example, in the area of corporate law and securities market regulation. All economies had much earlier enacted a company law and the basic framework for securities markets had been established decades before these markets took off in the mid-1980s. However, the rapid development of capital markets revealed the lack of effective investor protection and the need for market oversight.[3] In addition, the expansion of markets and the increasing complexity of market transactions created a demand for new laws and regulations. Evidence for this are the consumer protection and intellectual property laws, among others, that were enacted during this period.

The trigger, enhancing the role of corporate law and exposing weaknesses in the existing legal framework, was the expansion of the private corporate sector as indicated by the data on capital formation in the different sectors of the economy. There are also signs that the structure of corporate finance began to change during this period. Previously bank credits, often backed by a political commitment to support certain firms or industries, were the most important source of finance next to retained earnings; now firms began to raise external finance on the market, in the form of both equity and corporate debt instruments (bonds). Many of the market-allocative laws that were on the books barely addressed the legal issues that were now arising. One reason is that the markets were developing at a pace any legal system would find hard to keep up with. Another is that the existing laws including rules on shareholder protection and capital market oversight were

---

[3] This procedural aspect is further discussed below under the heading "Persisting Differences in Legal Development."

transplanted at a time when even in the West capital markets were only in their infancy. Given the speed of capital market development in Asia, existing laws were often outdated by the time they were finally put to use in the now rapidly emerging markets.

The legislatures often responded to these changes by improving shareholder rights and streamlining the governance structure over markets. The timing as well as the scope of this response differed across economies. Japan, for example, went through several amendments of its Company Law and revised the securities and exchange legislation in the early 1990s; so did Malaysia and India. Taipei,China had enacted a comprehensive legislative package already in the 1980s. By comparison, the Republic of Korea witnessed few legal changes that directly addressed the need for investor protection. Finally, the PRC only embarked on establishing the legal framework for capital market development in the early 1990s.

Changes in economic policies led financial institutions to reassess the role of collateral for lending activities. Previously, when lending decisions were based on state policies that targeted sectors for priority lending, taking collateral in the form of mortgages, pledges, and others was only a formality. It was often required by banking laws or internal guidelines. However, the economic function of collateral as a source of compensation should the debtor default was hardly ever realized, because policy rather than economic considerations determined whether or not enforcement was sought. In addition, the transaction costs for enforcement were often too high for security interests to serve the economic purpose. The best example is India, where enforcement could take up to 12 years. As the state control of lending declined, collateral became increasingly viewed as a device for reducing the financial risk of the lending institution.

Nevertheless, we find little evidence for increases in the rate of enforcement against secured assets even after policy change enhanced the economic function of this legal device. In part the reason for this may be that economies continued to grow. Carrying bad loan portfolios banks often inherited from previous policy periods was not damaging enough to force lenders to liquidate bad loans quickly by foreclosing against the debtor or the collateral. In times of economic downturn, however, these large bad loan portfolios put the banking sector at substantial risk. Another reason may have been that existing laws had not been adapted to the changing economic environment. In addition, deficiencies in the law conspired against formal legal rules playing an active role in reducing creditors' risk. The fact that several economies, including Malaysia and India, lack an automatic stay for secured creditors in bankruptcy may have prevented many creditors from filing for insolvency. This would have triggered a run on the assets by other secured lenders which in turn would have undermined reorganization attempts aimed at protecting the economic value of the firm as a going concern. Even where provisions on automatic stay existed, as in Japan and the Republic of Korea, for example, they were rarely used in practice. Finally, the choice of assets that were used as collateral often left the creditor exposed to substantial risk. This is most evident in Japan and Republic of Korea, where real estate served as a reliable collateral during periods of real estate boom, but could not cover the losses after the market had collapsed. Evidence from interviews with bankers in these economies suggest that overreliance on real estate as a security frequently led banks to extend credits against collateral without undertaking a more extensive feasibility study. As a result, the banks' monitoring skills remained underdeveloped.

From Discretionary to Rule-based Law

The process of legal change from state- to market-allocative law has been accompanied by a—somewhat weaker—trend from discretionary to rule-based law. Legal change curtailed the lawmaking powers of the bureaucracies and reduced their scope for discretionary decisionmaking. This trend has not been universal. Malaysia is a counterexample, where the discretionary power of the state increased rather than decreased during a period when economic policies shifted back from state centered to market based strategies.

The trend from discretionary to rule-based law is reflected in the establishment of legal procedures that allow non-state agents to hold the state as well as state officials accountable to the law. By 1995, all economies provided for administrative litigation, even though the scope of the courts' judicial review power differed considerably across economies. In Malaysia and India, the general courts have long had broad jurisdiction over cases involving state and nonstate parties. After independence, extensive judicial review processes were added, although their scope was reduced during subsequent policy periods that witnessed a strengthening of the discretionary power of the state. In Japan, Republic of Korea, and Taipei,China the possibility of seeking recourse against state acts was on the books as early as 1960. However, these processes were curtailed in the Republic of Korea and Taipei,China during periods of martial law and autocratic power, and in Japan litigation rates remained low and declined further after the early 1970s. In the PRC, litigation against state officials was first allowed in 1982, but the scope of such actions was considerably expanded with the enactment of an administrative litigation law in 1989.

In practice, the change from discretionary to rule-based law has not been straightforward. Where state acts are not based on law, where the underlying laws are vague or conflict with each other, the establishment of procedures for challenging the legality of state acts are only a half measure. Nevertheless, the procedures seem to have enhanced the awareness of formal constraints on arbitrary state power. An example is a recent case in a south PRC village in which a villager was jailed by local police because he posted a state council document against excessive taxation. When his lawyer challenged the police action, the court found that he had a legal right to post a lawful enactment and that the local authority must obey the document and compensate the villager. The court acknowledged the citizen's rights to challenge authority through legal process, albeit the legal basis for this decision remains unclear in the PRC's very fluid legal environment. Whether this case reflects an overall trend towards greater adherence to legal restraints on state power is, however, a different matter. The case may rather reflect a power struggle between central and local authorities of state power. Moreover, as formal independence of the judiciary has not been established and salaries remain woefully low, the judiciary is still a rather weak institution. In other economies, the discretionary power formally allocated to state officials by law has been curtailed over the years. An example is Japan, where the 1994 administrative procedure code for the first time legally defined the long standing practice of "administrative guidance." This is a necessary step in a formal legal review of the permissible scope of this practice. The formal legalization of the relationship between government and business may not fundamentally alter the tradition of settling disputes through negotiation, including negotiation prior to enacting rules that affect business, rather than through litigation. However, the availability of legal procedures and the use of litigation by at least some parties is likely to have important effects in signaling the trend.

We also find evidence that economic agents have increasingly used formal dispute settlement institutions to solve their conflicts. Litigation rates overall have increased with economic development and are higher now than they were 35 years ago. Moreover, disputes are more likely to end up in the courts even if they are first filed with mediation or arbitration institutions. These are signs that informal mechanisms for dispute settlement work less well in economies that are as complex as the Asian economies are today. Still, the relationship between economic development and dispute settlement is not straightforward. Litigation rates in Japan, which are low by comparison not only with countries in the West but also with less developed countries in Asia, remain a puzzle. We have not solved this puzzle, but the comparative dimension added by this research project has demonstrated that other Asian countries show stronger signs of convergence with the West than Japan in this respect. Finally, the case of criminal sanctions used in Taipei,China to punish the bouncing of checks shows that litigation rates for civil and commercial disputes alone may understate the extent to which formal legal institutions take part in enforcing private contracts. When Taipei,China abolished this provision, it embarked on a path similar to legal development in the West, where the role of criminal sanctions against economic misconduct, which has decreased substantially over time, used to be quite extensive.

Patterns of Legal Change in Six Asian Economies

If we take the observed trends of legal change along the allocative and the procedural dimensions of law together, the pattern depicted in figure 8.1 emerges. We have located the six countries at two points in time; in 1965 or five years into the period we are studying; and in 1995. The location of each country is based on a qualitative assessment by the authors of this report, taking into account differences across countries as well as relative change over time. The two points are connected with a straight line to indicate total change of the legal system between 1965 and 1995. In many countries, the actual development from a relatively more state-allocative and discretionary to a relatively more market-allocative and rule-based legal system was less linear than suggested in the chart.

Although the figure reflects a general trend in legal development in five of the six economies, it also shows that each started from different point in 1965 and as of 1995 all six still differ considerably from each other.

Figure 8.1   Legal Systems in Asia, Patterns of Change from 1965 to 1995

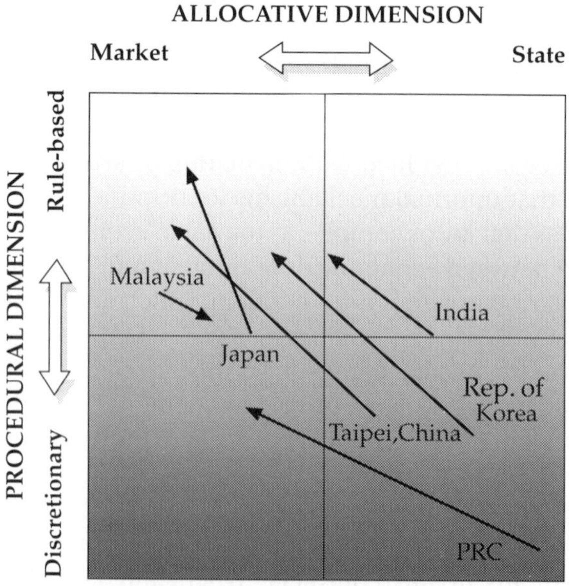

Source: Authors' compilation.

The location of the PRC in 1965 reflects a legal system whose formal constraints had given way to party policies, at a time when comprehensive state planning had been established. Thirty years later, a legal system had evolved that was much more rule-based and provided ample scope for nonstate economic activities. However, remaining gaps in the legal system and the extensive discretionary power state and party officials continue to have suggest that in 1995 the PRC was still more discretionary than the other economies. Along the allocative dimension, the legal system today places considerably more emphasis on markets, but has retained extensive state controls.

The Republic of Korea and Taipei,China shared many similarities and have followed a similar development path. In the Republic of Korea, the legal framework for the subsequent heavy and chemical industries drive was only in the early formatting stage as of 1965. But the principles of a state-allocative legal system with substantial discretionary power in favor of state officials had already been established. Thirty years later, legal change has resulted in a more market-allocative system and greater adherence to rule-based law.

The location of Taipei,China in 1965 represents a legal system under martial law, which vested the state with substantial power to intervene in political as well as economic affairs. In comparison with the Republic of Korea, the system appears to have been slightly more market-allocative in the mid-1960s, as it allowed for the development of the small-and medium-sized enterprise sector. By 1995, Taipei,China had moved decisively towards a system that accepted formal legal constraints, reduced the state's discretionary power, and supported market based activities.

Japan's legal system in 1965 differed from PRC; Republic of Korea; and Taipei,China in that it was already essentially market-allocative and adhered to formal rules. However, the extensive practice of administrative guidance, the vagueness of many rules, and the existence of financial control instruments suggest that Japan's legal system included features of state-allocative as well as discretionary law. Changes introduced since have reduced the scope of state interference on both dimensions and have resulted in a legal system that is essentially rule-based and more market-oriented.

In India and Malaysia, the legal system in 1965 was more rule-based than in most of the other countries. India had a well established rule-based system in 1965. However, the adherence to formal rules was combined with extensive powers for the state to intervene in and control economic activities. In the years since, India's legal system became at times considerably more discretionary and more state-allocative than it had been in 1965, but subsequently shifted back to a more rule-based and market-allocative system. The overall change from 1965 to 1995 shows a move towards a more market-allocative system. This trend has been accompanied by a reduction in the rule-making power of the executive. Moreover, the courts have begun to reassert the economic rights granted by the Constitution and to challenge the priority of social rights.

Malaysia is the only economy in our sample where a comparison of the situation in 1965 and in 1995 suggests a trend in the opposite direction towards more state controls and more discretion. In 1965 Malaysia was the most market/rule-based economy in our sample. State controls increased substantially in the interim period. Although many controls have been reversed after 1985, in comparison with 1965 state controls appear to have increased. In addition, the executive has assumed a strong role, which has left many legal rules with ample room for discretion. In contrast to the overall pattern observed in other economies, the trend towards a more market-allocative legal system since the mid-1980s has not resulted in a strengthening of rule-based law.

In historical perspective, these patterns of legal change suggest that the relationship between economic policies, legal change, and economic development has changed over time. The infusion of Western law to Asia would seem to have given Asian economies a head start toward economic development, but it proved at that time to be insufficient. The economic take-off, when it came, went hand in hand with economic policies that strengthened the role of the state in the economy. Law was used as an instrument of change and legal change often preceded economic outcome. An example is the adoption of licensing requirements and their subsequent implementation, or the establishment of SOEs or state agencies with the task of controlling trade in specific commodities. The policy change that shifted allocative rights from the state to the markets was implemented by repealing many of these laws. It is only during this period, which started for most economies around 1980, that we can observe the close interaction between legal and economic change that has characterized much of the legal evolution in the West.

Persisting Differences in Legal Development

Despite the major trend from state- to market-allocative, and from discretionary to rule-based law, we also find evidence for differences in Asian legal development that caution against concluding that legal developments in Asia and in the West are fully converging. PRC, India, and Japan, particularly, continue to differ in significant ways from the West.

In most cases where we see evidence of persistent divergence between East and West as well as among the six economies, this affects legal institutions and processes rather than substantive law. The process of drafting and formulating rules prior to their enactment leads to very different types of dispute resolution, compared with the West. An example is the making and application of state regulations that affect business practice in Japan. Members of the business community frequently participate in the lawmaking process through consultations and negotiations that go beyond the well known phenomenon of lobbying in the West. There is little if any evidence of litigation between large businesses and the state. Administrative litigation is largely confined to disputes brought by individuals or small entrepreneurs. The preemptive involvement of large business in rule making and the avoidance of legal conflicts in the implementation of rules provide a glimpse of a legal system that operates very differently from the West. Although there is evidence that Japanese business is increasingly demanding a hands-off policy by the state, and the recent Administrative Procedure Code has made attempts to regulate the use and extent of administrative guidance, this practice has not vanished.

Some economies differ from the West in the role courts play in settling disputes among private parties. Despite that fact that Japan is the most developed economy in our sample, litigation rates have remained conspiciously lower not only than in the West, but also than in the Republic of Korea or Taipei,China, and this despite the fact that all three economies use similar controls over the size of the legal profession. Japan, Republic of Korea, and Taipei,China still regulate the maximum number of candidates that may pass the annual exam, which is an entry requirement for the practice of law. Still, in recent years there has been a trend to relax the imposed ceilings. In addition, courts in some economies lack the capacity to deal with the new demand for formal litigation.

Finally, administrative agencies often function quite differently from similar institutions in the West, despite the fact that Western legal institutions often served as a model for institutions with similar functions that were established in Asia. The securities and exchange legislation in Japan, Republic of Korea, and Taipei,China, for example, has not adopted the concept of an independent securities and exchange commission. Japan even eliminated this agency, which had been put in place under the American occupation, and placed the supervision of capital markets under the auspices of the MOF. Similarly, antitrust agencies were often not endowed with the same degree of independence as their Western models, although their independence has been enhanced over time. And for consumer protection, most Asian countries evidently mistrusted market mechanisms and instead required regional and national governments to establish networks of consumer protection agencies.

India's legal development since independence has been quite idiosyncratic, and this affected both substantive law and legal processes. With respect to the expansion of state-allocative law, India differed from the other countries in degree, but not in substance. However, India's case is special with respect to the expansion of legal rights that became enforceable within the framework of rule-based law. The new Constitution of independent India combined the classic canon of fundamental liberal rights, including the right to life, liberty, and property with affirmative rights that obligated the state to take action in order to provide the right to a work place, housing, and equal pay for equal work. State actions to realize these affirmative rights took the form of laws that limited private entrepreneurial activities, imposed ceilings on urban land ownership, and protected tenants and employees against eviction or dismissal. These actions conflicted with the classic liberal right to property. The tension between the classic rights and the new affirmative social rights was increasingly solved in favor of social rights. A constitutional amendment passed in 1978 downgraded the right to property from a fundamental constitutional right to an ordinary constitutional right. This change confirmed a longer term legislative and judicial development that had enforced social claims against claims based on private property rights. Still, since the initiation of economic reforms, this trend has been partially reversed. Courts have increasingly upheld private property rights and have implicitly questioned the downgrading of its constitutional protection.

Causes for Divergence and Convergence of Legal Systems

The Convergence Hypotheses proposes that the major cause for convergence of legal systems would be economic development and the internationalization of markets. Our findings show that in the six Asian economies these factors have indeed played an important role in bringing about changes in economic policies that resulted in legal change.

The worldwide trend towards more market-based economic strategies and the growing internationalization of trade and commerce was important for the subsequent shift towards market-allocative law. Changes in world markets had to influence economic policies in countries that relied heavily on export-led growth. Pressure from bilateral trading partners and multilateral institutions, such as the General Agreement on Tariffs and Trade (GATT) and the World Trade Organization (WTO), reinforced this trend. Worldwide economic globalization was supported by the international harmonization of laws and legal standards. The movement towards international legal harmonization preceded economic globalization. Following World War II, international conventions on matters ranging from human rights to IPRs have proliferated and countries around the world have made efforts to ratify and implement them. The internationalization of law has also affected legal procedures. An example is the convention on the recognition and enforcement of international arbitral awards. The six Asian economies have taken part in this process of the internationalization of law. They have ratified many conventions and have become members of, or are seeking membership in, GATT, WTO, or the Organisation for Economic Co-operation and Development (OECD). In other areas, legal harmonization was the result of economic globalization. The effects of worldwide economic development, while giving rise to coordination in the area of environmental legislation, also promoted the development of standardized rules for international transactions. This has had its effects on the allocative as well as on the procedural dimension of law. However, as further discussed below, changes in legal processes have been slower to implement.

The policy shift that has promoted the process of convergence of legal systems has been similar in all six economies. For most it took place in the late 1970s to early 1980s, in Japan it began roughly a decade earlier. As the six economies differed considerably in the stage of economic development at the time the policy shift was introduced, this suggests that forces other than domestic events or stages in economic development played a role.

A major cause for diverging legal systems is differences in the institutional environment. This proposition is based on comparative historical research about institutions and institutional change (North 1990). It shows that institutions and the way they function are the result of a process of incremental change. Factors that promote change remain ineffective, because interest group behavior, cultural preferences, or simply historical accident create sufficient inertia to prevent far reaching change. In other words, institutional change tends to be path dependent. The concept of path dependency implies that even where more efficient alternatives are available, existing institutions prevail and continue to shape the process of socioeconomic change. Path dependency can result in continuous divergence of institutions. Even though some adaptations to a changing environment may take place, overall institutional behavior changes only at the margin. The results of our research project have indeed shown us substantial evidence for path dependency. This affects primarily legal processes and the functioning of legal institutions. Change is taking place, but change is considerably slower than in substantive law.

The legacy of legal transplants may account for some of the differences we observe across economies. The judiciary in India and until recently in Malaysia has been more independent and more outspoken than in the other four economies. This seems to reflect the different role the judiciary has traditionally played in common law as opposed to civil law economies. In common law economies the judiciary is vested with the power to make new law by way of establishing precedents, while its role in civil law economies tends to be confined to interpretation. This difference may have become increasingly blurred in the legal practice of the Western countries from which these common and civil law systems originated. However, in the nineteenth century when these legal systems were transplanted to Asia, an independent judiciary was still an issue of contention in continental Europe. As a result, administrative litigation was referred to a special court system, which at least initially was weaker than the general courts.

The process of transplanting these systems to Asia further underscored the difference between the common law and the civil law system. The transplantation of British common law to India and Malaysia involved not only a transfer of rules about legal procedures and courts, but also the establishment and running of the judicial system. The legal and bureaucratic elite that practiced and enforced the law was trained in England. By contrast, Japan copied the formal structure of the continental European court system, but the courts were staffed with personnel trained domestically and often long before the new formal structures had been put into place. Moreover, in the two common law economies, the Privy Council served as the supreme court until independence (in Malaysia appeals to the Privy Council were possible until 1985). As a result, in these two economies, the members of the legal profession became deeply familiar with the traditions that shape the common law system. Still, as the example of Malaysia in particular demonstrates, this has not prevented a reversal to more discretionary processes. The transplant of judicial procedure codes to East Asia, however, was limited to a transfer of formal rules and institutional structures. When transplanted, they became part of the legal traditions that existed in the law receiving countries. The economies of East Asia had a strong Confucian tradition, according to which law is an undesirable, but necessary, instrument for upholding order, and not a source of legal rights. Existing rules were often not known to the subjects. In fact, they were prevented from knowing the contents of rules, as it was believed that knowledge of the law would help them to circumvent the rules.

Regulatory agencies, such as securities and exchange commissions or antitrust agencies, provide another example of path dependent institutional development. These institutions were established at a time when in the receiving countries policies prevailed that favored state-led economic development and fairly extensive state controls. Despite subsequent change in economic policies, the design and functioning of these institutions has largely remained unchanged. This example bears important lessons for the timing of legal reforms. Where institutions are established in an environment that is not conducive to the economic activities they are to support, they are likely not only to be dysfunctional but inappropriate for their purpose; the chances are that they will be structured to comply with policies that exist at the time they are established. Because of institutional inertia, these structures tend to survive future policy change and may skew subsequent economic development.

CONCLUSION

The observed patterns of legal and economic change in Asia tend to support the Differentiation Hypothesis. This hypothesis predicts that different parts of a legal system behave differently, with some parts showing signs of convergence and others developing along a more idiosyncratic path. Indeed, while we find strong signs of convergence in the shift from state- to market-allocative law, the procedural dimension of law has proved to be more path dependent.

The difference in response between the two dimensions of law has important implications for drawing conclusions about the convergence or divergence of legal systems. Comparative legal theory supports the Divergence Hypothesis in suggesting that although the content of rules tends to converge over time and across economies irrespective of differences in legal traditions, the attitudes about law and the way in which a legal system operates has proved to be more path dependent (Merryman 1985). The norms governing rulemaking, rule enforcement, and court proceedings that we have referred to as the procedural dimension of law embody these basic attitudes about the role of law in society more than substantive law alone. If legal processes are primarily responsible for the nature of an economy's legal system, and the differences in legal processes are still substantial, this would support the Divergence Hypothesis.

The slower pace of convergence among legal processes and institutions is inherent, however, and does not justify the claim that legal systems in Asia persistently diverge from those in the West. Trends in recent years, in particular the changes in administrative and commercial litigation rates and procedures, suggest a remarkable potential for change with respect to legal processes. With the further strengthening of legal procedures this change is likely to continue. It may not change the behavior of all members of society and established patterns of behavior are likely to persist for some time. However, the legal rules that are even now in place will allow maverick firms or individuals to take action. To the extent they are successful, this may encourage others to follow suit and create further demand for institutions and processes that enforce rule-based behavior.

None of this suggests that Asia has already converged with the West in its legal arrangements or that it will do so in the near future. The comparative analysis of different legal systems in Asia has revealed remarkable differences even between Asian legal systems. One may argue that in some ways these differences have become even more apparent during the process of socioeconomic transformation. As countries go through a similar development process, country-specific factors that shape the path of socioeconomic development are being revealed. In this diversity, Asia's growth experience largely resembles the different paths of economic and institutional change taken historically in the West, where substantial differences in legal systems and the structure of economies remain to this day. The important point is that 35 years after the onset of high speed growth in Asia, differences in legal systems between East and West have diminished considerably.

REFERENCES

Asian Development Bank. 1997. *Emerging Asia: Changes and Challenges.* Manila.

Alford, William, 1995. *To Steal a Book is an Elegant Offense—Intellectual Property Rights in China's Civilization).* Stanford, California: Stanford University Press.

———. 1986. "The Inscrutable Occidental? Implications of Roberto Unger's Uses and Abuses of the Chinese Past." *Texas Law Review* 64 (5) 915-972.

Barro, R. J. 1994. "Democracy and Growth." *NBER Working Paper.* National Bureau of Economic Research, Cambridge, Massachusetts.

Barro, R. J. and J.W. Lee 1994b. *"Data Set for a Panel of 138 Countries."* Unpublished, Harvard University.

Bebchuk, L. and J. M. Fried. 1995. "The Uneasy Case for the Priority of Secured Claims in Bankruptcy." *Yale Law Journal* 105 (4): 857–934.

Beckerath, E. V., ed. 1956. *Handwoerterbuch der Sozialwissenschaften.* Stuttgart:Gustav Fischer; Tübingen: J. C. B. Mohr; and Göttingen: Vandenhoeck et Ruprecht.

Beller, A. L., T. Terai and R. M. Levine. 1992. "Looks Can Be Deceiving — A Comparison of Initial Public Offering Procedures under Japanese and US Securities Laws." *Law and Contemporary Problems* 55(4):77–118.

Bennett, A., C.Y. Tan and P. K. Loon. 1995. "A Study on Privatization in Malaysia: Impact on Competition, Productivity, and Efficiency." Restricted Document. New York: UN Department of Development Support and Management Services.

Bernstein, L. 1992. "Opting Out of the Legal System: Extralegal Contractual Relations in the Diamond Industry." *Journal of Legal Studies* 21(1):115–57.

Black, B. and R. Kraakman. 1996. "A Self-Enforcing Model of Corporate Law." *Harvard Law Review* 109(8):1911–82.

Blumberg, P. I. 1993. *The Multinational Challenge to Corporation Law.* New York, Oxford: Oxford University Press.

Buxbaum, D. C. 1996. "ISR – Taiwan." In R. C. Rosen, ed., *International Securities Regulation.* Dobbs Ferry, New York: Oceana Publications. Booklet 1 (Commentary).

Chandler, A. D. 1990. *Scale and Scope — The Dynamics of Industrial Capitalism.* Cambridge, Massachusetts: The Belknap Press of Harvard University Press.

Chiu, T., I. Dobinson and M. Findlay. 1991. *Legal Systems of the PRC.* Hong Kong: Longman Group (Far East), Ltd.

Chou, T.C. 1996. Article delivered at the 1996 APEC Meeting.

Clarke, D. 1991. "Dispute Resolution in China." *Journal of Chinese Law* 15(2):245–96.

Clarke, D. 1995. "The Execution of Civil Judgments in China." *The China Quarterly* 141 (March):65–81.

Cole, D. C., H. S. Scott and P. A. Wellons. 1995. *Asian Money Markets.* New York: Oxford University Press.

Corbett, J. and T. Jenkinson. 1994. *The Financing of Industry, 1970–89: An International Comparison.* London: Centre for Economic Policy Research.

Cowitt, P. P. 1986. *1985 World Currency Yearbook.* Brooklyn, New York: International Currency Analysis Inc.

Dalla, I. and D. Khatkhate. 1995. *Regulated Deregulation of the Financial System in Korea.* Discussion Paper 292. Washington, DC: World Bank.

Dipchand, C. R., I. C. Chang and M. Ma. 1994. *The Chinese Financial System.* Westport, Connecticut: Greenwood Press.

Durkheim, E. 1984. *The Division of Labour in Society.* Basingstoke, UK: Macmillan.

Edwards, J. and S. Ogilvie. 1996. "Universal Banks and German Industrialization: A Reappraisal." *Economic History Review* XLIX (3):427–46.

Edwards, J. S. S. and K. Fischer. 1994. *Banks, Finance, and Investment in Germany.* Cambridge (UK); New York: Cambridge University Press.

Fields, K. J. 1995. *Enterprise and the State in Korea and Taiwan.* Ithaca, New York: Cornell University Press.

Fleisig, H. W., J. C. Aguilar and N. de la Peña. 1997. "Legal Restrictions on Security Interests Limit Access to Credit in Bolivia." *The International Lawyer* 31(1):65–110.

Foote, D. H. 1994. "Evolution in the Concept of Contracts." In Y. Yanagida, D. H. Foote, E. S. Johnson Jr., M. J. Ramsayer, and H. T. Scogin Jr., eds., *Law and Investment in Japan.* Cambridge, Massachusetts: Harvard University Press.

Forbes, K. F. 1986. "Limited Liability and the Development of the Business Corporation." *Journal of Law, Economics, and Organization* 2(1):163–77.

Frye, M.J. 1995. *Money, Interest, and Banking in Economic Development* (2nd ed.). Baltimore and London: The Johns Hopkins University Press.

Goldsmith, R. W. 1969. *Financial Structure and Development. Studies in Comparative Economics.* New Haven, Connecticut: Yale University Press.

Goldstein, M. 1996. *The Case for an International Banking Standard.* Washington, DC: Institute for International Economics.

Government Statistical Yearbooks:

India: Central Statistical Organization of India. 1960–present. *Rashtriya Lekha Sankhyiki. National Accounts Statistics.* New Delhi: Nai Dilli.

Japan: Keizai Kikakucho and Keizai Kenkyujo. 1979. *Kokumin Keizai Keisan Nempo. Annual Report on National Accounts.* Tokyo.

Republic of Korea: Kyongje, Kihoegwon, and Chosa, Tonggyeguk. 1977. *Korea Statistical Handbook.* National Bureau of Statistics, Economic Planning Board: Seoul.

Malaysia: Kementerian Kewangan. 1977. *Economic Report.* Ministry of Finance, Kuala Lumpur: Malaysia.

PRC: China State Statistical Bureau. 1995. *China Statistical Yearbook (formerly Statistical Yearbook of China).* Beijing: China Statistical Publishing House.

Taipei,China: *Statistical Yearbook of the Republic of China.* 1975–present. Edited by Accounting & Statistics Directorate-General of Budget, Executive Yuan. Taipei.

Granovetter, M. 1985. "Economic Action and Social Structure: The Problem of Embeddedness." *American Journal of Sociology* 91 (3):481–510.
Hahm, P.C. 1996a. "Korea's Initial Encounter with the Western Law, 1866–1910." In S. H. Song, ed., *Korean Law in the Global Economy.* Seoul: Bak Young Sa Publishing Company.
———. 1996b. "Korea's Initial Encounter with the Western Law, 1910–1948." In S. H. Song, ed., *Korean Law in the Global Economy.* Seoul: Bak Young Sa Publishing Company: 61–74.
Haley, J. O. 1978. "The Myth of the Reluctant Litigant." *Journal of Japanese Studies* 4(2):366–89.
Hansmann, H. 1996. *The Ownership of Enterprise.* Cambridge Massachusetts: The Belknap Press of Harvard University Press.
Hooker, M. B. 1988. *Laws of South-East Asia—European Laws in South-East Asia.* Singapore: Butterworths.
Hu, M.W. and S. Chi. 1996. "The Market Shares of Small and Medium Scale Enterprises in Taiwan Manufacturing." *Asian Economic Journal* 10 (2):117–31.
IISMD. 1995. *"Conference Proceedings—Country Briefings."* Washington, DC: International Institute for Securities Market Development.
International Finance Corporation. 1996. *Emerging Stock Markets Factbook.* Washington, DC: International Finance Corporation.
Jin, H. and Y. Qian. 1997. "Ownership and Institutions: Evidence from Rural China." Development Discussion Paper No. 578. Cambridge, Massachusetts: Harvard Institute for International Development.
Jones, C. A. G. 1994. "Capitalism, Globalization, and Rule of Law: An Alternative Trajectory of Legal Change in China." *Social & Legal Studies* 3:195–221.

Jones, T. 1994. *People's Republic of China Country Report.* Paper presented at the Symposium on Legal Issues in Debt Recovery, Credit, and Security. Asian Development Bank. Manila, June 1993.

Jordan, Cally. 1997. "Family Resemblances: The Family Controlled Company in Asia and its Implications for Law Reform." *Australian Journal of Corporate Law* 8 (2):89–104.

Kahn-Freund, O. 1974. "On Uses and Misuses of Comparative Law." *The Modern Law Review* 37(1):1–27.

Kaufmann, D. and A. Kaliberda. 1997. "Integrating the Unofficial Economy into the Dynamics of Post-Socialist Economies—A Framework of Analysis and Evidence." In B. Kaminski, ed., *Economic Transition in Russia and the New States of Eurasia.* Armonk, New York: M.E. Sharpe.

Kelly, J. M. 1992. *A Short History of Western Legal Theory.* Oxford: Clarendon Press; New York: Oxford University Press.

Kim, K. S. 1996. "Chaebol and Corporate Governance in Korea." In S.H. Song, ed., *Korean Law in the Global Economy.* Seoul: Bak Young Sa Publishing Company.

Kim, S. C. 1993. *Republic of Korea Country Report.* Paper presented at the Symposium on Legal Issues in Debt Recovery, Credit and Security. Asian Development Bank. Manila, June 1993.

Kim, L. and J. Nugent. 1994. *The Republic of Korea's Small and Medium-Size Enterprises and their Support Systems.* Policy Research Working Paper 1404. Washington, DC: World Bank.

Kirby, W. 1995. "China Unincorporated: Company Law and Business Enterprise in Twentieth-Century China." *The Journal of Asian Studies* 54(1):43–63.

Knack, S. and P. Keefer. 1995. "Institutions and Economic Performance: Cross-Country Tests Using Alternative Institutional Measures." *Economics and Politics* 7(3):207–27.

Kodderitzsch, L. 1994. "Japan's New Administrative Procedure Law: Reasons for Its Enactment and Likey Implications." *Law in Japan* 24(**2**)105–27.

La Porta, R., F. Lopez-de-Silanes, A. Schleifer and R.W. Vishny. 1997a. "Law and Finance." Development Discussion Paper No. 576. Cambridge Massachusetts: Harvard Institute for International Development.

———. 1997b. "Legal Determinants of External Finance." Report No. 5879. National Bureau of Economic Research.

Landa, J.T. 1981. "A Theory of the Ethnically Homogeneous Middleman Group: An Institutional Alternative to Contract Law." *Journal of Legal Studies* 10:349–62.

Levine, R. 1997. "Law, Finance, and Economic Growth." Unpublished paper, 2 June 1997.

Levine, R. and S. Zervos. 1996. *Capital Control Liberalization and Stock Market Development.* Washington, DC: World Bank.

Lopez, L. 1997. "Malaysia Bars Circumventing Land Code." *Asian Wall Street Journal.* 9 June1997.

Lubman, S. 1995. "Introduction: The Future of Chinese Law." *The China Quarterly* 141(March):1–21.

Macaulay, S. 1963. "Non-Contractual Relations in Business: A Preliminary Study." *American Sociological Review* 28 (1):55–67.

Maddison, Angus. 1995. *Monitoring the World Economy, 1820–1992.* Development Centre Studies. Paris: OECD.

Maine, Henry Summers. 1977. *Ancient Law.* London: Dent; New York: Dutton.

Mauro, P. 1995. "Corruption and Growth." *The Quarterly Journal of Economics* CX (3):681–712.

McKinnon, R. I. 1973. *Money and Capital in Economic Development.* Washington, DC: Brookings Institution.

Merryman, J.H.. 1985. *The Civil Law Tradition: An Introduction to the Legal Systems of Western Europe and Latin America.* Stanford, California: Stanford University Press.

Merryman, J. H., D. S. Clark and John O. Haley. 1994. *The Civil Law Tradition: Europe, Latin America, and East Asia.* Charlottesville, Virginia: The Michie Company, Law Publishers.

Milgrom, P. R., D. C. North and B. W. Weingast. 1990. "The Role of Institutions in the Revival of Trade: The Law Merchant, Private Judges, and the Champagne Fairs." *Economics and Politics* 2 (1):1–23.

Milhaupt, C. J. 1996. "A Relational Theory of Japanese Corporate Governance: Contract, Culture, and the Rule of Law." *Harvard International Law Journal* 37(1):3–64.

Mitra, N. L. 1989. "Toil in Distrust." *Journal of the Indian Law Institute* 31(2):177–93.

Moore, B. 1966. *Social Origins of Dictatorship and Democracy; Lord and Peasant in the Making of the Modern World.* Boston: Beacon Press.

Ng Beoy Kui. 1985. "Some Aspects of the Informal Financial Sector in the SEACEN Countries." SEACEN Research and Training Center Staff Paper No. 10.

Nolte, G. 1994. "General Principles of German and European Administrative Law—A Comparison in Historical Perspective." *The Modern Law Review* 57(2):191–212.

North, D. C. 1981. *Structure and Change in Economic History.* New York: Norton.

———. 1990. *Institutions, Institutional Change, and Economic Performance.* New York: Cambridge University Press.

Oda, H. 1992. *Japanese Law.* London, Dublin, Edinburgh: Butterworths.

Patrick, H. T. and Y. C. Park 1994. *The Financial Development of Japan, Korea, and Taiwan: Growth, Repression, and Liberalization.* New York: Oxford University Press.

Phang, A. T. K. 1995. "ISR – Malaysia." In R. C. Rosen, ed., *International Securities Regulation*. Dobbs Ferry, New York: Oceana Publications. Booklet 1 (Commentary).

Pillai, P. N. 1986. "Securities Regulation in Malaysia: Emerging Norms of Governmental Regulation." *Journal of Comparative Business and Capital Market Laws* 8(1):39–73.

Pinto, B., M. Belka and S. Krajewski. 1993. "Transforming State Enterprises in Poland: Evidence on Adjustment by Manufacturing Firms." *Brookings Papers on Economic Activity*, Issue No. 1:213–70.

Potter, P. B. 1994. "The Administrative Litigation Law of the PRC: Judicial Review and Bureaucratic Reform." *Domestic Law Reforms in Post-Mao China*. Armonk, New York; London: M.E. Sharpe.

Pye, L. W. and M. W. Pye. 1985. *Asian Power and Politics: The Cultural Dimensions of Authority*. Cambridge, Massachusetts: The Belknap Press of Harvard University Press.

Qian, Andrew Xuefeng. 1993. "Riding Two Horses: Corporatizing Enterprises and the Emerging Securities Regulatory Regime in China." *UCLA Pacific Basin Law Journal* 12:62–97.

Rajan, R. G. and L. Zingales. 1997. "Financial Dependence and Growth." Draft Paper. University of Chicago and National Bureau of Economic Research, Chicago.

Ramseyer, J. M. 1985. "The Cost of the Consensual Myth: Antitrust Enforcement and Institutional Barriers to Litigation in Japan." *Yale Law Journal* 94 (3):604–45.

———. 1991. "Legal Rules in Repeated Deals: Banking in the Shadow of Defection in Japan." *The Journal of Legal Studies* 20(1):91–117.

———. 1994. "The Puzzling (In)Dependence of Courts: A Comparative Approach." *Journal of Legal Studies* 23(2):721–47.

———. 1996. *Odd Markets in Japanese History—Law and Economic Growth*. Cambridge, UK: Cambridge University Press.

Roo, Annie de and Robert Jagtenberg. 1994. *Settling Labour Disputes in Europe*: Boston: Kluwer Law and Taxation Publishers.

Rosen, R. C. 1979. "The Myth of Self-Regulation or the Dangers of Securities Regulation Without Administration: The Indian Experience." *Journal of Comparative Corporate Law and Securities Regulation* 2:261–302.

Sachs, J. D. and A. Warner. 1995. "Economic Reform and the Process of Global Integration." *Brookings Papers on Economic Activity* (1):1–118.

Savigny, Friedrich Carl von. 1814. *Vom Beruf unserer Zeit für die Gesetzgebung und Rechtswissenschaft*. Heidelberg: Mohr und Zimmer.

Schwartz, A. and R. E. Scott. 1982. *Commercial Transactions: Principles and Policies*. Mineola, New York: Foundation Press.

Scott, R. E. 1986. "A Relational Theory of Secured Financing." *Columbia Law Review* (901):265.

Scully, M. T. 1984. *Financial Institutions and Markets in Southeast Asia: A Study of Brunei, Indonesia, Malaysia, Philippines, Singapore, and Thailand.* New York: St. Martin's Press.

Semkow, B. 1994. *Taiwan's Capital Market Reform: The Financial and Legal Issues.* Oxford: Clarendon Press; New York: Oxford University Press.

Shaw, W. R. 1996. "Social and Intellectual Aspects of Traditional Korean Law." In S. H. Song, ed., *Korean Law in the Global Economy.* Seoul: Bak Young Sa Publishing Company.

Singh, A. 1995. *Corporate Financial Patterns in Industrializing Economies.* Washington, DC: International Finance Corporation.

Smart, M. 1996. "On Limited Liability and the Development of Capital Markets: A Historical Analysis." Working Paper. Department of Economics, University of Toronto.

Soto, H. de. 1990. *The Other Path.* New York: Harper & Row.

Stein, P. 1980. *Legal Evolution: The Story of an Idea.* New York: Cambridge University Press.

Stern, J. J. 1995. *Industrialization and the State: The Korean Heavy and Chemical Industry Drive.* Cambridge, Massachusetts: Harvard Institute for International Development.

Stiglitz, J. E. 1989. "Financial Markets and Development." *Oxford Review of Economic Policy* 5 (4):55.

Tam, On Kit. 1991. "Capital Market Development in China." *World Development* 19 (5):511.

Trubek, D. R. 1972. "Toward a Social Theory of Law: An Essay on the Study of Law and Development." *The Yale Law Journal* 82 (1): 1-50

Tsunematsu, K. and S. Yanase. 1997. "ISR-Japan," In R.C. Rosen, ed., *International Securities Regulation.* Dobbs Ferry, New York: Oceana Publications. Booklet 1 (Commentary).

Ueda, Kazuo. 1994. "Institutional and Regulatory Frameworks for the Main Bank System." In Masahiko Aoki and Hugh T. Patrick, eds., *The Japanese Main Bank System: Its Relevance for Developing and Transforming Economies.* 89–108. Oxford: Oxford University Press.

———. 1996. *Causes of the Japanese Banking Instability in the 1990s.* Discussion Paper No. 96–f–17, Faculty of Economics, The University of Tokyo, September 1996.

Unger, R. M. 1976. *Law in Modern Society: Toward a Criticism of Social Theory.* New York: Free Press.

Upham, F. K. 1987. *Law and Social Change in Postwar Japan.* Cambridge, Massachusetts: Harvard University Press.

VanderMay, M. C. 1996. "The Role of the Judiciary in India's Constitutional Democracy." *Hastings International and Company Law Review* 20: 103–33.

Wade, R. 1990. *Governing the Market: Economic Theory and the Role of Government in East Asian Industrialization.* Princeton, New Jersey: Princeton University Press.

Wang, Tay-Sheng. 1992. "Legal Reform in Taiwan under Japanese Colonial Rule (1895–1945): The Reception of Western Law." Ph.D. diss., University of Washington.

Watson, A. 1974. *Legal Transplants: An Approach to Comparative Law.* Edinburgh: Scottish Academic Press; London: Chatto and Windus.

Weber, M. 1980. *Wirtschaft und Gesellschaft.* Tuebingen: J. C. B. Mohr (Paul Siebeck).

———. 1981. *General Economic History.* New Brunswick, New Jersey: Transaction Books.

Weinstein, D. E. 1995. "Evaluating Administrative Guidance and Cartels in Japan 1957–1988." *Journal of the Japanese and International Economies* 9:200.

Wolf, H. C. 1993. "Endogenous Legal Booms." *The Journal of Law, Economics & Organization* 9(1):181–187.

Wood, P. 1995. *Comparative Law of Security and Guarantees.* London: Sweet and Maxwell.

Woon, W. C. M. 1995. "Regionalisation of Corporate and Securities Law: The Singapore and Malaysia Experience." *Australian Journal of Corporate Law* 5:356–63.

World Bank. 1989. *World Development Report for 1989.* New York: Oxford University Press.

———. 1993. *The East Asian Miracle: Economic Growth and Public Policy.* Washington, DC: Oxford University Press.

———. 1995. *Bureaucrats in Business: The Economics and Politics of Government Ownership.* Washington, DC: The World Bank.

———. 1997. *World Development Indicators.* CD-ROM, Win*Stars version 4.0. Washington, DC: The World Bank.

Yanagida, Yukio, Daniel H. Foote, Edward Stokes Johnson Jr., Mark J. Ramseyer and Hugh T. Scogin Jr. 1994. *Law and Investment in Japan—Cases and Materials.* Cambridge, Massachusetts: Harvard University.

Yoon, D.K. 1990. *Law and Political Authority in South Korea.* Boulder, Colorado: Westview Press.

Xiangmin, X., R. Caldwell and E. Epstein. 1996. "China's New Negotiable Instruments Law." *Butterworth's Journal of International Banking and Financial Law* 11(2):88–91.